Her Sacred Fire

The Fierce Love of the Dark Feminine in You

by Cassandra Eve

with illustrations by Kate Gold

Published 2022

The Fierce Love of the Dark Feminine in You

Cover design by Redsnapper Design

Dedicated to women's journey

of awakening within the

Dark Sacred Feminine

and to the men who love them

and Her.

Her Sacred Fire - Contents

Introduction to the Dark Feminine

The Spirit of the Valley never dies.

It is the unknown first mother,

the Dark Feminine

whose gate is the root

from which grew heaven and earth.

It is dimly seen,

yet always present.

It is there within us

All the whiles.

Draw upon it as you will,

it never runs dry.

The Tao Te Ching 6

The opening lines of any childhood story, 'Once upon a time', reveal a world of mystery and adventure. Who knows what we might discover in the realms of fairy tale or imagination? Tales of love and heroics, thrilling forays into danger, magical realms beyond our own and characters with fantastical powers. Often these tales have an element of darkness: the wicked queen, the witch in the forest, the sorcerer; or a journey fraught with danger from adversaries, seen and unseen. They demonstrate that life is always a synergy of the tensions between dark and light.

Stories prepare us for life in many ways. As a child we may model our self on a favourite hero or heroine; we discover the many ways to face challenge; we get a sense of potential victory over 'the bad guys', the triumph of good over evil. Sometimes we get spooked too. Then the shadows under the bed can invoke fear in us. How do we know the looming presence of the bedroom wardrobe doesn't house a monster? We become nervous of the potentials that lurk in the dark. Despite their good endings, stories cultivate in us a creeping recognition of the uncertainty of life. They inform us that life is equally thrilling and scary.

As we grow, our childhood fears get put to bed. Nonetheless darkness and our lack of capacity to see or know what's in it, can become a reality to be avoided, even for adults. Fear of the dark - and the thought that danger lurks there - is socially normal, but is it natural? It is wise, when walking late at night, to avoid dark alleys. For we live in a world where we are not always physically safe, but is it sensible to imagine a threat in every dark place? We have been taught in many ways to fear the shadows rather than recognise darkness is a natural aspect of life's rhythms as the absence of light. It is essential to our lives, as a time of rest and renewal. Our seasons fluctuate between maximum light and maximum dark, just as weather fluctuates between dry and wet. Perhaps we accept this more easily in nature than in human nature? For we have been conditioned to make value judgments that create division between the natural polarities of dark and light in ourselves and in our lives.

Conditioning is a natural aspect of our personal and social development. It occurs within childhood to support our growth in ways that are both healthy and damaging. As we mature it is wise (even essential) practice to become awake to the patterns we have inherited, to see if what we've been taught is relevant to our individuality and how we're evolving. As we explore what we have unwittingly taken on as belief, and as wounding, the potential is we consciously choose who we are becoming. This is the journey of healing integration and evolution, to learn to live within a framework of our own making and perhaps for some, to consciously go beyond it into a knowing of our innate divinity. Such exploration requires we not only question and engage our personal conditioning, but that we explore the social context of our beliefs. In such a process we discover the social programming that informs the collective psyche within our cultures and how that has been used as an intentional means of adaptation and control, to change our beliefs, attitudes, and behaviour. It takes a huge variety of forms, including peer pressure towards conformity and compliance, even towards obedience. It's generally fear-based and occurs through contact with perceived authority figures, information and the media, politics, and religion. Whilst some social conditioning is valuable to enable healthy connection within the collective sphere, some is distinctly unhealthy. A major aspect of our evolutionary journey is to sift, sort and discern what serves our growing awakened consciousness.

The Bible is one of the stories that informs our global culture. It has major influence in terms of how we see the ever-changing synergy of dark and light as good or bad. It begins by relating that in the beginning the Earth was void; empty, dark, and formless. Then God created light. We are told that the light was good, and it was separated from the dark. That the world was created only by God from nothingness, and that it will return to nothingness, within a straight timeline. This interpretation of a separative creation is common to Abrahamic and Muslim traditions too. Even the Big Bang, the scientific creation story, is described as an explosion of light. Light is the focus, separated from darkness.

Other more ancient creation stories do not create this split between light and dark. The creation myths of the Hindu culture relate that time is not a straight line. They believe there are eternal cycles in which universes are being created, exist, and are being destroyed, without beginning and end. Light and dark are essential aspects of this eternal cycle, unified yet with different functions within the whole. Buddhism has no belief in a Creator God. Instead, it teaches that everything depends on everything else: present events are caused by past events and become the cause of future events. Buddhism posits that life is both endless and subject to impermanence, suffering and uncertainty. Although Buddhist philosophy teaches that there are six realms, there is no split between dark and light, all realms are interlinked, in keeping with the Buddhist philosophy that mind and reality are linked. Time is not a straight line, there is no beginning and end. These realms are depicted in a diagram known as the Wheel of Life or Wheel of Becoming.

In diverse Chinese creation myths, light and dark are deemed to be essential features and forces of the Universe. Light (Yang energy) is seen as active, Masculine energy whereas Yin energy is dark, passive, Feminine energy. Yin and Yang do not relate to gender but to a cosmocentric theory of creation, human personality, and psychology. In Chinese philosophy it is the dance of Yang/Yin which gives birth to the Five Elements, and then the Ten Thousand Things. Rather than operating as separate forces, Yin and Yang are complementary. Each contains the seed of the other. Nothing is purely Yin or Yang. They are seen as fluid possibilities, always interchanging. Much like the natural flow of light and darkness every day.

The cultural perspective of light equalling good, and darkness meaning bad, undoubtedly influences our subjective perspective. Determining whether something is light or dark, positive, or negative is limited by our learned mindset and beliefs. The separation of light and dark, predominant within our western culture, has influenced our psychology whether we believe in the Bible or not. It permeates our culture in many ways. We see collective manifestations of this everywhere. Behaviour is influenced by the unconscious stereotypes and behaviours we associate with that labelling. Our simple judgments about another person's behaviour, without knowing the circumstances, are just one example of this polarisation.

Filmmakers are masters at depicting polarity in movies, where a light and a dark side exist as opposite forces, generally fighting each other. Life is not so simple, although we might try to make it so. The human tendency is to view people and their behaviour through the lens of 'good' or 'bad', rather than recognizing we are all moving in more subtle or gross frequencies of consciousness at different times. We fail to own that we all act in less than healthy ways on occasion. Looking a little deeper into the narrow duality of good/bad, we find that virtually nothing is completely one state or the other. Like the Chinese concept of Yin and Yang as differing forces at play within the Cosmos, both states contain the seed of its opposite. Wisdom recognizes that the dualistic view is essentially limited. It does not truly serve us in knowing what is true.

Polarity at play

What's really behind that old saying 'opposites attract'? Is it derived from the elusive yet potentially challenging chemistry of difference? There is no doubt, opposites do attract. Science is now proving there is a universal reality behind this experience. That the primary forces of the Universe move through attraction and repulsion. It's in the rhythms of the planetary bodies and the dance of the particles within the cells of our bodies. In astrology we see it too; the signs opposite each other have a natural affinity to move towards balance. It's like the Yin-Yang polarity in Chinese philosophy; each contains a seed of the other within itself.

In our lives and relationships, polarity can lead to curiosity or dismissal, to the urge to unite or reconcile, or towards conflict. When the opposing qualities are within our self (for example a need to achieve and to go with the flow) or in important relationships, their tension potentially leads to a stretch - growing beyond our known limits. Opposites within our self may lead us to go from one extreme to the other in our desires or actions; or we may become polarised by choice. In relationships polarity can lead to attraction, drama, and confrontation with another, or both. We all would recognise in some way the 'can't live with him, can't live without him' scenario.

In astrology, planets, and signs across the zodiac from one another have a push-pull effect. Human relationships are no different. The tension of difference is a catalyst for evolution. In astrology, perhaps also in life, one polarity has and needs what the opposite lacks. They have different means of expressing, acting, and manifesting but can learn from each other, with willingness.

Like astrology, with its roots in antiquity, the unity of life operating through polarity is a core foundation of many Eastern philosophies and religions. According to Taoist cosmology, Yang Qi and Yin Qi are opposing yet complementary forces - primordial Masculine and Feminine energies. They cannot exist without each other. In Hindu mythology, the Divine Union is expressed as Shiva/Shakti; our creative life-force being Shakti, who dances in pure erotic enjoyment as our expressive creative power for life. Shakti is impersonal; She, life, is in us all, in all forms. Her union with her consort, Shiva, creates the Universe. Her dance is free, fluid, ever-changing erotic flow, arising in a multitude of frequencies and forms, including our subtle and physical bodies. Whilst Shiva's steadfast, still presence completely permeates all forms of creation that are birthed from Shakti. Theirs is both the supreme partnership and the truth of life; consciousness and form in ever-flowing Divine Union. Shiva is pure Being in his stillness. Shakti is pure Becoming in her wildly sensual, raw expressive opening, flow. She is the infinite creative possibilities of life.

Shiva and Shakti are opposite yet equal and complementary forces. They are indivisible, dancing in union as reality behind all difference. Their dance of desire is the movement of the divine flowing erotically within all forms.

Both Masculine and Feminine consciousness are essential to our embodying wholeness. Working together they create the dance of evolution. It's both the tension of their polarity and the calling of desire towards union that is the play of life. It's a paradox. For life cannot be other than unified, held in the arms of the Great Mother, Adya Shakti, the primordial power devoid of all dualities. Yet here on Earth we experience duality, with the desire to know union. We are already always in the dance of Shiva, the unchanging ground of reality, and Shakti, the dance of life's expression, changeless Being and ever-changing, forming and dissolving Becoming, expressing as time and space. Yet we fail to know it mostly. In Being, life simply is. No contrast, no movement, no expression, without growth or expansion. In Becoming we must experience ourselves as 'other' than that. It's the play of the Mystery that calls us to return consciously to what we already are, Being.

Despite its more rational perspective, science is discovering the cosmic dance of unity known as Yin and Yang, Shiva and Shakti, in the smallest aspects of life: particles. Physicists may not call it such, but they are discovering desire, operating through attraction and repulsion, as the very basis of life. Physics reveals how attraction is a force moving between two or more dissimilar or unlike charges. Repulsion is a force between two or more similar charges. Atoms are constantly moving closer and farther apart, both within our bodies and in the furthermost reaches of the Cosmos. As above, so below; as within, so without. It seems strange to me that the more science is discovering about energy, the very basis of our lives, collectively we are more and more caught up in the material world. As this has happened, our relationship to both the natural world and its truly erotic nature, has become distorted. We have lost touch with the power of life within us. Yet paradoxically science is now witnessing that desire lies behind and within everything. Rather than being the drive to get what we want to satisfy our ego, desire is the very essence of life.

In our human self, desire is a driving force in our lives. Without it we would not survive or thrive. Yet desire sits behind all our conflicts too. We know this in the contrast of contradictory aspects within us wanting different things, or desiring different experiences, for example, freedom and intimacy. We experience it in the push and pull of facing change, in the desire for it and the fear of it. It's obvious in the conflicts we have within relationships too. Although having our desires fulfilled can make us happy and bring us comfort or security, desire also challenges us. It can put us on an edge where we must stretch. This is the play of polarity that either potentially grows us to express more of our beingness or keeps us on the egoic hamster wheel of more, more, more. We exist in a choice field of tension between comfort and security, risk, and growth. To be fully alive is to live on the edge where both interweave.

There is a concept in ecology known as The Edge Effect that wonderfully describes how the play of polarity fuels growth. It describes how there is a greater diversity of life in the region where the edges of two ecosystems overlap, such as land/water, or forest/grassland. This meeting of difference whether it's in two very different environments, substances, or individuals, creates chaos but also fertility. It is an alchemical process from which innovation arises. This is true in our human realm as well as the natural. The difference being, we have choice to allow the alchemy or not, to allow polarity to challenge, cripple and separate us from each other, or to discover fertility in its tension. The quandary is always: am I prepared to accept and evolve through difference, or create conflict from it?

This tension of polarity is further described in Hindu philosophy. It posits that there are three basic forces of life arising from Prakriti - the basic cosmic substance behind all forms. These forces are Tamas, Rajas and Sattva. Tamas is inertia or darkness, Rajas is activity or dynamism, Sattva is balance or beingness. The tension between the three, and the complexity of their constant interchange creates life; everything from the physical structuring of matter to human behaviour. For instance, minerals are basically tamasic, but at their core lies the chaos of their subatomic organisation. Perhaps this is where the theories of quantum physics and ancient Hindu philosophy are beginning to meet.

Polarity is a natural mechanism of life's unity at play. At different times of life, the interplay of its forces will be expressing and acting differently through us. Living in awakened wholeness, requires us to be consciously awake to the synergy of this duality within us. As individuals we have a natural proclivity more towards one polarity than the other. For instance, when Yang is emphasised, we express more through the fire and air energies of intellect and spirit. We are drawn outward and upward, towards the light. When Yin consciousness is predominant, we move in the earth and water of inward subjective consciousness: caring, nurturing, and feeling. We also move towards darkness, quiet and rest, ultimately towards death. Just like with electricity, polarity determines the direction of current flow.

In wholeness, both polarities are moving naturally and dynamically through each other, as unified consciousness. We may experience this internally or through relating, particularly in lovemaking, when polarity dances in constant interchange towards unity. Yet inevitably, in a human process of growth, we move out of balance, for this is the very tension that grows us. When Yang is overly strong, we become insensitive to others, dry, driven, potentially aggressive. If Yin predominates, subjective emotion and passivity can be over- emphasised, and the spirit of life within us becomes weakened.

It's not difficult to see how the time of patriarchy has over-emphasised Yang: the spirit of competition and conquest, intellect, growth without responsibility for its effects and a God remote from human life. The quest for power has dried out our more soulful Yin qualities, leading to a culture where domination rules. Intellectual power has taken over our lives, rather than it being in service to life. Collectively this has led to the suppression of our feeling nature, along with its denial and judgment. The Yin energies have either become dry and barren, or culturally undervalued unless paired with the patriarchal concept of success in a worldly sense. We can see how this way of being is decimating nature and our Earth. We all carry the responsibility for this, in the desire to fit in, or be comfortable. Collectively there is a growing need for the Yin aspects of our nature to be reclaimed, yet equally there is resistance to this change. We cannot heal the split in the way it was created – by trying to fix it, or through being reactive. This simply brings more Yang to the situation. We can only heal through reciprocity, through a reconnection to Yin that requires each of us coming to balance in the heart and sharing that in our lives.

Here on Earth the conscious dance of polarity occurs through compassionate response and action. Spirit, intellect and drive uniting with deep caring and compassion in the heart. Two different ways of being are then consciously unified. We must engage both the Yin darkness of feeling and emotion, and the Yang spirit of enterprise, engagement, and action. The tension between the two is where we grow. Our polarisation towards one or the other needs to dynamically move. When we are in touch with both, we can make conscious choices. When we favour one, our creative potential will always be lacking.

When we live as centred beings, connected to the spirit of life and embodying more fully in our humanness, we are Being immersed in Becoming. Through this ongoing process the value judgments about dark and light, good and bad, that divide us from ourselves and each other must go. It's not that there's no distinction between the two; it's about what's appropriate at different stages of evolution. For instance: through a patriarchal mindset, my life choice as a young woman to be living with a violent alcoholic man, is labelled bad, as is he. Yet compassionate response to both of us knows differently. It was an experience I needed to have at that time, until I chose differently.

As we awaken, as we choose to see consciously, both practically and philosophically, wisdom in us realises that our choices move naturally towards frequency of consciousness rather than value judgments. A more subtle recognition of heavy frequency (that is usually labelled 'bad') is that it distances and separates from its Divine Nature, and that 'good' is that which leads towards it. The tension between the two is the process of evolution.

The Dark Goddess

Nowhere is the split between dark and light more evident than in the realm of religion and worship. In our western culture, religion is a major source of the cultural perspective on the Sacred Feminine, women's nature, and sexuality. The goddess has been exiled through a supposed civilising process in our western world, wiped from mainstream culture. Although her existence can be seen in many of the ancient myths, archaeological discoveries, or obscure ancient texts, she is deemed irrelevant in our current culture, except to a few who keep her sacred flame alive.

Despite our lack of conscious connection to the Sacred Feminine energies now, it was not always so in human history. The fertile Feminine was an accepted, if not revered, aspect of daily life pre-patriarchy. goddess figurines unearthed in the Mediterranean, the Middle East, Egypt, Greece, Turkey, the Balkans, even in India, are dated between 38,000 to 14,000 years ago. These figures mostly have large breasts and bellies, are sometimes headless, have a birdlike head and wings, or are part-formed with animals. They appear to symbolise the fertility and abundance of the goddess as Earth Mother and a connection to both the natural and spirit world that we have mainly lost.

Archaeological evidence has also revealed that the oldest Shaman were women. So far as we know currently, the first people to routinely bury their dead, were the Natufians, based in present-day Israel. The oldest ritual grave there, dated to 12,000BCE, contained the remains of a Natufian female. Her grave is distinct from the others on the site, for she is surrounded by fifty complete tortoise shells, select parts of a wild boar, an eagle, a cow, a leopard, and two martens, as well as a complete human foot that is not her own. This suggests community engagement in ritual practice, given the task of gathering these grave goods. The internment rituals and grave seal strongly suggest that it is the burial site of a shaman.

Where is the Sacred Feminine in our cultures now? Her absence is obvious, and her qualities much needed. In the East, the dark-light nature of the Feminine is both well-established and revered. She is alive, openly acknowledged and honoured as the Great Mother of life. In India in particular, this aliveness has been retained through ancient scripture, where Devi (with her diverse forms) is portrayed as the Great Mother of all life, even the gods. Her forms and expression range from all-loving and bountiful, to death-wielding. She mirrors the powers we see in nature, dark and light, benevolent and beautiful, wild, and ferocious. She is both the Great Mother and creative aspect of the gods, the dance of life and energy in all forms, still celebrated in annual festivals throughout India. She flows through light and darkness, life, and death, holding all expressions of beautiful terrible life in her loving arms.

Kali is a goddess archetype from the Hindu tradition who carries the theme of destruction and rage. Commonly depicted with a fierce face, wearing a necklace of skulls, a skirt of severed arms and dancing on the body of Shiva, her consort, Kali reveals that the Dark Goddess archetypes hold potent keys to the mysteries of life and death. She stands for the life-giving and a life-taking energy of the Divine Mother, representing death and destruction as well as renewal and life. Blood drinking, death-wielding Kali lives on the edge of life. She expresses as the unacceptable dark force of the Feminine, untamed, and untameable. She is the Keeper of Time, wherein everything disappears. She takes all forms back into herself, just like Mother Earth. Her fierce force of love burns through all illusions. It knows no bounds. She is the constant letting go that time imposes, invoking death of egoic attachments.

Similarly in Tibetan Buddhist systems, the Dakini is a primordial female wisdom energy. Known as 'Skydancer'. She is completely free, able to travel between worlds and dimensions, free of the mind's entanglements, intimate with life's nature of impermanence. The name Dakini is used to refer to different emanations and frequencies of the Great Mother as a tantrika, spiritual practitioner or demoness i.e., expressing both dark and light energy. Dakinis dance both in limitless luminous space and in the graveyards, adorned with skulls and bones, wreathed in flames. They are fierce and wise, primal yet deeply compassionate, for they intimately know all aspects of life and death. The great passion of the Buddhist Goddess Vajrayogini is another aspect of the Dark Feminine within Buddhism. She is the Cosmic Feminine Mother, who births all and destroys all. She fluctuates between blissful and wrathful, both fierce and a source of ultimate compassion. The dark nature of some human qualities feed her sacred flame of passion. Her fire is of a purifying nature. It facilitates rebirth.

In our western cultures, the dark face of the Great Mother is denied except in more palatable, yet ultimately mysterious forms such as the Black Madonna. Her statues began to appear in the western world in the eleventh and twelfth centuries, through contact with the Muslim culture. They are believed to have originated from the figure of Isis, the Egyptian Great Mother Goddess of fertility. Yet the gift of life she represents, expressed through women's wombs, was somehow forgotten in this transfer of imagery to the West. The Christian religion denied and distorted the gift of creation happening through a woman's body. It was purposefully negated in the myth of Eve's 'sin'. This conscious misdirection meant the mysteries of death and renewal held by the Dark Goddess were forgotten, perhaps hidden intentionally. Through religion, the darker elements of the Feminine became confused with women's sexuality. She was portrayed as ultimately devouring, causing men to transgress from their moral and religious codes. How did this happen? How did She, revered as an essential aspect of life in the East, become held in fear and judgment? How did our naturally erotic sexual nature become distorted into the belief in woman as the originator of sin? To understand how the Feminine disappeared from our collective field, we must look at the biggest picture, history as written mainly by men, and our evolutionary processes over eons.

The vast ticking clock that is evolution

Current research into ancient history, along with archaeological evidence, now points towards a transition from what may have been a primarily matriarchal to patriarchal culture starting around 3000BCE. The astrological timeline, in terms of human evolution, known as the 'Astrological Ages', also points towards this shift. It mirrors the developmental transitions of humanity.

The Astrological Ages reveal some of the main themes of evolution for humanity and its cultures. The astrological themes of this system align with discoveries from palaeontology and archaeology going back to the 10th millennium BCE megalith temples in Turkey, even to goddess figurines dating back 35,000 years. The time frame 4000BCE to 100CE is particularly relevant to the matriarchal to patriarchal culture shift. It is represented by the astrological ages of Aries and Taurus. Yet it has continued through the Christian era of the Piscean Age and into the Age of Aquarius, that we are entering now.

The astrological ages last approximately two thousand years with a transition period between each lasting several hundred, or even a thousand years. These ages reveal a transition that changed culture and the lives of human beings, sometimes dramatically.

Age of Cancer: 8000-6000BCE approximately

Humans began to move from nomadic to settled cultures and develop agriculture. This is the Age of the Mother Goddess. It is believed human beings lived in participation mystique with the Earth as giver of life, nurturer, and sustainer. There was no sense of separation from nature and its tides, no established egoic individuality. Many Earth Goddess figurines have been discovered from this era. In astrology Cancer is the zodiac sign representing the mother-child relationship, the family, home, roots, belonging, emotional sustenance and food.

Age of Gemini: 6000-4000BCE approximately

Settled communities developed into cities in this era. Trade between cities began. The development of writing started. The first written texts appear from this time, in the form of stone tablets. In astrology Gemini represents oral and written communication, learning and teaching, business, and commerce.

Age of Taurus: 4000-2000BCE approximately

A time of mainly peaceable creative cultures without weapons or armies, where matrilineal descent was the norm, the role of the priestess and temple was central to culture, distributing food, taking care of the weak and elderly, as well as providing a focus for worship, ritual, and celebration. In astrology Taurus is the sign of the bull. Many bull statues have been discovered from this time. Creativity thrived, as seen in ceramics, jewellery, and other art forms from this time. Taurus represents earthly abundance, material security and comfort, enjoying the fruits of the Earth, creativity, and the arts.

Age of Aries: 2000BCE-1CE approximately

During this age great military civilizations arose and invaded the settled cultures of the Balkans, Middle East and Mediterranean. This is when the takeover of patriarchy began, where the 'right of might' rather than the good of the people began to take precedence. This is the age of the warrior and the hero, where domination of the power of nature and women's roles in the culture begins to appear. It is a time when environmental disasters took place on a huge scale also, leading to the destruction of established Mediterranean cultures, such as the Minoan civilisation on Crete. Aries is the first sign of the astrological zodiac. It is the sign of the warrior, the ego, courage, passion, individuality, and self-determination.

Age of Pisces: 1CE-2000CE approximately

Pisces is the age of organised religion, the age of the saviour. Christianity, Buddhism, and Islam appeared during this period, all with male gods. Suffering, victim consciousness, guilt, and sin were all promoted through the control of Mother Church in this age. Women became categorized through the labels Madonna, mother, or whore. Natural healing arts became hidden, and the true nature of sexuality was forgotten or actively denied as witch-hunts thrived. Pisces is the zodiac sign of dissolution. It is where the soul and suffering, spirituality and compassion reside. It is the zodiac sign of endings, where what was formed becomes formless, as such it symbolises physical or psychological death.

Age of Aquarius: 2000CE-4000CE approximately

The era of higher consciousness, when innovation through technology and science may provide the answers to our global dilemma, working with and for nature. Potentially an age of individuality, equality and global community is dawning where technology becomes the servant to abundance for all. Aquarius is the zodiac sign of the humanitarian, rebel, and pioneer. It is the sign that symbolizes inclusivity of difference. It can be seen as gender neutral, androgyny being an Aquarian trait. We can see its energy emerging in recent changes in gender, as well as the genetic engineering involved in traditional medicine. Aquarius symbolizes originality, ingenuity, connection into utterly new frequencies of potential that may serve the collective through new technology. But it is also where the tools of the mind may hold sway over the heart. Aquarius is where the top-down model of hierarchy, the patriarchal system, potentially makes way to a community orientated grass-roots system. The focus of innovation comes through going beyond the current social, cultural norms, including those of gender. Perhaps the emerging Age of Aquarius will bring us the awakened state of unified consciousness, realizing and expressing the qualities of both Sacred Feminine and Masculine from within ourselves.

In western culture time is viewed as linear, with the future evolving from the past. In India, however, time is viewed as cyclical. The Universe is known through living experience, whereas in the West, the cultural norm, especially through science, is to reduce all life and its forms to objects, to be used as a resource. The implications of this difference are immense. In the Eastern worldview, individual souls slowly evolve, then slowly devolve, only to slowly evolve again. They are part of life, flowing through what is known as the 'Yuga Cycle' divided into four different yugas or epochs: the Ages of Materialism, Energy, Thought and Spirit.

The entire cycle Yuga Cycle lasts for 24,000 years, with the last Satya Yuga of Spirit ending in 6700BCE. There are different theories as to whether we are currently in Kali Yuga (Materialism) or Dwapara Yuga (Energy) or moving between the two. Some schools of thought believe Dwapara Yuga began in 2012, coinciding with the Mayan calendar's 'End of Times'. As with the astrological ages, transition between ages takes hundreds of years. Both the chaos of our materialistic ways and the potentials of energy awareness are evident in our current times. We are moving between a collective concept of the world made up of objects (including nature, animals, and human beings) to be manipulated and exploited, that may lead to us destroying the world and a growing understanding of all life as energy.

Exploring this bigger picture of humanity's growth process, it may seem we have gone backwards in terms of evolution, particularly regarding our connection to the natural world. Yet in some ways our intelligence and our consciousness have evolved. We have moved through the states of tribal dependence and participation mystique into independence, from polytheism to monotheism, and are now potentially travelling towards interiorized spirituality rather than religious belief. We have moved on from expressing solely as an instinctual self to an egoic self, and for some, to an evolving self. The emerging potential now is for our sense of self to be derived from soul and spirit and to know that in each other.

Collectively our sense of self derived in ancient times from immersion in nature, that through patriarchy became power against nature, is now called to evolve towards power with nature. A significant evolutionary aspect of this current process is held in the shadows of transition from matriarchy to patriarchy. Denial of the Great Mother and women's role within life, still play out in our relationship to the Earth and to women's power of creation through sexuality and physical birth. It is these shadows calling for redemption now. It is these shadows, held in the Dark Feminine, that are keys to transforming our relationship to body, instinct, sexuality, and our Earth.

Patriarchy - a takeover? Or evolution at work?

In these current times we are faced with the fact that the development of human beings, with our agricultural, industrial, then technological advances, may also lead to our collective demise. The Astrological Ages may give us clues to the energies of our potential evolution but not to the circumstances. We live on a planet of choice. It is our choices that also dictate our potential future. Does humanity's past also provide clues to our collective future? Perhaps it depends on the eyes we view it with. Some would say, we must keep repeating our karmic lessons until we learn the way of balance and respect for our home, the Earth. It is clear, as technology enables us to go beyond our beautiful planet to other planetary worlds, that we must learn to respect and engender care for life in all its forms here.

The seeds of our current crisis are held in our western history. Whether they are the seeds of extinction or evolution remains to be seen. Clues to our current cultural model lie in the period represented by The Age of Aries, expanded by that of Pisces. Aries was the age of the conqueror. This period brought irrevocable change as warring tribes from the north invaded the peaceable cultures of the south. As they overran these temple-based, community-orientated cultures, the role of the temple as the spiritual and caregiving centre of the community was destroyed. A nature-centred and community-based egalitarian way of life was shattered.

Aggression is one way to establish power. Changing the culture is another. As the invaders settled in their new lands, the centre of power shifted. Firstly, it became devolved from kings and male leaders in a hierarchical way. The god of the invaders was generally a single solar figure, Divine Masculine, a hero, that gave rise to the many hero myths of this time. This strengthened the concept of a single powerful male figure as both leader and 'caretaker' of the culture. To appease the old ways, the invaders 'married' their god to the existing goddesses, just as the Christian church built on pagan sites in later times. Eventually divinity became separated from the Great Mother Goddess and the Earth, centralized in a solar deity, and on Earth in a king or male leader. The gifts and cycles of the Moon and Earth, connected intimately to human lives, particularly those of women, were denied. Human beings began to look away from the Earth that gives us life, towards the Heavens.

As humanity disconnected from the Earth, the role of the Mother Goddess forgotten, we neglected our gratitude for her abundant nature. Over hundreds of years as worship of a solar deity became the norm, as the king, or tribal chief, was deemed the centre of secular power, the move towards the male right to own and control women, children, and nature, became a basis from which to create personal wealth. The control of woman's sexuality was a major element in this, deemed necessary to disempower women and encourage dependence on the male provider. It was during this time that the blood sacrifice of bulls (that tended to be male) began to replace the sacred mystery of menstruation and ritual bleeding, the return of menstrual blood to the earth. In this shift our life-force was deemed to come only from the divine, and so was offered to the Heavens, rather than back to the Earth. Women's menstrual cycle became shamed, labelled as unclean, rather than a holy gift of life potential. Spirit was separated from body. Creation deemed to come only from God.

Well before the Christian era, both Greek and Roman culture had established the Patriarchal shift in everyday life. After the destruction or takeover of the temples, this was strengthened by the ending of matrilineal inheritance. The cultural shift to the ownership of property by males became established as the norm. Women and girls came to be seen as material goods, owned by their father or the male householder. In Roman culture, only the priestess and the prostitute were independent. The priestess retained her strong social and political role initially within the culture as Vestal Virgin. Yet the demand that she remained a virgin sexually (on pain of death) grew the split between spirit and sexuality that we see so strongly marked in our cultures now. It was a convenient dismissal of the fact that a woman's womb is the portal between spirit and matter, of her role as the creatrix of human life.

It is in these cultures that we find the main body of mythology that informs our western psyche. Yet many of the Greek and Roman myths have their roots in more ancient traditions, many from the Egyptian and Sumerian cultures. In these more ancient tales, the goddess is alive, honoured for her creative participation in human life. For patriarchy to rule, her-story, held within these ancient Goddess-honouring tales had to be distorted or destroyed. The control of woman depended on the hiding of truth, so women's wisdom and power were assaulted in every way.

In the Greek culture, the longstanding unity of Maiden-Mother-Crone goddess as guide to the human cycles of life was eventually split. The Triple Goddess, alive in ancient culture, was responsible for the entire cycle of life and death. As such she was mother, nurturer, and, as crone, death-wielder. In ancient Greece, for more than 2000 years, people went to Eleusis to participate in rituals known as the Eleusinian Mysteries. It was Persephone, the Maiden and daughter (see Chapter 4) who became Queen of the Underworld, who was the guide through the Underworld and out again. Before her in Sumerian culture was Inanna (see Chapter 1), who also journeyed to the Underworld, was stripped bare, killed, hung on a hook for three days, then resurrected. Sound familiar? For patriarchy to succeed, the energy of the ancient crone goddesses particularly had to be suppressed by culture and religion, for the crone's power overruled even the will of the supposed Heavenly

Father God, Zeus. Ancient mythology had to be replaced or distorted to relate stories more suitable to the patriarchal agenda. Compounding this, a change to the measuring of time, ensured the further demise of our connection to the Earth's natural rhythms.

As humanity moved further away from the ways of the Sacred Feminine in the western world, the invention and imposition of a solar calendar, was perhaps the death knell to a lunar and Earth-based culture. The Solar calendar (known as the Julian Calendar) was introduced in 45BCE, seemingly on a whim, by Julius Caesar. It replaced the Lunar calendar and is still used to this day. Our Earth-Moon connection, so naturally reflective of our lives as human beings, reflected through the ocean tides, our feelings, and women's menstrual cycle, was broken. Prior to this, the rhythm of life was known through the waxing and waning of the Moon from darkness to light and back again, as well as the Solstice sunrises and the Earth's seasonal cycles. Through the Moon's links to women's menstrual cycle, the nature of woman's womb as ultimately life-giving was evident. The Moon cycle mirrored the life cycles of human beings through woman, the time of sowing seeds and harvest, the ocean tides, the tides of women's blood, nature's rhythms of plenty and lack through the seasons.

The Julian Calendar was not the first solar calendar, but it was the first to have a more global impact. The Mayan calendar included solar as well as other cosmic calculations. For millennia the Egyptians also had been using the annual sunrise reappearance of the Dog Star, Sirius, in the eastern sky, as a basis for their calendar. This coincided with the annual flooding of the Nile so was a form of timekeeping aligned with nature. Their calendar began to drift gradually into error though, so in 25BCE Augustus imposed the Julius calendar on the Egyptians too. The calendar alignment in the west with a solar cycle, and therefore a solar deity, was complete.

With the rise of Christianity, the devolution of power to males and the dishonouring of women's sexual creative power became further established. The story of Adam, Eve, and the serpent in the garden (often portrayed as Lilith - see Chapter 6) encouraged this. Some sources state that this myth - man and woman created in pairs, with woman emerging from man's rib – was created for political purposes. Whether this is true or not, the outcomes are evident. The story of Eve and serpent power as evil, strengthened the idea of woman's nature as sinful, to be suppressed or feared. In the temple cultures serpent power was known to represent the power of life present in our sexual energies, not just for the creation of a child, but for purification of the body, to opening a living experience of unity with the divine. As woman was thrown out of the Garden along with her naturally sensual, creative nature, the serpent was also judged, vilified as evil. Christianity retained the Sacred Feminine only as Virgin and Mother. It eliminated her role as sexual being, creatrix of life (except as Virgin) and wise woman crone, guardian of the Mystery. Woman was demoted from creatrix to an animal body for producing heirs or providing service to male demands. With the suppression of women's sacred role within creation, the suppression and control of nature was inevitable.

The world as we know it now is based on these misunderstandings or outright distortions and control of the female role as creatrix. They arise from ignorance – perhaps wilful ignorance - about our innate unity with, and dependence on, nature. This has led to the abuse of our creative power, evident in the decimation of our Earth and her creatures. If we are to survive, a huge rebalancing is needed. A deep understanding of how we use creative power is crucial. Every aspect of life stems from that. We are responsible. A myth from the Hindu culture reveals how the Sacred Feminine is essential to that understanding, and a pointer towards the shift of consciousness needed for us to evolve.

Before time began an asura called Mahishasur thought to himself, 'If only I could grow so strong that even the gods couldn't touch me. If only I could become the most powerful being in all creation.' He became obsessed with gathering power. Then one day an idea came to him, 'Everyone knows that strict fasting and prayer can make a person very strong.' So, he began his spiritual practice. He stopped eating; he meditated; he began to pray to Brahma, the creator.

Many years passed. The longer Mahishasur practiced, the more strength he gained. Soon his practice spread through all the three worlds. Even Brahma the creator felt its presence. 'He deserves to be rewarded,' thought Brahma.

Brahma set off for the place where Mahishasur, the asura, was fasting. When he saw Brahma standing there, Mahishasur knelt at his feet, 'Lord, you have honoured me greatly. You have recognised my devotion and answered my prayers', he said. Brahma raised his hand in blessing, replying, 'I am, indeed, very impressed by your long and devoted practice. I want to grant you a boon. Ask for anything that you desire.' Mahishasur's heart leapt with joy. 'All I ask is that I should become immortal,' he cried. Brahma smiled and shook his head. 'What you ask for is not possible,' he said. 'Every creature that is born must die. Think of something else. I will be happy to grant you a boon.' Mahishasur was disappointed, but also wily; he thought quickly and replied. 'Lord, if you cannot make me immortal, can you grant me the boon that I cannot be killed by either a man or a god? If I must die, it should only be at the hands of a woman.' Being a tough demon, he was confident that no woman would be strong enough to kill him. 'It shall be as you ask,' Brahma said. 'You will meet your death only at the hands of a woman.' Mahishasur bowed low before Brahma. 'I thank you for this great boon, Lord,' he said.

As Brahma departed, Mahishasur bellowed with triumph. 'Now I will show these weakling gods who the true ruler of the three worlds is!' he yelled. His terrible laughter rang throughout creation, and he lost no time in unleashing his reign of terror. He gathered a huge army of fellow asuras and began to torment the inhabitants of the Earth. If people fought back or tried to stop them, they were killed. Soon, all the inhabitants of the Earth were living in fear of the demons. The news spread everywhere that Mahishasur was invincible, and that no one could harm him.

After violently subduing all mortals, Mahishasur decided to challenge the gods. Brahma's boon meant no man or god could harm him, so he gathered his generals and prepared for battle. Meanwhile the gods had heard about the coming attack and were concerned. They consulted Brahma. 'There is little I can do,' he said gravely. 'I was the one who granted the boon of invincibility to Mahishasur. If only I had known his intentions!' Nonetheless he entered the battlefield, with his fellow gods Vishnu and Shiva. Mahishasur had taken the form of a huge buffalo and was leading the demons.

As battle commenced, to the horror of the gods, all their holy weapons proved useless before the asura's strength. Vishnu hit him with his powerful mace. The demon was stunned but rose again, taking the form of a lion. Then Vishnu threw his chakra to cut off Mahishasur's head, but it bounced back. As a last resort, Indra hurled his thunderbolt Vajra at the demon. But Mahishasur stood there, laughing as Indra's mighty thunderbolt simply passed over him. Mahishasur now took the form of a giant buffalo again and redoubled his attack. The gods began to flee in despair. With shouts of delight, the asura army drove the gods out of Heaven. There was no one able to curb Mahishasur's oppression now. He did what he wanted, and the people of the Earth suffered terribly.

For years the gods, homeless, wandered over fields and mountains. Finally, tired of being in exile, the trinity, Shiva, Vishnu, and Brahma, got together to resolve the situation. There had to be a way to destroy the demon so they could return to Heaven. They began by focusing on Brahma's exact boon to Mahishasur. Eventually they came up with a solution. Vishnu said, 'Right now not a single woman living in all three worlds is strong enough to destroy this evil creature. Let us use our combined powers to create one.'

In desperation, the gods closed their eyes and began to concentrate all their powers on creating an invincible woman. A fiery pillar of light appeared in the sky. It was so bright that even the gods found it impossible to look. Yet they continued to combine their powers. Shiva created the face of a goddess, Vishnu gave her arms, and Brahma created her legs. In this way, all the gods gifted her, until she had ten arms, each carrying different weapons. Finally, Himalaya, the god of the mountains, gave her a tiger to ride on. Then they named her Mahadevi (Great Mother) Durga. With the blessings of the gods, Durga mounted the tiger and set out to destroy Mahishasur. She approached the asura's dwelling place, letting out a mighty roar that shook the mountains and created huge waves in the seas. Mahishasur asked his soldiers to find out what was happening. When he heard that a woman on a tiger was challenging him, he laughed, 'Tell her that I will be happy to marry her' he said.

When Mahishasur's messengers brought the proposal, Durga laughed and replied, 'Tell your king that I am no ordinary woman who would be eager to marry him. I am Mahadevi. I have come to ask him to return to his place below the world. If he doesn't go, I will destroy him!' When he heard this reply, Mahishasur flew into a rage. He sent his leading warriors out to fight with Mahadevi, but to their astonishment and horror, one after the other the boastful warriors were killed. The asura king became even more furious. 'Cowards and weaklings! They could not stand up to a mere woman. I will settle this wretched female once and for all!' he thundered.

Cunningly (or so he thought), Mahishasur assumed the form of a handsome man to woo Mahadevi. 'Beautiful lady, why do you want to fight like a man?' he said. 'Why not marry me? Throw your weapons aside, come and live like a queen.'

When Durga rejected him firmly, Mahishasur attacked the goddess along with his terrible army of asuras. Durga immediately created a multitude of soldiers from her breath. Mahishasur tried all the tricks he knew. He kept changing shape: from a man to a lion, then an elephant. But each time, Mahadevi wounded him severely with her weapons. The battle raged for nine days. Finally, Durga beheaded Mahishasur, who had once more taken the form of a huge buffalo. Durga had freed the world from Mahishasur's tyranny. Indra and the other gods returned to the Heavens again, and all was well. Since then, Durga is worshipped as the Great Mother Goddess who vanquishes all.

To me, the relevance of these myths to our times is without question. The powers of the Great Mother and other aspects of the Dark Feminine in her many forms, are crucial to defeating the 'demons' of our current times. What are these demons? The desire for ultimate power in this Hindu tale is telling, isn't it? Don't we see this at play in our world now? That dark demand seems voracious. Like the gods we may become paralysed in the face of collective power-grabbing, greed, and overwhelming need, mystified by what we can do to make a difference. Yet this metaphorical play of gods, goddesses and demons exists inside our psyche too. We can address it there, as well as in activism in our world. It resides in our lack of honouring our Sacred Feminine nature, in ignoring her whispers, in lacking love for our self and our own self-care, in withholding our wisdom or withdrawing in the face of patriarchal demands. It plays in denying the fierceness of our feelings. It is essential for each of us to play our part in reclaiming the Divine Feminine, is it not?

Was patriarchy a takeover? Or is it evolution at work? Did we choose the left-brain route of science and rationale as part of our evolution? Did we choose to seemingly separate from our Source and the Earth to make a free-will choice to return to it consciously? We cannot know really. Yet we can commit to making a difference.

From inclusivity to division

The way of patriarchy is to emphasise a division between divine and human, soul and instinct, spirit, and matter, good and bad, especially through organised religion. Its establishment forced many of the ancient goddess archetypes, rooted in the entirety of the Moon cycle, into an assimilation labelled 'unholy' or 'dark and devouring'. Where did that leave women? With our cyclical nature, primal emotions, dark wombs, and messy menstruation?

The denial of our wholeness has permeated our lives since patriarchy grabbed power. As mankind disowned the fertile creative power of desire, negative projection about the nature of female sexuality grew and became the norm. Understanding of the sacred nature of menstruation and fertility, sexuality, women's role within creation and birth, the cycles of nature and the truth of death as part of that cycle, disappeared from the cultural perspective. The Mother disappeared (except through virgin birth), the Dark Goddess became feared and abhorred rather than venerated as an innate aspect of the whole cycle. As what is naturally dark was named 'evil', women's choice was to be 'good' and therefore perhaps taken care of, or to be ostracised. Through this, woman's sense of self-worth or security has come to be based on compliance, accommodation, and compromise. Or be shamed, abused, and hounded.

We know little about how matriarchal societies operated in practice. Simply that the Goddess was venerated. This is shown through archaeological evidence and some ancient texts such as The Hymns of Inanna (explored in Chapter 1), or the more recently discovered Gospel of Mary Magdalene. There is conflict amongst scholars as to whether matriarchal societies are simply myth. Yet there is evidence in places such as Crete, ancient Sumer (now Iraq), Celtic Ireland, the Baltic regions, along with Asia, in both Neolithic and Bronze Age periods. Matriarchy is still alive now in tribal cultures including the Mosuo tribe on the borders of Tibet and China, the Hopi in America, the Bribri in Central America, the Umoja (meaning oneness or unity) in Kenya, the Akan in Ghana, the Garo in India and Bangladesh, and the Minangkabau in Indonesia. If we were to explore our collective human roots through multiple threads, rather than just the history written by men, we would perceive an entirely different picture. To do so, we must follow the threads we find, whether documented, through oral tradition, or intuitively.

One of the most well-researched systems that demonstrate the role of Feminine power is in the Old and Middle Kingdoms of Ancient Egypt (2375 BCE -1650BCE approximately). It reveals exactly how strong the goddess influence was on culture, beyond the more commonly held theories of female land ownership, the roles of priestesses and queens, and matrilineal inheritance. This period of the Egyptian culture operated under the Laws or Principles of Maat, Goddess of Truth. These principles are Truth, Justice, Balance, Order, Compassion, Harmony, and Reciprocity. They also included 42 ideals, such as all life being held sacred, non-violence, and gratitude. In its abstract sense, the Principles of Maat affirmed that human life be aligned with the cosmic order and rhythms established at the creation, reaffirmed with the accession of each new king of Egypt as its caretaker. Pharaohs are often depicted with the emblem of Maat (an ostrich feather or a goddess figure with an ostrich feather for a head) to emphasise their roles in upholding the law. The pharaohs were believed to only rule through Maat's authority.

The goddess Maat's primary role in ancient Egyptian religion comprised the ritual known as Weighing of the Heart that took place at death. She travelled in her father, the Sun God Re or Ra's boat between the Underworld and the Heavens. Her ostrich feather was the measure that determined whether the soul (considered to be in the heart) of the departed would reach the heavenly afterlife or not. Maat's scales rested on a long vertical pole with a hawk-headed bird at the top (representing spirit) and a crocodile (representing instinct) at the bottom. These two symbols can support our understanding of the split cultivated between spirit and instinct prevalent in the patriarchal age. To do this, we must enter the world of mythology, stories that provide clues to the evolutionary process and purpose of the times. It is mythology that portrays the underlying meanings of our evolution beyond recorded his-story.

Truth and lies

Mythology is not solely comprised of stories of a fantastical past; it's alive. It arose from the collective unconscious as a means of describing human impulses and motivations, making meaning of our lives in particular ages. It's still alive now in our story-making, albeit through different forms such as novels, movies, and computer games. The ancient storytellers had no conscious knowledge of psychology, or the unconscious layers of our humanness, yet they expressed them through story and passed them on. As Platonic philosopher Synesius of Cyrene put it, 'Myths are things that never happened but always are'. Myths express that which is difficult to put into words in any other way. They passed through different cultures and generations, often by word-of-mouth, because they were meaningful. They provided a map of our inner landscapes, affirming our common human experience, using symbolism as a means of understanding.

As myths were related in different cultures, the stories people told transformed. As they were told and retold through the ages, they naturally changed, sometimes naturally, sometimes with agenda. Nonetheless as living templates of our human experience, they generally retained the core resonance and meaning of a particular human theme. Mythologist Joseph Campbell described their function as four-fold: inspiring awe; explaining the origin and nature of the Cosmos; supporting the social order; and awakening individuals to their divine potential. Of these functions, it's easy to see how supporting the social order took precedence, much as happens now through the media. Myths were changed to suit the purposes of those in power.

We are living mythology today. For mythology is alive, fluid, a map for self-expression and sharing, the making of meaning, and for evolution. Myth provides us with the means of accessing the 'Gods' in our unconscious. Those 'Gods' are our inner drivers, desires, and emotions. We recognise them, as they express personally and collectively. For instance, the ancient god and goddess archetypes are now expressed through the cult of celebrity. We worship them (if we do) in similar ways that the Greeks worshipped Zeus, Aphrodite, or Athena. We project energy onto them; they have influence. Maybe we want to be like them.

We can see how these archetypes change through history; the goddess for one generation was Marilyn Monroe or Amelia Earhart, now it's Lady Gaga or Greta Thunberg. The characters may change, yet we can identify with the meaning they make as timeless.

Myth provides us with maps of living frequencies that we energise and express both personally and collectively. Myths are inside us, speaking to us symbolically. They bypass the rational, logical, scientific perspective. Myth is multi-layered; symbolic, prevailing over the either-or, black-white perspective of the rational mind. It takes us into the world of both-and, paradox, and synchronicity. Myth belongs in the world of the right hemisphere of the brain, in oral tradition, where there are multi-layered versions with the same archetypal theme. We cannot neatly box and label these themes expressed through myth, but we can connect with them, for they are already alive within us.

Myth evolves through different eras of human history and through different cultures, many of which have creation myths with similar themes. The story of a Christ figure is presented in like ways in different traditions. Most of the myths underpinning the astrological and Sacred Feminine archetypes we are exploring here arise from the Greek and Roman cultures. Figures of Roman mythology were largely appropriated from the Greek tradition and given new names. Yet if we travel deeper into history, before the Greek culture, we find these myths are based on even older stories. Not only that, but we also discover the Feminine archetypes as portrayed through Greek or Roman perspectives have been sanitised. Her-story has been changed.

Understanding the rise of these cultures, the changes they brought to the lives of human beings, especially women, and what they destroyed in a quest for power, is vital to understanding our current gender power plays and politics. Deep in the unconscious we know there's been an appropriation and distortion of women's natural way of being. Even now, the archetypes and myths of patriarchy are still playing out. In connecting with them, understanding how they influence us still, deconstructing the patterns and receiving their gifts, we not only reclaim what's been lost, but we evolve.

One myth in particular - the Greek myth of Gaia and Uranus - holds profound keys to the unfolding takeover of patriarchy in the Age of Aries and beyond it. It is the generally accepted version of a creation myth held by the ancient Greeks. It relates how before the world came into existence, there was a confusion of elements named Chaos. Eventually these elements coalesced into a lighter substance, forming the vault of the sky, known as Uranus, and a more solid one we would call Earth, known as Gaea or Gaia. In some versions, such as Greek poet Hesiod's Theogeny (750-650BCE approximately), Uranus is the first offspring of Gaia. Uranus, represented the light and air of Heaven, with its qualities of brightness, heat, purity, and omnipresence, whereas Gaia, the firm, life-sustaining Earth, was worshipped as the all-nourishing mother. She was the Great Goddess of the Greek culture; there being scarcely a city in Greece without a temple erected in her honour.

Whether her son or not, eventually Uranus joined with Gaia, and their first-born child was Oceanus, the ocean, encircling the Earth. Other offspring, that occupied the intermediate space between the sky or Heavens, and Earth, came along next: Aether (Ether) and Aer (Air). Aether and Aer were separated from each other by divinities called Nephelae, nymphs of clouds and rain, floating between Aether and Aer. Gaia also produced the mountains and Pontus (the sea), along with sea-deities. Co-existent with Uranus and Gaia were two mighty brother and sister powers who were also the offspring of Chaos. These were Erebus (Darkness) and Nyx (Night), worshipped by the ancients. From the union of Uranus and Nyx came Eos (Aurora), the Dawn, and Hemera, the Daylight.

As creation ensued, Uranus and Gaia generated two distinctly different races of beings called Giants and Titans. The Giants had brute strength alone, but the Titans combined great physical power with bright intellect. The three Giants, each of whom possessed a hundred hands and fifty heads, were known collectively as the Hecatoncheires, meaning with a hundred hands. These mighty Giants could shake the Universe and produce earthquakes. The Titans were twelve in number and included some gods and goddesses we may be familiar with, such as Cronos (Saturn), Themis and Thea.

As creation unfolded, a subtle but telling change began to occur. Uranus, the bright light of Heaven, repulsed by his crude, coarse, offspring, the Giants, began to abhor them. He feared that their force might eventually overthrow him. In his disgust and fear, he hurled them into Tartarus, a lower world of Gaia's, and locked them away. Gaia, displeased with Uranus's action against his own children, began to plot with her other children, the intelligent Titans. Their son, Cronus took on the task of revenge. Killing his father by cutting off his genitals and throwing them into the ocean, he de-throned him. Aphrodite, Goddess of Love, was born from his sea foam. Cronus became the Father of Time, ruling over his siblings. Nonetheless he suffered the same fate as his father, eventually being killed by his son Zeus. This act ended the rule of the Titans and brought in the more familiar Olympian pantheon.

Exploring this creation myth in the light of our current knowledge of life on Earth, it's possible to see a certain truth within it. The offspring of Uranus and Gaia are active elements of the alchemical process that created the Earth. We live in both light and darkness, under the over-arching sky. Uranus represents not only sky but Heaven. This myth, as others, represents where the first split between the light of Heaven and the dark of Earth begins to appear. Uranus's act of disowning his uncivilized children and locking them away, was a judgment. He actively created separation from his children. This was seen by Gaia as an act of betrayal, for she accepted all her children's unique natures as aspects of creation. She had created a realm called Tartarus for the Giants but Uranus, in his fear, imprisoned them there. Unwittingly, his action was the cause of his demise. Much as experience teaches us, what we try to hide away, or run from, will come back and bite us. Uranus had introduced judgment into the natural system of life expressing itself through differing frequencies. The seed of judgment creating the split of consciousness between spirit (light, bright and therefore good) and the instinctual aspects of form (coarse, reactive, and therefore bad).

In contrast to this myth from the foundation of western civilization, the myth of Shiva and Kali, reveals an utterly different perspective on dark and light.

A legendary battle is taking place between the demon Raktabija and the Great Mother Goddess Durga. As the situation threatens to become overwhelming – for every drop of blood spilled by the wounded, Raktabija becomes a clone warrior - Durga manifests the dark Goddess Kali. Kali is the guardian of time as destroyer. She rules over the processes of death and dissolution. Her emergence turns the battle around, as she drinks Raktabija's blood before it touches the ground and devours his existing warrior clones. In a frenzy, her blood lust becomes unstoppable. Shiva, who is the power of supreme consciousness, steps in to stop her. He lays his body before Kali, bringing her to awareness. Dark and light work together to defeat the demons and end the chaos. Peace and stability are established once more.

The alliance of dark and light in this Hindu tale reveals a key to our own evolution now. As we face the demons of this current age, both internal and in our world, we need the capacity to fight our demons, to take in and transmute their energy as they emerge. And we need to know when to stop, when to become awake to the deep still presence that lies behind all expression, to rest in it as the ground of all experience. We need strong commitment to face and embrace our shadows. Expansive consciousness – Shiva presence - acts as our witnessing space in this. We need the fierce Feminine and the supreme Masculine to work together within us, to change our lives and our world.

Life forming itself as patterns of consciousness

What were once known as Gods and Goddesses, are still active in us now as archetypes. They are patterns of energy that lie deep within our collective and individual psyche. When we hear of them, we recognise them as meaningful. Jung claimed that archetypes exist in the collective unconscious, as pre-established models of behaviours, thoughts, and feelings. He suggested that these energy patterns are innate, universal, unlearned, and hereditary. For instance, if I use the word 'warrior', you recognise that the word represents a model of a certain way of being and behaviour. It works similarly with 'mother', 'villain', 'victim', 'witch', 'lover', 'jester' and so on. The archetype holds the core energy of a particular form of expression that speaks to us symbolically.

Archetypes cover all realms of experience. We recognise the main ones when presented to us through story, song, theatre, and film, through reading novels or the ancient myths. Yet many of the inner maps we need lie buried in the unconscious, particularly the shadowy ones. We may recognise that they're there within us, but not claim them as an aspect of self. Often, we experience them through reaction, much like a software program; press 'button a' and 'b' happens. Or we may notice them in others.

Many of the ancient archetypes, particularly those that women would relate to, have been lost through patriarchy, denied a place in a culture that focuses on progress and control of nature. They have disappeared from culture due to lack of acknowledgment of their relevance, let alone value, in our world. Or they have been denounced as morally wrong and thrown out of mainstream culture as relative to our lives. Yet these archetypes are valuable mirrors for forgotten aspects of self, buried deep within us. We merely need to be reminded of their existence to become enriched and empowered in connecting with them.

According to Jung, archetypes are innate universal pre-conscious psychic patterns or predispositions. They form the basis from which the collective themes of human life and experience emerge. The Greeks first developed theories about these patterns of human behaviour; Plato described them as ideas and forms that are imprinted before birth. The gods and goddesses of the Greek culture displayed these archetypal energies not only through their mythology but through their temples. They were a valued aspect of everyday life. Nowadays we can discover these archetypes as sub-personalities through psychology, or in an astrological birth-chart, as planetary energies. The planetary bodies represent energetic frequencies that we live through. These patterns have a certain density and momentum, depending on how much validity we give them personally and collectively.

Jung's exploration of the human psyche and the nature of consciousness opened the inner world to us in new ways. As did that of the early psychologists, attempting to map our inner world. Jung's writing led to a revival of interest in astrology too. His words 'Astrology represents the sum of all the psychological knowledge of antiquity' reveal his deep understanding of the inner workings of human beings and the Universe. Jung likened the planetary bodies not only to archetypes but to gods and goddesses that loom large as symbols in our collective unconscious. These symbols act as guide, mentor, protagonist, and catalyst within our inner world and in our relationships. They provide us with maps for ways of being and expression, along with our evolution in individuality. They open us to the expansive mystery of what it is to be consciousness playing in the human realm.

The language of the universe

Astrology is considered weird by many individuals, irrelevant to our lives other than as entertainment. Popular astrology, with its limited predictive expression, doesn't truly serve the depth of this ancient esoteric science. If we take time to explore it, we discover astrology has been informing humanity of our innate connection to the stars, and our place within it, for more than five thousand years. Similarly, structures such as Stonehenge, the Pyramids, and other ancient sites worldwide, can broaden our perspective on our human selves. They help us see that there is much more to human history than we currently know. At some point, perhaps they will open our connection to the Cosmos and its rhythms in ways we cannot imagine now. That humanity is but one aspect of life in an intimate link between the Earth, Moon, Sun, planets, and stars. That we are interdependent, not only with nature and the animal kingdom, but the Cosmos. That its rhythms affect our human lives just as the rising of the Sun, or the flow of the seasons.

Science walks the provable path. It seeks to define not only the nature of life, but its mystery. Traditionally spirituality and science have been at odds. Yet current thinking reveals the gap between science and spirituality is closing. The understanding of life's natural unity held by tribal and some spiritual traditions, is now becoming available through science. New physics reveals that behind all matter lies energy that can express both as form and energy, particle, and wave, even appearing in two different places at the same time, yet always unified at its source. Just as in Hindu philosophy, it is now known that forms may change but energy cannot be destroyed. Life is infinite as energy, expressing through ever-changing forms, including our human ones. The boundaries between science, philosophy and spirituality are blurring. Perhaps we are beginning to understand that our focus solely on the physicality of life is limiting. We must discover the language of energy and what lies within it.

Astrology is an energetic language. It gives us a framework through which to explore the rhythms and play of energy on planet Earth and within ourselves. Our Universe is both physical and energetic, expressing through diverse astronomical forms and on many different frequencies. Planetary bodies certainly have physicality: either material or gaseous. Their movement through space, orbiting the Sun and aligning with other planets, creates diverse energy fields in which Earth (and humanity) is immersed. These energy fields have tangible effects on Earth and within us. Scientific experiments in the early 1940s revealed that certain alignments of the Sun with Earth and other planets affected radio signals. Just in a practical sense, it was a valuable discovery during a world war, when stable communication systems were needed. Yet it also paved the way for further understanding of our place within the Universe. More recent scientific discoveries, especially in new physics, expand on that knowledge. Coming back to astrology, if we accept that each planetary body has an energetic resonance that we are receiving on Earth constantly, we begin to see that our potential for experience goes way beyond mere physicality and the five senses. Just like the Moon affects our ocean tides, women's menstrual cycle and our moods, other planetary bodies exert subtle influences on our minds and body-beings. How we respond or react to these frequencies is the free will aspect of our existence.

Just as life on Earth has seasonal rhythms so does our Universe. As the planets radiate at different frequencies within rhythmic patterns, our consciousness acts as a receiver, subtly picking up and responding to the universal language of frequency. It's simple to understand this through our physical connection to the Sun and Moon cycles. We see them moving through their phases, day to night, dark to bright. We might notice how they affect us daily. Their longer rhythms - New Moon to Full Moon, or the flow of the seasons – are an accepted aspect of our human lives. We can also see the stars and planets Mercury, Venus, Mars, Jupiter, and Saturn physically without the aid of a telescope. When we do so, the wonder and beauty of the Universe we're part of can astound us. What we fail to recognise perhaps is that we are not separate from this universal system, that at some level we are immersed in their energies too. The ever-moving rhythms of the planetary bodies are an intricate aspect of our life rhythms. The only difference being that the energies of most stars and planets are invisible to us. Collectively, we don't yet understand that we not only receive, but we are, the energy of the Universe.

How does this work? The phrase 'as above so below' is apt to describe this. Just as the Sun radiates as a huge source of light and life for our planet and humanity, other planets transmit energy. We are immersed in a universal field of energy, constantly changing. We could consider this to be like walking through a field of invisible rays, much as we are living in background radiation, mobile phone signals, radio waves and so on without seeing them. Our consciousness is subtly aware of this energy flow. Yet consciousness itself is still a mystery to the scientific mind. Generally, it is defined as the state of being aware of and responsive to one's surroundings. It is seen as a product of the brain. But is it? Or is this merely a scientific theory yet to be verified. Spiritual belief systems suggest the opposite; that the brain is an instrument of consciousness. This broader definition suggests that consciousness is all that is, formed and formless. Within the field of infinite consciousness, human beings have individualised consciousness. Astrology acts as a bridge of language and understanding between the energy of the universe and every human being.

The innate connection between universe and individual is demonstrated through an astrological birth-chart. The chart operates as a map of consciousness. Having just taken physical embodiment, a birth chart can be considered as the individual's soul map for life. Not as a static or fatalistic way of being – for the universe is infinitely expanding. Planetary bodies, even our Earth, are always moving. The chart acts as a map of individual potential to evolve in a way of response, expression, choice, and consciousness through a lifetime. Charts work for countries too, and for human evolution. For as new planets are discovered, they mirror the potential of our growing consciousness here on Earth. They indicate readiness for a shift of consciousness on a global scale.

A cosmic pointer to the Dark Feminine

Science now knows that a dance of energetic particles lies the at the core of all matter. Sub-atomic particles are constantly interchanging, creating dynamic patterns that we see as solid. These interactions give rise to the apparently stable world of form, yet the truth of the sub-atomic world is chaos in flow, albeit with an underlying set of principles. These very smallest aspects of life are mirroring the cosmic dance of black holes, stars, planets, moons, asteroids, and other cosmic phenomena. The rhythm of these interactions is the dance of life and death, chaos, and creativity. It is the dance of life itself, vastly mysterious, infinite, ever-expanding. This is the world of the Dark Feminine, the Mystery of chaos from which order and form appear.

For me, there is an intimate connection to the presence of the Dark Feminine in the discovery of dark matter in our universe. Astrophysicists are aware of this invisible subtle energy, yet as with many of the Dark Feminine archetypes within us, it essentially remains a mystery. Dark matter cannot be seen directly. It is only known through some of its effects. It neither emits nor absorbs light. Its existence is inferred only by its gravitational effects on light and visible matter in the form of planets, stars, and other bodies.

To see the potential link between dark matter and the Dark Feminine, we must explore the correlation between the initial discovery of planets and global social movements, such as the American and French Revolutions. Over centuries of astrological research, it has become apparent that a connection exists between the discovery of planets, mass social movements, major advances in knowledge and inventions that change our human lives. It's as if different forces of the universe become available consciously to us here on Earth on their discovery and as we evolve. Their discovery is a mirror for new ways of being for us here on Planet Earth.

The discovery of Uranus (the planetary frequency that we receive as high frequency 'electrical' energy) broadly aligns with breakthroughs in electrical inventions: the lightning rod, the battery and electric motor. The discovery of Pluto (the planet symbolizing the Underworld, power, and the processes of death and rebirth) coincided with the splitting of the atom and the rise of fascism. World War II followed, with the building of the atomic bomb, the use of concentration camps and other horrors, calling into question our responsible use of power and force here on Earth. It could be said that we entered the Underworld at this time. Eventually this also led to the development of atomic power stations, and yet more questions on the same theme of power that we are still facing. The discovery of Chiron, known through mythology to represent the archetype of the Wounded Healer, heralded the start of the New Age Movement and alternative therapies becoming more widely accepted in mainstream culture. The existence of dark matter, unknown until the 1930's and not verified until the 1980's, points towards another potential shift for humanity. Scientists now know that it plays an important role in the formation of galaxies i.e., in creation. What it means in our human lives is yet to be seen. My gut feeling is it's connected to the Dark Mother. For just like Dark Matter, she is behind all forms of life including cosmic bodies, holding everything together.

Contrary to the esoteric belief that the universe is filled entirely with light energy, astronomy tells us that about 84 percent of the matter in the universe does not absorb or emit it. Dark matter came to be known as a universal force through its effects on light, not through its own visibility. This was verified in 1998 by two teams of astronomers, who measured light coming from exploding stars. Theoretical physicist, Stephen

Hawking, also linked dark matter with black holes at a similar time. His theories shocked the scientific world, as they created a paradox of two fundamental theories. To cut a long and very scientific story short, the contradiction of theories was resolved through discovering what are now known as 'hairy black holes.' Can you believe that name! On discovering this, my fascination with the Dark Feminine was seriously piqued, for my intuition had already linked Black Holes with the creative power of the Dark Mother. I have long intuited, black holes to act like cosmic vaginas.

Through their vast gravitational fields, black holes both take in and digest planetary bodies, even gigantic stars, and eject ingested material to form new universal systems. They take in, gestate the material taken in, birth and create. For me, this play of energies in the universe is a vast mirror for our sexual creative energy here on Earth. It's the natural power of death and life, in our tiny human bodies and the most massive forces of the universe, some the size of over one billion suns. If this is indeed so (and I wonder how science might even begin to prove this) the term 'hairy black holes' would be apt indeed. Furthermore, it is now known that black holes act via a process astrophysicists are calling superradiance. When this occurs, a black hole boosts any nearby light into intense levels of energy. It's an interaction where dark seems to feed light, energising and expanding it. To me, it's symbolic of our transformative processes, where we release our darkness, evolving and expanding our consciousness. I cannot help but get super-excited when I make these correlations, and even that state is a mirror of what is happening at the sub-atomic level. Physics now knows that an electron enters what's called 'an excited state' when it temporarily occupies an energy state greater than its ground state.

The mystery of black holes is just one of many ongoing discoveries within the field of astrophysics. Scientific research often generates contradictory theories as part of the unravelling process of discovery. This is the energetic realm of dwarf planet Eris (see Chapter 2). The discovery of Eris, first seen in 2005, generated conflict within the scientific community about the nature of planetary bodies. Eris is known as the Goddess of Discord. She symbolises what happens when something unexpectedly disrupts an existing system and how disruption has potential to bring new life. In 2005, Eris's new presence as part of our universe generated a seemingly insoluble conflict of contradictory theories. This conflict was resolved not through an either/or battle, entrenched in the duality of opposing viewpoints. Rather it was approached from the perspective of paradox and the need to go beyond it. Theoretical physicist Stephen Hawking grappled with the contradictions, invoking controversy through his courage to challenge the status quo. He was unafraid to disrupt the current system of scientific knowledge and his discovery evolved scientific understanding. It's a profound mirror of Eris energy in action.

Disrupting existing forms i.e., the necessary process of change, is a primary quality of the Dark Feminine. In her realm, resolution does not come through the either/or paradigm but through holding the tension of both/and in a process of discovery. It's the embrace of all elements of life, dark and light. A simple example of this in our lives is learning to walk; it is both difficult and exciting. In embracing the contradiction of our desire to explore and challenge of that growth point, we evolve. Strangely enough, recent new discoveries about black holes show that their deep black density is equalled by their light, which can span the entire electromagnetic spectrum, from X-rays to radio waves. They reveal to us: nothing is at it seems. Dark and light are always in interplay. The nature of life is revealed as our consciousness expands to encompass it.

Wholeness embraced

If we desire to know ourselves as whole, the embrace of both dark and light within ourselves and life is the path. This is the way of the Dark Feminine. She guards the threshold of new consciousness emerging, the conscious unifying of disembodied spirit and unconscious matter, of the divine and instinct. This pathway involves reclaiming the energy in us that has become distorted as a force of separation. It's the journey of rediscovering and reclaiming the light in our shadows, and the shadows in our light.

Our cultural and personal tendencies towards labelling experience, other individuals, or our self as 'good' or bad' is a habit of perspective. Perhaps it is time we grew out of it. Not in the denial of what is healthy or not, what is conscious or unconscious, but to grow the realisation that life is constantly expressing through differing frequencies, all with a potential to evolve and expand. Is it wise to label experience 'bad', when studies on the effects of adversity reveal it makes us both stronger and happier? Through its challenge we are forced to question and uplift our beliefs, create new life meaning and stretch into more fulfilment. Is it wise to judge others as wicked without considering what lies behind their behaviour, or recognising that only wounded people hurt others? This doesn't mean that we don't need laws and boundaries, or that we don't discern what's appropriate for our self and take action to protect our self where necessary. It doesn't mean there are not beings whose desire is create pain or suffering. It means we choose to stop being victims of our shadow, of others, or the dark side of life. It simply means we understand that life is both dark and light, without judgment, without projection, but with appropriate action. The appearance of darkness, its perceived ugliness or mystery, is just the way it looks and feels. Potentially it's a doorway, a portal to awakening.

I invite you think about a natural compost pile – full of rotting material, dark and steaming. Now consider that compost pile once it's fulfilled its process. It becomes dark, rich, fertile food for new life, full of goodness.

Our perception changes, doesn't it? The Dark Feminine invites us to go beyond appearances, to be free of reaction to appearance and to recognise that everything has its place, its timing, and its purpose in life. We have choice in our perspective. Be like Uranus, the Sky God, and thrust what we don't like into the bowels of the Earth in the attempt to forget it (much like we do with our rubbish), only to find it comes back to bite us. Or face it, discover what lies behind its appearance, within its mystery, and evolve.

Embracing the Dark Feminine is not for self-improvement, or to fix what we think is wrong with us, but to discover that the divine permeates the whole of life no matter how ugly or distorted it seems. It's a paradox. The darkest, seemingly unacceptable, aspects of our/Her nature offer us stepping-stones into deep dimensions of our souls. Without embracing the shadows of our darkness, we cannot embody fully, we cannot feel deep enough, we lack understanding and compassion. When we don't know the full intimacy of our presence as Sacred Feminine, we close in fear instead of remaining open hearted whilst acting from wisdom. She is the entry point to the full eroticism of our desire nature, to engage the deep participation with the whole of life that brings fulfilment. She is shrouded in mystery, behind the scenes of our lives and yet tangible, only known through feeling our way in the dark. She cannot be boxed or conceptualized. At best, we can only discover how to be with Her energies in us and align as willingly as possible with Her life-death-life cycles as the truth of our being in form.

Tantric philosophy states that life force is more concentrated in a female body so we may fully be the dance of birth, life and death creating form on Earth. We are like the black holes in our universe, filled with the power to birth, create and destroy. Our understanding and respect of that power in ourselves as women is fundamental to the shift that needs to take place in collective consciousness now. The Sacred Feminine is calling to emerge in her purity and power in all of us. To unveil her we must travel through her shadows both personally and collectively. It starts with each one of us. The time is now! Understanding the collective patterns that have arisen over eons and how they are operating through our consciousness now, we may transmute them. In transmuting them we connect with their great gifts. We reclaim the innate power of Sacred Feminine wisdom, caring for each other and our Earth. In the reclamation of ancient wisdom, in the evolution of finer frequencies of consciousness, we engender deeper values.

The potentials for the evolution of our collective consciousness are both potent and vast. Yet, without our participation in our own fullness, however that appears in the moment, nothing happens. The fact is: darkness exists. The biggest question is: how do I relate to it? To be the evolving wholeness we are, we must visit this question consciously. We must choose to enter the gates of the Dark Feminine consciously. There's a myth from the Hindu tradition that describes the necessity of passing through this gateway.

The God Shiva and his wife, the Goddess Sati, are arguing furiously. Shiva (who finds his bliss in the deep stillness of meditation) has had enough. He heads for the door in an endeavour to escape Sati's chaos. As he does so, she grows fangs, blood starts to come from her mouth, her body begins to shine with deep blackness yet the light of ten thousand suns radiates from her.

Shiva runs. She multiplies. Wherever he turns, she faces him in forms both beautiful and terrible. Shiva realises he cannot escape. He faces one of her forms, with the question, "Where is my beautiful wife, Sati?' She responds, 'Don't you see? There is only I'.

Shiva realises this as truth. He sees he cannot escape Her; He can only go through Her – and so he surrenders.

She is everywhere, in everything, in us. Try as we might, we cannot avoid Her. To know our evolving wholeness, we must go through Her.

Chapter 1

Strip Away Your Old Skin –

Queen of Heaven

&

Earth Inanna

Death's hand
caresses my heart,
squeezes then
wrenches open,
quenches
with sweet
honey
that pours
as pain roars.
Duality
has no place here
for as I journey deep,
I discover
they walk
hand in hand.
An ecstatic edge
wherein death
births
new Life
and Life
inevitably
contains the demise

of what has been
including
this self.
Gaia
is our greatest teacher
in the natural rhythms,
life and death,
light and dark,
walking hand in hand
in every moment.
Inanna,
the Queen
who dares
to go deep
is our greatest teacher.
Revealing
heavenly light
and earthy dark
as Her,
as our,
fullest nature
of Feminine.

Cassandra Eve

Queen of heaven and earth

Archetype: The Queen of Heaven becoming the Queen of Heaven & Earth.

Symbols: Eight-pointed star; the planet Venus & her orbit; the lion; a crown & sceptre; gold, carnelian & lapis; apples & dates; a hook-shaped twisted knot of reeds, known as Inanna's knot, representing the doorpost of the storehouse & symbolising plenty.

Message: Be willing to go deep. Strip away your old skins. In your nakedness lies renewal.

Inanna themes: Descent and ascent; risk-taking; courage & sacrifice; an initiation into spiritual maturity; death & rebirth as an evolutionary passage to embodiment.

What the Inanna archetype calls for: Willingness, courage, sacrifice.

Also known as: Syncretised with Astarte and Ishtar.

The goddess Inanna appears first in the ancient land of Sumer, around 4000BCE. Her existence was discovered through a series of epic poems written in cuneiform on clay tablets, the earliest written artefacts so far discovered. Inanna is an early goddess form associated with both the planet and the goddess Venus. She carries similar symbology: love, beauty, and sexuality but also war, justice, and political power, yet being a more ancient archetype, she has deeper roots. Inanna was venerated by the Akkadians, Babylonians, and Assyrians, under the name Ishtar or Astarte. She is one of the group of deities named Anunnaki by the ancient Sumerians, Akkadians, Assyrians, and Babylonians.

The ancient Sumerians created one of humanity's first great civilizations. Their homeland in Mesopotamia, called Sumer, emerged roughly 6,000 years ago along the floodplains between the Tigris and Euphrates rivers in present day Iraq and Syria. In the earliest Sumerian writings, the Anunnaki are descendants of An and Ki, the God of the Heavens, and the Goddess of Earth. Some modern sources suggest they were an alien race that came to Earth and interbred with humans. Certainly, these early cultures were responsible for rapid advances in agricultural technology, inventing the plough and canals. Their culture was abundant. They also invented wheeled chariots and the first known form of writing, cuneiform.

What we now know about Inanna comes from epic poems written around 2300BCE, depicting what is known as The Cycle of Inanna. These stories, originally written in cuneiform on clay tablets, were discovered at Nineveh (modern Iraq) in the mid 19th century and are written in the form of poems or hymns. The discovered tablets comprise different fragments that have been named 'The Huluppu Tree' (we will explore this one in the chapter on Black Moon Lilith); the deeply erotic 'Courtship of Dumuzi and Inanna'; perhaps the most well-known, 'The Descent of Inanna'; along with seven hymns of praise. It appears these were all composed by the high priestess Enheduanna of the Sumerian city-state of Ur, in about 2300 BCE. How remarkable that we know so much about a woman who lived over 4,000 years ago in what is present-day Iraq! The Hymn to Inanna is 700 years older than the Egyptian Book of the Dead, more than 1,000 years older than the I Ching and 1,500 years older than the Greek epics, The Odyssey, The Iliad, and the Hebrew Bible. How come it is not more widely known?

The Descent of Inanna describes, as the title suggests, the Sumerian goddess Inanna's descent into the Underworld. It predates and certainly establishes a foundation for later stories of similar descents. This poem is particularly poignant because the Akkadian civilisation would decline not long after this poem was composed. Inanna's descent is a profound teaching story, clearly relevant in its time and even more so now. Through the alchemical process of Inanna's journey to meet her dark sister Ereshkigal, she becomes the Queen of Heaven & Earth. Inanna represents not only the gateway to our shadow realms but gives us keys to the entire process of death and rebirth, however it appears in our lives. She is the gateway to the Dark Goddess. As such, she represents for us, the evolving journey of integrating light and dark aspects of the self, to attain fuller embodiment of our divine potential.

Her-story

In the epic Descent of Inanna, Queen Inanna descends into the Underworld, the realm of her sister, Queen of the Dead, Ereshkigal. Before we explore that potent myth however, we must encounter Inanna differently, in her youthful role as Queen of Heaven. For firstly she appears in tales named 'The Huluppu Tree', 'Inanna and the God of Wisdom' and 'The Courtship of Inanna and Dumuzi'. These epic poems reveal a maiden queen testing her power, maturing in service, and entering womanhood. It is the journey through the archetypal maturing cycle of feminine energy through the phases of maiden, mother, queen, and crone, as is also reflected in the Moon's waxing and waning, the seasons of nature and our menstrual cycle.

The Huluppu Tree could be considered a Sumerian creation myth. It relates how in the beginning times, Heaven, Earth, Man, and the Underworld were separated, each with their own guardian or ruler. In this time, a tree, the Huluppu Tree, was first planted on the banks of the Euphrates River. We might consider this tree, this first tree, representative of the Tree of Life. It was nurtured by the river and held by its banks, until eventually a storm carried it away.

The young Inanna came across the tree as it floated down river. She plucked it from the river, planted it in her garden and cared for it. Yet she did not do this without an agenda. Constantly she was wondering: how long will it take this tree to grow? How long will it be before I have a shining throne to sit upon; how much longer before I have a shining bed?

Many years passed. The tree grew and strengthened. Over time a serpent nested in its roots; the Anzu bird nested in its branches and the dark maid Lilith (explored in Chapter 6) built her home in its trunk. Inanna wept at their presence. She wanted rid of them.

First, Inanna appealed to her brother Utu to help her. He would not. Then she approached the warrior Gilgamesh for his help. Gilgamesh, being a warrior and intent on pleasing Inanna, immediately cut down the tree. He struck the serpent; the bird flew off with its young and Lilith fled into wild, uninhabited places. Gilgamesh then proceeded to carve a throne and a bed for Inanna, whilst she created for him, a mukku and pikku (symbols of royal power). They served each other in their quest for power.

In the next tale, God of Wisdom, Enki, and Inanna are having a party. The texts state 'Enki and Inanna drank beer together. They drank more beer together. They drank more and more beer together...... They toasted each other, they challenged each other.' In his drunken state Enki passes more and more roles, gifts, qualities, and benefits, including the crown, the holy shrine, the role of Priestess of Heaven, and many symbols of power to Inanna. To each offer, Inanna replies 'I take them!'. Having received all these windfalls, she left for home.

Emerging from his drunken state, Enki enquired of his servant where were the crown and all his regalia - all of which he had freely given Inanna. He was horrified to realise what he had done. Seven times he sent his servants in various forms – monsters, sea serpents, demons, giants - to claim back the gifts. Each time Ninshubur, Inanna's servant, retrieves them from the aggressors. Eventually, realising she had to stop this conflict in some way, Inanna takes all the gifts and even more offerings to the city of Uruk. Here she holds a great celebratory feast for the people and places the symbols of power in a temple. Enki, moved by her actions, relinquishes his claim on them. He realises that Inanna has shown her growing maturity and sovereignty through this act of sharing and service.

Many of the tablets of Inanna's mythology are fragmentary or lost. There is one more tale that relates her growing womanhood though: The Courtship of Inanna and Dumuzi. The story begins with the Sun God, Utu, telling Inanna he is preparing a bridal sheet for her. When she asks who will take her to her marriage bed, she is horrified to hear her bridegroom is the shepherd Dumuzi. She feels he is beneath her. Eventually Dumuzi begins to woo Inanna, stating that despite his being a shepherd, his breeding is as good as hers. They talk. Love begins to arise. Inanna's mother, Ningal, also commands Inanna to bathe, prepare herself and take Dumuzi to her bed. The story then unfolds in erotic verse, relating their lovemaking and passion, connecting it to the fertility of nature and their lands. After many nights of passionate loving, Inanna states Dumuzi is her king.

Finally, we come to the 'Descent of Inanna' tale. Having claimed both her sovereignty, her role in service to the community through her connection to Enki, and her womanhood, Inanna is ready for something more. She is drawn to enter her sister Ereshkigal's realm, to claim her right to the title, Queen of Heaven & Earth.

Ereshkigal is the older sister of the goddess Inanna, named Queen of the Dead who rules the Underworld. Her name translates as 'Queen of the Great Below' or 'Lady of the Great Place.' She was deemed responsible for both keeping the dead within her realm and preventing the living from entering, thus preserving the integrity and truth of the afterlife.

The introductory passage of another ancient Sumerian epic poem, 'Gilgamesh, Enkidu, and the Netherworld,' suggests Ereshkigal was abducted and taken down to the Underworld by the Kur (demons or dragons from the Underworld. She was forced to become Queen there against her will). In certain tales it appears that Inanna is somehow to blame. Although the gods tried to rescue Ereshkigal, they were not able to do so, as no one, not even the gods, were able to return from the realm of the dead. As we shall see from both Inanna's descent and the chapter on Persephone, this is a tale that repeats throughout history and different cultural mythology, yet with a different ending for both these feminine archetypes.

Ereshkigal is known as a formidable goddess of great power yet also one who forgives an injustice in the interests of the greater good. She has accepted her role as Queen of the Underworld although her great pain persists. She therefore represents the power to transmute and acts as a role model for human beings. If Ereshkigal could suffer injustice and yet perform her role in accordance with the will of the gods, then human beings could do no less. Her deeper significance as Queen of the Underworld was to keep the dead in the realm where they belonged and the living out. The seven gates of the Underworld were constructed for this purpose. Even Inanna must face these locked gates and adhere to Ereshkigal's ruling in her own realm.

Despite the rules, and the seven locked gates, Inanna decides to go into the Underworld to observe the funeral rites for her sister's husband. In the opening lines of 'The Descent of Inanna', we are told Inanna abandoned the realm of Heaven and her earthly life to make this descent. Despite her sacrifice, she is not welcome in her sister's realm. Inanna must intuit this coming lack of welcome, for she adorns herself with her queenly garments and objects of power in preparation for her journey. She also commands her minister Ninshubur that if she does not come back within three days, Ninshubur should seek help from the gods to ensure her safe return.

Meanwhile, in the Underworld, Ereshkigal is not happy to hear of her sister's descent towards her realm. She instructs her gatekeeper Neti to make Inanna remove her crown, jewellery, and ornaments of power at each of the seven gates, before admitting her to the throne room. So, when Inanna stands before Ereshkigal, she is naked. At this point, before the sisters even meet, the Annuna, judges of the Underworld, pass judgment against her, saying she is responsible for the death of Ereshkigal's husband. Ereshkigal kills her sister and hangs her corpse on a hook on the wall.

After three days and nights waiting for Inanna, Ninshubur follows her queen's command to instigate a rescue. Here we encounter yet another reference that links with the Christian crucifixion story, mentioned in the introduction chapter. Ninshubur pleads with all the gods to bring Inanna back, but they refuse her; all except Enki. Enki takes the dirt from under his fingernails to create two galla – tiny, sexless demon beings. He gives them the food and water of life to revive Inanna, then sends them down into the Underworld with precise instructions on how to rescue Inanna.

The galla enter the Underworld like flies and, following Enki's specific instructions, they attach themselves closely to Ereshkigal. The Queen of the Dead is in much distress, experiencing profound pain. The galla empathise with Ereshgikal, simply by mirroring her cries of agony. In gratitude for their empathy, she offers them whatever gift they ask for. As commanded by Enki, the galla respond that they wish only for the corpse that hangs from the hook on the wall. Ereshkigal gives Inanna's body to them, and they revive her with the food and water of life given them by Enki.

When Inanna rises from the dead, the galla immediately escort her out of the Underworld. As she rises, she reclaims her ornaments of power at each gate. But there is a price for Inanna's return; the galla must take another down into the Underworld in her place. They drag Inanna's husband Dumuzi – who in her absence has been abusing her throne - down to the Underworld as her replacement. Dumuzi is eventually permitted to return to Heaven for half the year, while his sister Geshtinanna remains in the Underworld for the other half. We see a similar theme in Greek mythology through the archetype Persephone, another Queen of the Underworld, who must descend and return every year (see Chapter 4).

Why does Inanna choose to go into the Underworld? Apparently, it is for the funeral rites of Ereshkigal's husband. The hymns of praise also speak of her wiliness, her determination and selfishness, along with the capacity to trick other rulers and Gods so she could accumulate their powers for herself. So it could be that Inanna has mixed or hidden motives and is trying to take over her sister's queendom. Yet as we shall discover in the section on astrology, through an association with the planet Venus's orbit, descent into the Underworld is a natural part of the cycle of wholeness. Whatever her motives, unwittingly Inanna was fulfilling her evolutionary calling, the opportunity to become the queen of both Heaven and Earth.

Inanna's descent mirrors what we might now call the quest for soul retrieval, or a challenging and painful initiation. It certainly lends itself to a Jungian interpretation of a journey to wholeness by confronting one's darker half. In this tale the dark half is mirrored by Ereshkigal and her actions. Each sister is one half of a whole. We might know a similar initiation in the calling to face our shadow, in relationship conflict, or in life circumstances that challenge us beyond measure. As we awaken, we all reach a point where we must choose, as Inanna did, to enter the darkness willingly.

Inanna's Place in the Universe – Astronomy & Astrology

Inanna is associated through ancient astrology and mythology with Venus, the Morning & Evening Star, visible in our morning and evening skies shortly before dawn or after sunset. The appearances of Venus are not stars, but aspects of the Venus orbit with the Earth around the Sun. Like Inanna, Venus is known as Queen of Heaven & Earth. Her phases reflect the different aspects of Inanna's mythology, including descent into the Underworld. We now know that the Venus orbit when mapped with the Earth's orbit around the Sun over an eight-year cycle, creates what can be seen either as a pentagram or a Flower of Life symbol. Inanna's passage through the seven gates refers to the Venus-Moon conjunctions in both her ascent and descent phases. A Venus-Moon conjunction is a gateway in transformation and healing our connection to the Sacred Feminine energies. I explored this in depth, along with its links with creation and the template for physical life in humanity and on Earth, in the Venus chapter in my book 'Sacred Pathways – Discovering Divine Feminine Archetypes in You'.

The cycle of Venus was recognised and revered by many ancient cultures. The people of Inanna's time, the Sumerians, and Babylonians, celebrated the cycle of Venus every eight years when she rose as a morning star near the Spring Equinox. The Mayans calculated the Venus cycle with incredible precision too. To them, the Morning Star phase of Venus revealed the dark face of the Goddess and the Evening Star phase, her beneficence. They even planned their conquests and wars through these phases. The Neolithic peoples of Ireland clearly had sophisticated methods of astronomical alignment too. Newgrange in Co Meath was built to track the Winter Solstice and the once in eight-year heliacal rise of Venus half hour before the Sun. At Newgrange, the long dark passage that leads to the inner altar is lit annually by the Winter Solstice Sun and once in eight years, also by Venus. Clearly these ancient cultures were intimate with the Venus cycle despite their lack of sophisticated star-gazing equipment.

Astrologically, the phases of Venus – and so Inanna, as the ancient face of this archetype - Morning and Evening Star, her conjunctions with the Sun, plus her retrograde movement, point to differing faces of the Divine Feminine. As Venus's orbit is so intricately linked with the Earth's, they symbolise our evolutionary potential here on Earth. The ancients portrayed Inanna as a Goddess with two sides, reflecting humanity: love, beauty, and sex, but also war, combat, and political power. The Morning & Evening Star reflect these two aspects. Venus's retrograde journey and inferior conjunction with the Sun close to the Earth, and exterior conjunction with and disappearance behind the Sun, representing the Underworld journey and the potential development of new qualities within our individual (Morning Star) and collective (Evening Star) creative nature.

Through the different Venus phases, we are called to pass through the seven gates of the Underworld, just like Inanna. In doing so, we are called to surrender what no longer serves our growth and potentially realise new frequencies of fertility, with the potential to embody finer potentials. We die to our old self, to be born anew. In this evolutionary death and rebirth process, the Inanna archetype invites us to access, transmute and embody the Dark Feminine aspects of our nature, reflected in her sister Ereshkigal. This journey carries Venus/Inanna themes of relationship, beauty and creative power, balance, harmony, and sovereignty, in service to collective social themes of service, peace-making and unity. Inanna unifies dark and light aspects of both Goddess archetypes as Queen of Heaven and Earth.

The Venus placements in an individual's birth-chart, along with the specific Venus phase at birth, can reveal intimate keys to our capacity for self-love, and the ease or challenges of our relationship connections, intimacy, and creative potency. Venus is representative of our capacity to give and receive freely and to create. Depending on her phase, she reflects our willingness or resistance to let go our current creation, to journey through the dark places of our psyche so we may serve collective evolution.

My journey with Inanna

Death is a great teacher. We face it psychologically whenever change arrives at our door; often when we least expect it, and mostly when we least want it. Yet, if we look deep, we might realise that in predictable ways, we are familiar with death as natural. Each day we travel between day and night; nature's seasons reflect this flow between light and dark too. Both are essential elements of life on Earth. We travel similar processes within our psyche. Both the light of joy and the grit of unexpected challenge are a natural rhythm. They arrive seemingly out of the blue, activated by events and circumstances, or sometimes simply descending on us for no apparent reason. If we're honest, we know we cannot avoid this rhythm of change, despite our preferences. For life is always moving. A psychological journey through the Underworld, through loss, is inevitable at some point. Despite its challenge, it has the potential always to bring us new life. Like Inanna, to discover what that new life is, we must be willing to go through the darkness.

I visit the beautiful island of Crete regularly, both to visit friends there and to facilitate retreats. My experience of this Greek island and its culture has always been very earthy. The land is wild, a wonderful mixture of rugged mountains, wildflower meadows, olive groves or vineyards, and glorious beaches. Nature is still mostly untouched or worked with in harmony and balance. The locals remain intimately connected to place, nature, community, and the bounty of Mother

Earth. Despite being invaded many times, the Cretans welcome strangers. It is a natural part of their way of life. I feel at home there.

I've had many profound sensual experiences of Earth connection when in Crete. The Snake Goddesses and huge phallic idols so common in this culture represent this possibility. It's as if Gaia herself is calling deeply to humans for embodiment through sexuality or a deep journey into the body in this land. I experienced a tangibly different earthy connection on one autumn visit though. It had a flavour of Inanna's descent that was surprising, yet with hindsight, completely natural. It revealed to me how intimately connected I am to the land, wherever I am.

A Cretan friend had collected me from the airport and taken me to my apartment. As always, simply being in his presence, opened my body tangibly. I knew Divine Masculine consciousness vibrating in every cell; my body was fully enjoying the penetration. Having arranged to see him the next day, I settled in, surprised to notice that there was a large group of workmen in the park area between my apartment and the sea. I saw mechanical diggers, mounds of earth, large holes; clearly there was a major reconstruction happening in what I knew to be a small war memorial garden. I wasn't initially disturbed by this disruption, as I would not be spending much time in my apartment. As the evening progressed however, I became aware of layers of emotion opening and rising through my body. It was profound grief, with no apparent reason.

I know myself well enough to simply allow and feel with presence whatever is moving through my consciousness. As I closed my eyes and dropped inside, layers of deep grief kept rising. Tears came in waves, until I found myself sobbing. As this was happening, I was aware of the mind questioning: what is this? I simply ignored it, allowing the waves of loss to move through until they naturally subsided. After this release I felt exhausted. I simply let the experience go and went to sleep.

Over the next few days my mind kept going back to what had been released, seeking understanding. Experience has shown me that if I need to know, insight will simply occur, so I kept letting go of the mind's questions. Revelation came along quite naturally further into my stay. Having been at the beach, I came back to my apartment to find the blinds fully drawn. I could not move them so called on the manager, Georgios, for help. As he opened the blinds, we both stepped out onto my terrace for a chat. 'What are they doing over there?' I asked him casually, pointing to the workmen. 'They are creating a children's playground' he said. Then he proceeded to tell me what had happened on the site.

In the Second World War German invasion of Crete, Rethymno (specifically the area where I was staying) was one of the first coastal areas where German troops parachuted in. As they did so, locals with guns and whatever weapons they could find, naturally defended their homes. Days later, the Germans, who had now invaded Crete en masse, began their reprisals. They gathered a large group of locals, including women and children, on the very land we were looking at and gunned them down. Immediately I knew what had passed through me. It was collective grief that had been held in the land since those days. The movement of earth to create the children's garden and play area had disturbed it. In my openness to simply allow the darkness of grief held in the land to move through, I had been an available vessel to transform it. My life experience of transforming grief was a training for this. Inanna and Ereshkigal were working naturally through me. It was yet another, albeit somewhat different, Underworld descent.

Inanna's Message: Be willing to go deep. Strip away your old skins. In your nakedness lies renewal.

The willingness to take a risk

The question that haunted me when this book first appeared in my consciousness was: does Inanna belong in a book on the Dark Feminine? As I stayed with the reflection, it came to me clearly: yes, she belongs here. For she is the bridge that takes us from Venus's beauty and creative power into the deep, towards our shadows. Inanna teaches us; be willing to go deep. Strip away your old skins. In your nakedness lies renewal and deeper embodiment.

Inanna as Queen of Heaven has reached the peak of her Venusian expression; one could also say, her self-centred creation. She is a youthful Goddess who has thrown herself into life, expressing her sexuality and her fullest self-expression. Inanna knows she is a queen already; she takes what she wants; she gives freely too. She asserts her power. She has sovereignty. She is not deeply rooted though. For that, she must descend.

Why did Inanna choose to take the journey into the Underworld? Was she really going to mourn her brother-in-law? Or was this merely a ruse? Was she bored, looking for an adventure? Perhaps she was curious about death, not knowing an encounter with her dark sister would mean her own demise? Had her role as Queen of Heaven lost its glamour perhaps? Maybe she intuits that there is more to life and wants it, without realising the cost. Was Inanna consciously seeking to take over her sister's realm? Was she arrogant enough to think it would be possible? Did she really know what she was undertaking when she decided to enter the gates of the Underworld? So many questions, and we cannot truly know her motives. Curiosity or hubris can take us exactly where evolution does its best work on and through us. Our part is to say, 'Yes', or at least be willing to look a little deeper.

In the text translation of The Descent of Inanna by Diane Wolkstein and Samuel Noah Kramer, it is said 'From the Great Above she opened her ear to the Great Below. From the Great Above the goddess opened her ear to the Great Below. From the Great Above Inanna opened her ear to the Great Below.' Here we can see a further perspective on Inanna's descent. This text seems to indicate that Inanna heard a calling. As some of us know, that mysterious calling cannot be denied if we are awake. It nags and niggles us. Call it intuition, a knowing, or something more clearly defined, there is an impulse in a certain direction without fully knowing why. The 'why' is extraneous, only to be discovered with hindsight, if at all. The alluring potential of the unknown is upon us.

Whatever Inanna's calling, or perhaps her whim, there is no doubt she begins the journey willingly. She is also wise enough to know she cannot go unprepared. It's interesting that in Sumerian 'ear and wisdom' are the same word. Inanna's ear is also attuned to her wisdom. Perhaps this is the moment of truth when she realises her experience as Queen of Heaven is incomplete as Feminine, without the knowing of what's beneath, deep in the earth.

As Inanna prepares, she ensures support for her return, from her minister Ninshubur. She empowers herself with all her regalia. As a sky goddess, Queen of Heaven, she has the overview. She certainly has no experience of the dark realm though. Yet she is willing. She has courage, or arrogance, or a mix of the two. Perhaps she is being provocative, simply wanting what she wants without sensitivity or respect to her sister's feelings. Yet without doubt, she is compelled to go, stepping into the unknown. As such, she represents in us, the knowing to take a risk, to step beyond our known experience and enter the Mystery. In doing so, the potential is that we discover this journey is not something we do, it is the journey that does us, through our willingness to be undone.

Entering the unknown

When we take a step into the unknown, although the mind may project certain expectations as a means of security, we truly have no idea of what is to come. Sometimes we receive intimations though. As Inanna prepares for her journey, she receives a taste of what the journey will bring. She has already abandoned her queendom and her temples, leaving her earthly responsibilities in the hands of her minister Ninshubur. As she moves towards the first gate of the Underworld, the seriousness of her quest becomes more apparent. She is challenged by Neti, the chief gatekeeper, 'Who are you? Why have you come?', he asks. For Inanna not to be immediately recognised and honoured is unusual indeed. Nor is she is given admittance. Neti goes to Ereshkigal and is told 'one by one, open each gate a crack. Let Inanna enter. As she enters, remove her royal garments. Let the holy priestess of heaven enter bowed low.' (from the Descent of Inanna) That she must 'enter bowed low' gives us clues to the ensuing journey.

At this first gate Inanna's crown is removed. She immediately reacts. She is not used to being questioned or being treated with such indignity. She is told to be quiet, with the statement, 'The ways of the Underworld are perfect. They may not be questioned' (from the Descent of Inanna). At each gate as she questions, the response is the same. At the second gate, small lapis beads are removed from Inanna's neck (in some versions of the myth, these are earrings). At the third gate, she is required to surrender her double-stranded lapis beads. At the fourth gate, her breastplate is taken. At the fifth, her gold ring is removed. At the sixth gate, her lapis measuring rod and line are taken from her hand. When Inanna enters the seventh gate her robe is removed. Finally, she enters Ereshkigal's throne room, naked and bowed down.

Inanna's passage through each gate symbolises our journey of letting go, descent into the unknown and unknowable. The circumstances of our descent will always be different, but the actual journey is represented energetically by the body's major energy centres (also known as chakras) from crown to root - also seven - into the darkness of earth. Throughout our life we accumulate experience, knowledge, roles, and possessions. These form, at least in part, our identity. Identity is not just rooted in the mind; it's held in each of these energetic centres. They are the energetic building blocks of our sense of self. Periodically we are called to clear and cleanse them of what no longer serves our growth, just as we are challenged to let go of different aspects of our life.

We arrive on this earth naked; we leave it similarly. At the point of death, every way we know our self, including our body, must be let go. Sometimes through our lives, we go through a psychological death experience: divorce, a loss or redundancy, a serious illness, or a major life change. Inanna's descent reveals to us that the demise of what we think, have, own, and know – the death of our existing forms and ways of being - is an aspect of life's natural cycle. There is no doubt this is challenging, yet it's fact of life. Whether we willingly surrender to this fact is another matter, for we live on a planet of choice. Resistant to the fact or not, the truth is life moves. Inanna's journey symbolises this. Her descent indicates what must be released at each energy centre in this process. The potential is we eventually come to a point of renewal. But first we must be stripped bare of our creation, our attachments, our identity.

Gate 1: The Gate of Authority

At Gate 1 Inanna is forced to remove her crown. She has no choice if she desires to go further into her sister's realm. We can understand 'crown' as both literally and spiritually symbolic. Inanna is entering the domain of Ereshkigal's queendom; her authority has no place there. This is the Gate of Authority, where Inanna must surrender the Shugurra, her Crown of the Steppe. She is stripped of her authority, her majesty and her connection to Heaven, her divinity.

93

In our own lives this gate symbolises the crown chakra, our self-knowledge, identity, role, or image in the world, along with our spiritual identity, our divine knowing, or beliefs. When we face this gate in our lives, we are called to let go of our preconceived ideas, even our connection to, or experience of, our divinity. This is also where we must surrender what is most of value in our lives. Just as at physical death, we must leave everything, even what is most precious.

Gate 2: The Gate of Perception

The second gate into the Underworld corresponds to the brow chakra, also known as the third eye. At this gate Inanna's small lapis beads are removed. Some sources suggest these are her lapis earrings, some her beads. The gemstone lapis lazuli represents truth and wisdom, having some of the oldest societal uses. It is found in numerous ancient artifacts including Tutankhamun's sarcophagus and was widely used by renaissance painters. Throughout the ages, Lapis Lazuli has been viewed as a stone of royalty. Its energy promotes heightened mental capacity and inner visions, particularly when used in meditation. It opens the third eye, enabling access to higher knowledge and truth. At this gate Inanna is stripped of her wisdom, along with her capacity to journey psychically, her sensitivity to see and hear beyond the norm.

In our own lives Inanna's sacrifice at this gate symbolises the falling away of intuitive knowing and wisdom, as well as our capacity to depend on any of the minds' tools. Our religious or philosophical attachments disappear, as we realise, we are entering the unknown. Our arrogance at thinking we know anything is challenged. We cannot know what this journey will bring, however it looks. We are offered the opportunity to simply live each step of the journey as it unfolds, without foresight or control.

Gate 3: The Gate of Self Expression

At the third gate Inanna is forced to remove the double strand of beads at her breast. The third gate corresponds to the throat chakra, the seat of self-expression and will. At this gate, Inanna surrenders her existing ways of expressing the truth and authenticity of her being, along with habits of self-determination, the right to ask or demand anything.

In our own lives this can represent our need to let go of how we like life to look and be, our imposition of personal will through control. Our old ways of self-expression and communication are being called to evolve – the habits of speech we have inherited, whether our own or another's words; the ways we adapt our self-expression to fit in; being nice, being accommodating or inauthentic.

Gate 4: The Gate of the Heart

The fourth gateway requires that Inanna surrenders her breastplate, that which shields her heart. As her regalia is removed, Inanna is more and more naked. In this act Inanna becomes truly exposed. The fourth gate is also known as The Gate of Compassion, for it is only with an open heart that we know the true balm of love.

The fourth gateway in our lives represents the release of all the ways we don't love our self or allow love to reach us. This is accomplished through letting go of our emotional armour. There are many ways we protect our hearts, believing that our defences will protect us from hurt. Exposure can leave us feeling alone and insecure, fragile, and exposed, yet armouring always disconnects us from the potential of a real heart connection. At this gateway the ways we withhold or push for love are challenged; our strategies of playing safe, manipulating through affection or affectation; the feelings of failure in love that cause us to protect our hearts. This fourth gateway calls us to open, become vulnerable and tender in order that we may experience true intimacy with our deeper self, and potentially with another.

Gate 5: The Gate of Power

At the fifth gateway Inanna removes her golden arm-rings. The arms and hands represent our capacity for giving and receiving, actioning, holding, and gripping. We can push and pull with our arms; we can hold on with our hands. Here at this fifth gateway, representing the solar plexus centre, Inanna is challenged to give up another element of her sovereignty. She is stripped of all the ways she uses power to acquire, control and dominate through strength of will and a sense of purpose.

The solar plexus chakra is like an internal sun. It is where we experience self-esteem and confidence. Here we face questions such as: what is it you most hold onto about yourself or your life? Where is your grip tight? What makes you feel power-full? Or where do you have habits of being powerless, or avoid action? Our strategies of power or powerlessness must be let go to enter at the fifth gateway.

Gate 6: The Gate of Creativity

At Gate 6 Inanna is asked to release her lapis measuring rod and line. These represent ways of measuring the value of what is already here in form. Inanna's lapis rod and line are used to measure land, to settle disputes. They indicate how creative power may be used in here in the ways of the Sacred Feminine and Masculine – to measure, to define and legislate as well as create and nurture. They suggest new possibilities of creative potential when we are able to measure or define 'what is'. The rod and line, as symbols of creative power, indicate the capacity to order, direct, control and create, using our capacity for discernment.

The sacral chakra is another gateway of power, relating to our human potential for physical creation. In the body this gateway corresponds to the womb, the vessel for human creation. In our lives, this gateway calls us to surrender the ways we create or navigate our lives materially, how we may strategize, measure, or use force in our attempts to create and control life rather than allowing our natural creative potency and its rhythms to manifest in right timing. The powerful potential of our Sacred Feminine and Masculine creative capacity lies in this chakra, how we receive and relate to direction, how we gestate new form and discern its potential ripeness.

Gate 7: The Gate of Physicality

At Gate 7, symbolising the root chakra, Inanna is finally stripped bare. She must remove her royal robe, also referred to as the Garment of Ladyship. Her identity has been dishonoured and taken from her; her body is naked. The symbols of her power have been stripped away; symbolically her life power has been removed too. She is utterly vulnerable, in her sister's hands.

In our lives, the seventh gateway represents our attachments to the material world, even our body. The root chakra is where we feel grounded and secure, both physically and emotionally. It's where we meet our most basic needs for food, safety, and security. It represents where we experience stability. At this gateway we must let go everything, to face the void. This comes at physical death. For many of us, especially in these times, it comes psychologically and spiritually long before death. We are left with nothing to hold on to, in the hands of Life, naked.

We have explored the map of Inanna's descent. The map is not the experience though. The knowledge of it is not the journey. It is the journey that brings us wisdom. We must live the experience fully to claim the wisdom of it. The journey is one of sacrifice – the ultimate sacrifice – identity and every aspect of one's life. As Inanna descends to the Underworld, she is dying to her old self, slowly but surely. When she arrives, she exists in utter uncertainty, at the mercy of her sister, in her sister's realm, the Underworld. The Queen of Heaven is in the hands of her sister. The Dark Feminine. She is entering a realm that is utterly unknown.

The void of unknowing

In her descent to her sister's realm, Inanna has been stripped of her vestments, the symbols of her power. She has also been stripped of her inner world, her attachments, ideas and ideals, beliefs, and strategies. Yet she has not been without choice. She has let go of her roles, masks, clothes, and her power with good grace. She could have turned back. Why did she not? Perhaps she intuited that in so doing, she would have missed the opportunity for growth. She was compelled to continue, as are we when we follow our knowing. Inanna has been made small. Soon she will be non-existent. Yet at each gate, she persisted. She needed to experience her sister's realm.

Within Ereshkigal's kingdom, there are different rules. All that is of the world above, does not matter here. None of Inanna's symbols hold power here. To even be in Ereshkigal's realm, Inanna had to be taken apart. We cannot enter the Underworld without being lost. Hope is nowhere to be seen. To be in this place is uncomfortable but it is right. We are in the death realm. How we respond or react here is crucial to our growth.

When faced with challenge, we think we have choice and sometimes we do, but in the biggest challenges, perhaps our only choice is to be willing, or to resist. Willing for what? To be willing to be stripped seems a painful choice. Yet being taken apart is an essential aspect of the dark journey, as is losing whatever we lose. We are constantly being undone. Being undone is not just an aspect of the journey, it is the journey. For it is only when we are truly unravelled that new life may find us. In such a state, it is willingness that creates an opening for new life to find us. When we resist, we suffer. When we allow the undoing, we become an empty space; we are made humble by life's inexorable processes. Humility is linked to the word humus. Its root 'humus' is Latin, meaning 'earth, soil'; also 'humi', meaning 'on the ground'. When we are on the ground, we have reached rock bottom. There is nowhere left to go, except fully into the void of unknowing.

Inanna was required to die to who she believed herself to be. On entering the realm of Ereshkigal, she was quickly taken to death. Yet is death the end? We may think so, or not, yet we cannot know for sure. In our own lives we all face this at some point. On the way to physical death, we encounter the Underworld initiation of death and potential rebirth. The old life makes way for a new expression. Yet initially, stripped bare of all we know, we encounter the void. It is a space of both emptiness and potential - a womb, where what has been shed awaits the seed of new life. Here, in this dark space, if we are wise, we may experience life's great pause, the quiet before the wheel turns once more towards a new season. It's potentially a place of deep rest, a crucible. As in winter, the buds of next spring are already there, yet we must wait.

The paradox of this process is that death and birth are inextricably linked. They are gateways. The birth of a child is the death of a woman into mother. During pregnancy she experiences the void, a process beyond her control in which she must wait, rest, take care of herself. The mother does not replace the woman fully but rests and grows within her foundation of experience. She makes a journey into the Underworld, into the unknown, potentially through great pain, yet birth is inevitable.

Change and death are the business of the Underworld, the realm of the Dark Feminine; yet they cannot be separated out from life. Just like the mystery of seeds appearing from the earth after being buried for weeks,

101

or even years. Certainly, the potential is our death leads to a resurrection, yet nothing is certain in this realm. We cannot rely on the potential of birth. We are in the void of unknowing. Mystery resides in the Underworld; it is a cauldron of transformation.

Encountering the Dark Queen

What was Inanna expecting from meeting her sister Ereshkigal? We cannot know. The tablets relate how immediately Inanna enters her sister's throne room, the Annuna – judges of the Underworld - condemn her. Without pause, Ereshkigal kills Inanna with her eye of death. Then she hangs Inanna's corpse on a meat hook. It seems shocking does it not? Ereshkigal gives Inanna no breathing space, no opportunity to state why she has come. She simply acts or reacts. We cannot truly know which it is. Perhaps Inanna's light triggers deeper layers of pain within her dark sister; perhaps this is simply the way of the Dark Feminine. Clearly, Ereshkigal has no time for sisterly bonding.

The Ereshkigal archetype within us represents raw instinctual pain, the primal forces that simply act and react without rationale. When we are in this place, the intensity of those forces consumes any intelligence. We simply become the raw burning intensity of our grief, our jealousy, or whatever dark suffering we are wrapped up in. These forces in us are primal. We cannot negotiate with them, just as we cannot bargain with death when it arrives. We cannot control, manage, or fix our self in this place. We are simply overwhelmed, consumed by feeling. In this state of being, Ereshkigal, along with those dark forces within us, demands complete submission. Inanna is in her realm. There are different rules here – no politeness, accommodating, no civilising boundaries. Ereshkigal is portraying the raw storm of life that we see in nature and know at times within ourselves – it decimates everything. In its seemingly cruel face, we may recognise that our human niceties have little value; they are inconsequential to life's natural forces.

What does Ereshkigal's reaction represent in our own experience? When we are in the darkest experience of despair, grief, or rage, often light is not experienced as a comfort or for its healing potential. Light amplifies the intensity of the pain that we must go through. When I was in the Red Centre of Australia, I directly experienced how this works in nature. It was a mirror for my own experience. The light in the desert is so intensely bright, it makes the shadows so black they appear solid. When in raw pain, our experience can feel similar. Despair can be tangibly dense and visceral. In mourning for her dead husband, Ereshkigal's pain is such that she cannot abide Inanna's presence, for she is a representation of 'Heaven'.

Is Inanna Ereshkigal's victim? It would seem so. Yet in the tale, Inanna is told at each gateway, 'The ways of the Underworld are perfect. They may not be questioned'. This statement reminds us that nothing is at it seems on the path of initiation. This may seem a brutal perspective, yet truth often is. Its clarity can be shocking, especially to our small self. Ereshkigal has, through the act of killing her, initiated her sister into the mysteries of the Dark Feminine. Like nature, she simply is Life no matter how brutal it feels. Through striking her sister down, Ereshkigal gives Inanna the opportunity to meet her own shadow, her own death. In encountering the descent, and death itself, she opens the potential of evolution, of Inanna becoming Queen of Heaven and Earth. Here we glimpse the possibility of wholeness that comes from descent. The story of Inanna's journey prepares us for our own inevitable descents. The potential is then to realise, as in nature, dark and light are two halves of one whole, that Ereshkigal and Inanna are simply different faces of one Feminine.

The Grace of Liberation

Inanna's descent calls us to redefine what spiritual maturity is. We cannot predefine our own or foresee our turning point. It simply arrives. Liberation never appears as we expect it to look. We cannot make it happen through effort or struggle. Often a turning point arrives even without our conscious awareness of it. For such is the nature of Grace that liberates us from pain, even in death. We find it simply happens through us, in startling ways. We might have to break the rules to discover the turning point – our own rules, or those of our family or culture. We may need to step out of a role, as Inanna did. We may have to say an emphatic 'No!' to someone or something. When everything has been exhausted, including our struggle, attempts to heal or fix our self, strategies, prayers and the like, Grace appears, like the miracle that is spring's emergence. It is simply the right time.

Liberation finds Inanna too. Her body is hanging on a meat hook, whilst Ereshkigal is moaning and groaning as though in the great pains of labour. It appears to be the end of the story, that nothing can be done. Yet if we return to the start of the tale, we may see that Inanna's preparation for the descent was not without reason. This is where Ninshubur steps in.

When Inanna does not return, Ninshubur knows the perfect time to act. Firstly, she laments the loss of Inanna in all the public places. Then she goes to Enlil and Nanna, the Father Sky Gods, to request their help. Her pleas were to no avail. Their statements were given with dispassionate rejection – Inanna broke the law (by descending); she's made her bed, now let her lie in it. They claimed that no-one returns from the Underworld, therefore Inanna was beyond help. The Sky Gods were cool and dispassionate. They reflect how rationale and logic, in its detachment or desire to fix, is of no use in this initiation. They reveal how the values of patriarchy cannot help in the Underworld journey. Just as Inanna is constantly reminded, there are different laws in this realm.

Ninshubur then goes to Enki, the Father God of the Waters, to plead his assistance. Enki being connected to the waters, meets Ninshubur's plea with receptivity and compassion. He represents open, fluid consciousness, representative of movement from a stagnant state. He knows what is needed. He knows only the elements of the Underworld may enter the Underworld unseen. Enki fashions two tiny androgynous creatures – a Kugarra and a Galatur – from his fingernail dirt. He gives one the food of life, the other the water of life, and bids them 'Enter the door like flies.' When these tiny beings reach the depths of the Underworld, they must empathise with Ereshkigal in her pain, purely by reflecting her words of loss back to her. Then, when she expresses her gratitude for their compassion, he instructs them to ask Ereshkigal for Inanna's body.

When the Kalatur and Karugurra fully bear witness to Ereshkigal's pain, she is miraculously restored. She has been acknowledged in her dreadful state. She has felt witnessed and so her heart has opened. In gratitude, she gives Inanna's body to Enki's emissaries. As instructed, they revive Inanna with the water and food of life. She is resurrected and begins her ascent. Yet before she goes, the galla, judges of the Underworld seize her once more. They tell her she must provide someone to take her place in the Underworld. As she begins her return journey, she is accompanied by demons to ensure this takes place.

What can we discover from this enlightened plan to rescue Inanna from the Underworld? What insight does it present that may support our own painful initiations?

In our own lives, Ninshubur represents the awakened state of consciousness that can hold us through a dark night of the soul, the support from other frequencies of our consciousness whilst we descend. Ninshubur has a warrior-like clarity; she acts; she has perfect timing. She symbolises aspects of our consciousness, higher frequencies of our being, that hold us whilst we're in the Underworld. She represents the loved ones who may support us through chaos. Or she may symbolise both – that which cannot travel with us but stays above ground, holding a bright light of love for our return.

When we enter the Underworld, the usual ways of the world cannot help us, for the Underworld has its own mystery. It is the qualities of mystery that we need: spaciousness, listening, intuition, subtle knowing, and waiting. Enki is a Father God of the waters. He naturally dwells in, and has dominion over, the collective unconscious, where all aspects of psychic mystery reside. This ocean of possibility is where the solution to Inanna's resurrection lies, not in rationale, not in trying to work it out and certainly not in judgment or blame. Ninshubur's initial request to the sky Gods is rebuffed. This reveals to us we must be wise and ask for help in the right places. Rationale, the mind's detachment, or spiritual bypassing does not help us when in the realm of the Dark Feminine. Support is found in the fluid realm of water: listening deep, allowing keys to the situation to flow into conscious awareness.

Timing is an important aspect of this kind of process. In our own lives we cannot force key elements of renewal to arise; they open naturally as we fully let go into 'what is', as we feel the depth of what is arising. Renewal may be discovered in following subtle nudges and seemingly irrational impulses that arise when we are actively listening for them, or when we are simply waiting without wanting out of the situation. To be in this state of active listening we need to cultivate the quality of receptivity that is a natural aspect of the water element. Water dissolves everything; it takes everything in and eventually dissolves it into itself. When presented with a seemingly impossible task, this initiation requires we awaken deeply to the gifts of reflection, stillness, and receptivity. When in a dark place, it is wisdom to recognise these qualities are our supporters.

When Enki is approached to support Inanna's return, he simply reflects. He intuitively knows that dirt is the element needed to create Inanna's rescuers. It is not simply dirt from the earth but dirt from his fingernails. This contains facets of Underworld energy – it is decaying, in a process of composting. It holds aspects of his wisdom as a Father God, as it comes directly from his body. It is like humus, of the earth, and therefore humble. With this dirt, he fashions the smallest creatures. Herein lies a profound key too, for when we are in the emotional states of an Underworld journey, the smallest thing has significance. In my experience, when I am most raw, it is the simplest blessings that touch the deepest: the Sun's rays through dark clouds, the fresh smell of rain, a kind word or touch. It may sound like a cliché and yet it's true. Enki's wisdom knows that the food and water of life are contained in these simplest elements of Life. To be touched by them is to be in a truly healing communion with Life.

On encountering Ereshkigal the Kalatur and Karugurra also act in the simplest way. They become mirrors, reflecting Ereshkigal's pain and suffering back to her. They do not act as advisors or fixers; they aren't interfering in her suffering. They are simply being with her in warmth, with compassion. Perhaps in this response, Ereshkigal experiences kindness for the first time. The Kalatur and Karugurra are witnessing her trauma, meeting her pain with empathy, acknowledging her exactly where she is. There is a profound key in this way of being. When we are suffering, in simply giving permission to our self to moan, to complain and simply utter 'what is', to voice our pain, rather than suffering in silence, a potential door opens to its release. Used wisely, this action of acknowledging and expressing without indulging, heals our hurt and anger. When we can name and witness our pain without judgment or a need to fix, change it or make it be different than what it is, true healing may occur. Like mourners at a funeral, the Kalatur and Karugurra, hear and acknowledge Ereshkigal's grief. This not only calms her; it honours her strength of feeling and her anguish. She is not hiding her pain, managing it, coping with, or controlling it; she is fully in it.

As Ereshkigal's state of being is acknowledged, her heart softens. She becomes ready to release her sister. Then Inanna's body is revived by the food of water and life. This act of resurrection presents another element of our own healing. What is the food of life? The water of life? For each of us that will be different. Asking our self: what truly nourishes and sustains me, is essential when we suffer. Such questions arise when we are ready to move beyond our suffering through acknowledging it, when we are turning our face towards the light of new life rather than away from it. As the the Kalatur and Karugurra represent in their smallness, what deeply feeds us can be discovered as the smallest impulse towards renewal.

Inanna now retraces her steps. Revived and renewed, she ascends through the seven gates of the Underworld. She appears the same as when she descended, but she is not. She is utterly changed. She knows life beyond death. She knows the depth of who she is beyond all her roles, regalia, and identity. As Inanna ascends, she collects what was sacrificed, yet what she lost has a new value now. She sees what she had possessed previously with new eyes. The forms of her queenship haven't changed but her identity with them has.

At the first gate, which was the last gate she passed through on her way into the Underworld, Inanna retrieves her royal robe, her Garment of Ladyship, reclaiming the healthy potency of her own life force, her relationship to her body and sexual renewal. In our own lives as we rise through this gate, we discover how new life force is available to us through having faced death in the Underworld. We inhabit the body in a new way, claiming the uprising of new energy, vitality, and sexual vigour. Our root to life, to earth, is grounded in new ways, available as a support to the embodiment of higher frequency creativity.

At the second gate Inanna retrieves her lapis measuring rod and line, symbolising a new connection to her creative potency and material life. At this gate, representing the sacral chakra, we arrive at a renewal of creative power, the gifts of the womb to both create and expel. Renewal at this gateway indicates a new integration of Sacred Feminine and Masculine qualities of expression, creation, and destruction. We are renewed in the potential of both ways of being and acting, unified as a creative force. Available, just like the sperm and egg, for new creation.

At the third gate Inanna reclaims her golden arm-rings, her capacity to give and receive, to act through the truth of her wholeness. Here we can claim a new integration of giving and receiving, actioning, holding, and gripping. We claim the power to act through new frequencies of will and purpose. The internal sun, where we experience self-esteem and confidence, shines brightly.

The fourth gate delivers Inanna her breastplate, signifying heart healing and a renewed capacity for vulnerability, intimacy, and love. When we arise through this gateway, the heart chakra, we recognise the truth of vulnerability, that nakedness is where our true strength and heartful capacity for love lie. Having encountered the ultimate state of fragility and surrendered into death itself, the truth of our own demise, we have become tenderised, open, and available for new frequencies of deep intimacy. We recognise and live from the knowing that an open heart is the true balm of love.

At the fifth gate Inanna retrieves her double- stranded beads, reclaiming the authentic self-expression of truth. Life and death are the truth of life in a human body. We cannot avoid that, try as we might. Having passed through the Underworld willingly, this fifth gate, the throat chakra, the seat of self-expression and will, is now available for a refined truth of life. We recognise the futility of control. We begin to know the truth of divine will. We are renewed in expressing the truth and authenticity of a deeper alignment with that.

At the sixth gate Inanna's lapis beads and/or earrings are restored to her. She reclaims her psychic and intuitive senses, enhanced. The second gate into the Underworld corresponds to the brow chakra, also known as the Third Eye. As we rise through this gateway, we become more readily available to receive truth and wisdom, mental acuity, and inner vision. Having journeyed through the Underworld, our ways of seeing and hearing into the unseen realms, are utterly transformed. Where before we had a partial perspective, the journey from light through dark, and our return, has equipped us differently. Our perception is expanded to encompass the whole of life, with its many shades. We are offered the opportunity to live more fully in the unknown, with the knowing that what we need to see or know will arrive in right timing.

At the seventh gate, which was the first, Inanna retrieves the Shugurra, the Crown of the Steppe, symbolizing her queendom, her role in the world, her reconnection to Heaven and her divinity. Here at this gate, on our own journeys, we fall into the arms of the divine once more. Realising fully that the divine is indwelling everywhere, in every experience, light or dark. We come to recognise that our former ideas about divinity are simply that, ideas, or ideals.

As Inanna ascends, she reclaims her place as Queen of Heaven, but now with the wisdom embodied from being stripped, from dying into darkness. Now she embodies Queen of Earth too. She appears the same but is not the same. It is equally true of us when we make this journey. We are reborn.

As Inanna returns to her physical realm, renewed, the saga does not end. For she is accompanied by the galla from the Underworld, who demand the next traveller into their realms. Firstly, they ask for Ninshubur, who appears as Inanna returns. Inanna refuses. Then they spot, each in turn, Shara & Lulal, Inanna's sons. Again, she refuses to let them be taken. Eventually the galla find Dumuzi, Inanna's husband, sitting on her throne, indulging in all the pleasures of Inanna's absence, unmoved by her return. At this point Inanna sees him for who he is. He has not grown in her absence; he has self-indulged. She also recognises in his behaviour, elements of her former self. 'Take him' she cries. She has taken on her sister Ereshkigal's detachment. She sees what is necessary, directly through her own experience. She may seem ruthless, yet her motivation is not revenge, it creates the same journey for her husband: death and rebirth.

Dumuzi escapes twice from the galla but eventually he is captured. He cannot escape his destiny as the consort of Inanna. He has enjoyed her love, their marriage bed and now he too must evolve. The grief of Dumuzi's sister Geshtinanna and his mother, Sirtur, at his plight is so great that eventually they come to agreement. Dumuzi will spend half the year in the Underworld, his sister, the other half.

The truth of this ending is such in our own lives. None of us can avoid the Underworld, even though we may desperately try to. Inanna has been transformed. Her consort must take this journey too. Without that, they can no longer relate. He must also face initiation in the Underworld. The demons that accompany Inanna back from the Underworld represent those active parts of us that won't allow us to return to what was, our former way of being. They guide us and goad us when we try to find comfort in our old ways of being, when we discount our direct knowing. They require those close to us to take their own initiatory path also. For we can no longer relate in the old ways. Death becomes a constant companion in this place. If we are wise, when faced with the descent, we go as willingly as we can, even at the final gateway. For who knows what new life death has in store for us?

There is juiciness here

Inanna's journey reveals to us the gifts of wholeness available to us when we are present with what is. Her courage and willingness demonstrate that if we're awake, we cannot stay in our comfort zone. If we desire our own wholeness, alignment with consciousness, to live as evolving wholeness, we must make the journey into the Underworld.

There is no doubt that the dark path is messy. We are called to let go of all the masks. The illusions of 'getting it right', being spiritual, looking good, being the light, all fall apart on this journey into the Underworld.

We must be willing to be stripped bare. In Inanna's story we've been given the map. The map is not the experience though. It is only in walking the path step by step that the territory reveals itself. Walking in the dark we cannot see ahead. We do not know what awaits us. We would approach it differently though, if we simply trusted the impulse to take the journey, just like Inanna.

Inanna appears to be Ereshkigal's victim in this journey. Is that the truth? Or is the truth that they both move into greater wholeness through their encounter? There is a rebalancing, an empowering integration that takes place, where both receive a gift. That gift is born through pain, just as in physical birth, where both mother and baby undergo the transition. Pain is the crucible for renewal, just as winter is the womb in which spring gestates. Inanna receives the wisdom of spiritual maturity. She deepens. Ereshkigal is immersed in unconditional acceptance. For both, brokenness is the doorway to alchemy. As it can be in our own lives.

For alchemy to occur, we must simply be willing. This is Inanna's gift to us. Being willing to face our pain, our disconnection and the void that follows when we let go. The willingness to go deep within, to be stripped naked, is powerfully cleansing. As we are told in The Hymns to Inanna, the ways of the Underworld are perfect. Yet we cannot know that for sure unless we go there. It is often only with hindsight that we know this. This is the initiation; it delivers the potential of wisdom.

As women we are constantly changing. That is our deep nature, just like the natural world. The wisdom of the cycles is already in us. We travel between dark and light in our own unique rhythms, at different times of life. Just as the planet Venus moves from Morning Star to Evening Star towards, behind and then away from the Sun from our perspective on Earth, representing the Underworld journey, we also make Inanna's journey. Just as the Moon cycles the Earth monthly, moving our tides, we make our own Moon journey, releasing our eggs and their protection, our unmet potential for new life. We also endure pain to birth new life. We know the journey from light to dark intimately in our bodies. We already are the fullness of the cycle, and its demise, constantly in a process of death and rebirth. Yet Inanna reveals to us how to be that consciously. In fully embracing our shadow, our pain, our disconnections, we embody the fullness of life.

Inanna resurrected is wholeness. Yet even the word is misleading. For wholeness is not a static state; it is ever evolving and expanding. Through Inanna's descent both her sister, Ereshkigal and her own life were utterly revitalized; Dumuzi was thrust into his own journey of evolution. Inanna renewed reflects to us a state of spiritual maturity. Following the thread of life in which everyone is naturally served in their own evolution. She appears the same as when she descended, but she is not. She is utterly changed. Now she knows who she is beyond all her roles, regalia, and identity. Yet can she define it? My experience says not. This is true strength of beingness; this is the journey of embodiment, to bring the mystery of who we are to life. Without the darkness, there is no embodiment. Both light and dark are necessary for wholeness. We see this in many Goddess pairs or trios in western mythology, for instance Athena and Medusa, Moon Goddesses Artemis, Selene and Hekate. In the East, the Dark Goddess reflects both supreme love and death. Kali Ma is known for her bloodlust and cutting detachment, yet also for her fierce boundless love. To live as evolving wholeness, we must encounter and engage both within ourselves, for in truth, they are not separate. Like Yin and Yang, they are inextricably linked.

Inanna's authenticity as Queen of Heaven was partial, as is ours until we make the Underworld descent. We are narrow even in our brightness and zest for life. It is only in traversing the darkness that we claim our true juiciness. Passing through the darkness is renewal. Just as the quiet restfulness of night's deep sleep revitalises us, the deep stillness of the empty void that is present when we've fully let go is regenerating. Staying in touch with it guarantees our resourcefulness, our depth, our fullness. Like Inanna we become deeply rooted in the knowing of earth cycles, the flow of life to death to life. More than this, we come fully in touch with our own body, engaging our lower chakra energies, our humanness, the creative potency of the womb, our grounding on Earth, as well as the density of our shadows. The energy held in the chakras below the heart are key not only to embodiment, our own renewal as women, but to the power of our erotic sensual presence here on the Earth. To be made whole, truly holy, we must make the journey from the fake holiness of the Gods of light into the darkness; we must make the full cycle, for we are that. We may be made small through this journey. In that, like Inanna, we learn humility. Through being made nothing, we open into our true state of magnificence, one with Life.

Chapter 2

The Uninvited Guest – Disruptor Eris

Ears plugged
with personal preference,
a Universe clothed
in human form,
they ride the
9 to 5 train.
Oblivious to
open connection,
the potential
to meet companions
of life
ignored.

Faces
reveal the drudge,
the painful sleep
of forgetting.
Foregoing
aliveness
for deadness of comfort,
creative riches
lost to money,
mortgage,
mortality.

Denying the call
to fully live,
evolve
as Life in life,
they ride
the train of self
from birth to death,
in the comfort
of unknowing, uncaring,
whilst fuelling the machine
of the grey
we have formed
from infinite light.

I see
their passion denied,
lifeforce throttled,
chaos feared,
and I weep
at their plight.
What will it take
to awake
the Bright?

Cassandra Eve

Written on a commuter train
in Melbourne, Australia

Archetype: Disruptor

Symbols: The Golden Apple

Message: Go beyond the conflict and competition of difference, and the chaos of change, discover the truth behind all appearances.

Eris themes: competition; strife & conflict; our instinctual reactions to change; the evolutionary demand; victim or growth orientation; truth and cosmic law; being an agent of social change; living with paradox

What the Eris archetype calls for: truth-telling despite the potential consequences

Also known as: Discordia (Roman), Enyo (Greek)

Eris, sister to God of War Ares, is a challenging figure in the Greek pantheon. Known as the Goddess of Strife or Discord, she is said to revel in chaos, war, and bloodshed. Yet, as always with goddess archetypes, there is more to Eris than meets the eye. To meet her, we need to go beyond the patriarchal overlay.

Daughter of ancient goddess Nyx (Night), Eris's origins come from darkness. Nyx is one of the primordial goddess figures in Greek mythology birthed from Chaos, existing before the Titans and their offspring, the Olympians. Hesiod (Greek poet, circa 700BCE) named these primordial figures as 'first-born' from Chaos - we might recognise this now as the primordial soup that science says followed the Big Bang. With her consort Erebus (Deep Darkness) - some myths state it was Ouranos - Nyx birthed beings such as Aether (Air), the Moirae (Fates), Hypnos (Sleep), Thanatos (Death), Nemisis (Retribution) and Eris. Some of her offspring came purely from her own body without the aid of a father. It is said Eris went on to bear numerous children, with names such as Lethe (Forgetfulness), Limos (Starvation), the Neikea (Quarrels), Ate (Ruin), the Pseudo-Logoi (Lies), the Amphilogiai (Disputes), and Dysnomia (Lawlessness). It looks and feels like a plethora of human ills. Another version of Eris's origins, gives her a less primal nature, born from Zeus and Hera's union, as sister to Ares. As we shall see, these two versions of Eris's birth give rise to the mystery and complexity of her meaning.

In her mythology Eris is commonly known through the myth of the Golden Apple that gave rise to the Trojan War. She is seen as a troublemaker, yet her medicine is really that of a catalyst. Eris exposes what is out of alignment. She carries an energetic frequency that is often unwelcome in our lives, for she challenges us. It is interesting that there were (as far as we know) no temples to Eris. Nor is there any record of people praying for her goodwill. Greek myth relates that the gods and goddesses chose to ignore and exclude her. Eris carried an energy that people would rather avoid, much like the changes that challenge us. Although she has no known origins in the ancient Sumerian goddesses, I cannot help but link her energy with Ereshkigal, Inanna's sister, as a queen of darkness. It's interesting that her name is similar.

Culturally, we come across Eris in the paintings of Rubens, The Wedding of Peleus and Thetis, and The Judgment of Paris, along with a more recent painting, The Feast of Peleus by Edward Burne-Jones. In his epic poem The Illiad, Greek poet Homer (circa 750BCE) equated Eris with the war-goddess Enyo. This adds another layer to her complexity. The common thread for Eris in art, music, and literature, is blame for the Trojan War, despite the reactions of the gods and goddesses being far more pertinent to this event. Eris had thrown the Golden Apple into a wedding feast, acting as a catalyst to reveal underlying competition amongst the goddesses.

Eris's action added fuel to religious and secular mythology that women with apples are troublemakers. Look at the stories built around Eris, Eve, Lilith, and Snow White's stepmother. They have all been labelled 'wicked' or 'evil', yet invariably there is a deep wisdom to be seen beyond a dualistic judgement of their actions. Interestingly, the word 'wicked' has its origin in 'wicca' meaning 'witch' or 'wizard', describing those who practised a nature-oriented way of life. The apple is the fruit of the Tree of Life, implying there is a deeper life-enhancing meaning to these stories.

Her-story

Before we explore the direct mythology of Eris, it is pertinent to explore her ancestry, as it relates to the overthrowing of the ancient goddess-based ways by patriarchy.

The mother of Eris, Nyx, primordial night, exists in the very first intimations of mythology. Homer, in his Theogony, regarded Nyx as one of the great goddesses. She came out of the void with Earth; Eros, the spirit of love; and Erebus, the personification of darkness. From the union of Nyx and Erebus came Aether (upper air or light) and Hemera (day). Erebus and Nyx were soon deprived of their power by their offspring Aether and Hemera. From them came Gaia and Uranus, whose mythology I shared in the introduction. In the very earliest mythologies, the darkness of night and the Moon (Feminine) had precedence over the light of day and the Sun. Gradually however the light took precedence. As I described previously, eventually Uranus denied the existence of his dark children, strengthening this shift from dark to light. The Solar Gods began to reign and the mysterious Dark Feminine was abandoned. Fear of her Mystery, rather than reverence, became the norm. Eris was born into this movement from darkness towards light. With all of Nyx's children, she was labelled 'bad', along with all the mysteries of life that human beings could not understand (including the nature of women as child bearers). In the emerging patriarchy, darkness and everything that came from it was now labelled evil. It is with this background that we approach the mythology and the mystery of Eris.

There are two myths associated with Eris, the first of which is commonly known. Her mythological origins come mostly from Greek poets Hesiod and Homer (circa 700-800BCE). Hesiod states that there are two Eris's. They have separate natures, one who is a troublemaker; the other, more approachable when you understand her motivation. 'She pushes the shiftless man to work' says Hesiod, affirming her role as a catalyst and motivator. He also associates Eris with all the ills that plague mankind, released from Pandora's jar. In the Iliad, Homer assigns the name Enyo to Eris. He calls her 'the sacker of cities', related to her role as the apparent instigator of the Trojan wars. Yet later in this epic tale states she is 'strong Eris, defender of peoples. It's useful to be aware that these Greek writers were creatures of their time, voices of a growing patriarchy in western civilisation. They were also the entertainers of their age. As always, what is the truth and what is fiction is lost in the mists of time and history's perspective.

Eris is most often associated with the myth 'The Golden Apple'. This symbol appears in myth and folk tales from many cultures; Russian, Irish, Romanian, Bulgarian and German, as well as Greek. Apples are commonly associated with knowledge or fertility. In the Garden of Hesperides, owned by Hera, they are reputed to gift immortality to whomever eats them. This is where we encounter Eris. Uninvited to the wedding of Peleus and Thetis because of her reputation for troublemaking, Eris decides to play a prank. She steals a golden apple from the Garden of the Hesperides. It is inscribed 'Kallistei', meaning 'to the fairest'. Sneaking into the wedding feast, Eris lobs the apple amongst the guests. It immediately ignites a contest between the Goddesses Hera (Juno, explored in Sacred Pathways), Athena, and Aphrodite. They all want it, and its label 'to the fairest'.

The myth continues with an attempt to resolve the discord caused by Eris's action. To avoid a fight, Paris, son of Priam, King of Troy, is chosen to be the judge of who is most beautiful. Each of the three goddesses immediately attempts to bribe him, each promising Paris a wonderful gift if he chooses them. Hera promises him great power; Athena offers him great wisdom and Aphrodite pledges she will give him the most beautiful woman. Whilst Greek culture placed a great emphasis on heroism and power, Paris chooses for love. He awards the apple to Goddess of Love Aphrodite. She ensures that the beautiful Helen, wife of Menelaus, King of Sparta, is available to Paris, despite her marriage.

Following the wedding, the couple run away together to the home of Paris in Troy. In this one act he dooms his city, for it was destroyed in the war that ensued.

Inevitably Eris was blamed for the event that initiated the Trojan War, just as fingers point towards any 'awkward woman' nowadays. Various theories have been suggested for Eris's action: feeling snubbed, jealous, or simply mischief-making. As we will discover through our exploration though, it's so much more than human emotion. The Eris archetype cannot abide hypocrisy. She has been snubbed because of her reputation as disruptive, yet most of the gods and goddesses readily wield their shadow sides, especially when thwarted. Eris knew the vanity, pride, and underlying competitiveness active in the Olympian Goddesses. She saw that how they portrayed themselves and acted wasn't consistent with being divine. Perhaps her action was one of exposure? Perhaps she knew what would ensue? For the goddesses clearly reveal their shadows, the darkness that was being projected onto Eris. Eris is reputed to have started the war, but its causes were more deeply rooted in what followed her action. She was merely a catalyst.

The Trojan war was not the only outcome of Eris's golden apple. As we know in our own lives, one small action can bring forth numerous unforeseen outcomes. At the end of the Trojan War, Aeneas, a member of the Trojan royal family, left his destroyed city and sailed for Italy. He became the founder of the Roman Empire, a civilisation that lasted a thousand years. From the chaos of war, a new culture was born. As we will discover, Eris's part in this unfolding introduces one of her major themes: chaos birthing evolution.

The second myth involving Eris is lesser known, but equally potent in the wisdom we can derive from it. It is especially pertinent to our recent collective experience.

In this myth two brothers, Atreus, and Thyestes, are in dispute over the throne of Mycenae. Zeus, who favoured Atreus as king, suggests he bet his brother that the Sun would rise in the west on the following day. The prize was the throne. Zeus then works with Eris to persuade Helios, the Sun God, to move backwards in the sky on that one day, thus reversing the laws of nature. Atreus claims the throne and banishes his brother Thyestes. The meaning behind this myth will become clearer as we explore collective experience since the discovery of Eris: her correlation with events in the natural world and her contra-nature orbit.

Eris's Place in the Universe – Astronomy & Astrology

In the early 2000's discoveries of planetary bodies (including Eris) in the Kuiper Belt - a region of the solar system beyond Neptune's orbit - shook up astronomical and astrological communities. Eris's appearance caused not only the chaos she is renowned for, but a shake-up of planetary classification.

Any object in our Solar System that orbits the Sun at a greater average distance than Neptune is known as a Trans-Neptunian object (TNO). The most well-known TNO is the dwarf planet Pluto, discovered in 1930. It was not until the 1990's that further TNO's were found. Then in January 2005 Eris was discovered (from data obtained in 2003) by Mike Brown, a professor of planetary astronomy at the California Institute of Technology, Chad Trujillo of the Gemini Observatory, and David Rabinowitz of Yale University. Larger than Pluto, Eris was initially called the tenth planet (after a short period named Xena, the fictional warrior princess). This led to Pluto's initial demotion from planetary status.

Eris's discovery led to heated debate about who discovered her, and about the nature and definition of a planet. In August 2006 the IAU (International Astronomical Union) came to a new definition of what a planet is. Under this new ruling, both Eris and Pluto became dwarf planets. All dwarf planets are a little smaller than our Moon. Yet dwarf is a misnomer for the influence of their energies. The reclassification decision was therefore considered controversial by astrologers, due to Pluto's significant themes and influence. Asteroid Ceres was also reclassified as a dwarf planet, along with other TNO's; Haumea, Makemake, and Sedna. Despite the controversy, this reclassification of planetary bodies was long overdue. We see the seeds of her themes - exposing systems or circumstances where an overhaul is needed - at her discovery.

Eris spans deep space in her orbit, twice the distance of Pluto to the Sun. She has an elliptical erratic orbit, taking 500 years to orbit the Sun. Her unusual orbit means she spends over 120 years in the sign of Aries (her longest period) and only 15 years in Leo, with varying times in other signs. As Eris has been in Aries since 1922 and remains there until 2048, she is in this fiery first sign of the zodiac for all active birth charts.

Astrologically, Eris's extreme eccentric orbit is a clue to her radical nature. Planets with this type of orbit can bring awareness from the far reaches of space, i.e., distant realms of consciousness, into our consciousness on Earth. Such planetary bodies cut through the norms of our existing perceptions of reality, necessitating change, as the circumstances of her discovery reveal. Eris's deep space presence and eccentric orbit strongly suggest that her qualities will be deep, far-reaching, and chaotic. Furthermore, as she is beyond Pluto, she represents what lies beyond our current power structures.

At the point Eris was discovered, dark matter and dark energy were coming to the fore in science. Both expand as an anti-gravitational force to grow the Universe i.e.; they are contra nature as we know it (this fact is suggested in Eris's mythology). As such, Eris calls us to go beyond what is familiar or comfortable in order that we expand our consciousness. She is relentlessly in service to the discovery of deeper truth.

Named by astronomers after the Goddess of Discord, Eris was misinterpreted by some astrologers as a negative archetype. Yet Eris's orbit, far beyond that of Pluto, reveals she operates at a high frequency, highlighting outworn structures to bring finer awareness to them.

In an individual's birth chart, Eris will reveal where that individual will fight for their rights (or those of the collective) revealing deeper, often controversial, truths. She shows what kind of battles the individual takes on. Her strength and aspects reveal how effective these battles are. Eris plays through situations where we are called to adapt, to individuate fully and carve our own paths. She also reveals where and how you experience yourself as an outsider, or a maverick. She governs both a personal sense of emergence - spirit to body, self to the divine - and service to the collective through exposing what requires deeper truth. Eris provokes change by upsetting the status quo, opening awareness to dishonesty, masks of politeness and egoic plays, social mores, or unacceptable behaviour driven by excessive ego. She calls us to see beyond current perceptions, to redefine our inner maps and embrace cosmic reality.

Well-known individuals with prominent Eris placement include Charles Dickens, who wrote about the dispossessed of his time; Barack Obama, the first Black American President; Pope Francis 1, a crusader for the poor and marginalised; Copernicus, the astronomer who proposed the heliocentric perspective view of the Universe, against the established power of the Church; Galileo; Sir Isaac Newton; Joan of Arc; Steven Spielberg; William Shakespeare; Albert Einstein; and Masaru Emoto. All were pioneers, often provoking controversy in their chosen field.

My journey with Eris

I wrote about how I encountered and came to live in Tantric community with a Tantric Master, in my book 'Sacred Pathways – Discovering Divine Feminine Archetypes in You'. Without doubt, I was led by Grace to the most challenging yet fulfilling evolutionary path. For thirteen years I walked the fine line between devotee and disruptor. It is only now that I recognise Eris at play during that incredibly evolutionary time. She would not let the unquestionable authority of the Master's awakened awareness diminish my questions or doubts, or my inner knowing when it comes to our human challenges.

At this time in my life Eris was clearly awakening in me, acting in her primary role as disruptor. I found her energy particularly challenging to my need to belong, yet I could not stop myself expressing her. She particularly played out during satsang, the times when as a group we were invited to sit together and enquire into truth. In these sessions I was like a dog with a bone. My deep need was to understand how what I knew without doubt to be divine truth being expressed, was relevant to our ordinary human lives. One aspect of myself could simply sit with the abstract nature of what was being spoken, receiving the transmission. Yet another aspect, (that I know now to be Eris) when aroused, would question, question, question. It was Eris at her best and worst, drilling down, not allowing any escape from the demand to know how the Divine plays out here in seeming ordinariness. I was relentless. I would not allow my teacher to rest until that demand in me was satisfied.

This energy of disruption in me was not easy to accept and hold lovingly at the time. I felt like I was always rocking the boat, being 'unspiritual', persistent, and dissatisfied. I saw how I disrupted what the community felt should be a peaceful space for enquiry. I had yet to recognise the impersonal function of Eris as disruptor, never a comfortable role. I was aware that my focus was on embodied truth though, i.e., not truth as an abstraction, but relevant to what seem to be ordinary human lives. Eris's appearance in me reflected my growing recognition to not use spirituality as an avoidance of being human. I would feel ashamed of my demand for my enquiry to be met, my need to receive pure insight, yet as I've come to know Eris more intimately, I recognise it was both my love of humanity and of the deepest truth that was the catalyst for my relentlessness.

Eris is a mirror for our deepest values. At that time, she was acting through me as catalyst for deeper truth, more relevant material, calling my teacher to greater depth and clarity about how enlightenment looks here, alive in all our human challenges. Eris is the one who will go beyond what is considered comfortable or acceptable, to reveal what is hidden. She is a catalyst. I had no choice but to allow her free rein. I could not hold her back, even if I wanted, for just as her planetary body lies beyond Pluto and therefore current power structures here on Earth, she takes us beyond the norm. She rattles the cages of what is comfortable, demanding to be set loose, to expand beyond all normality, to discover clear deep truth.

Eris's message: Go beyond the conflict and competition of difference, and the chaos of change; discover the truth behind all appearances.

The uninvited guest in our lives

Eris is a goddess of extremes. She highlights the polarities of conflict within us that underlie all processes of change. Change is often unexpected and unwelcome in our lives. Often, it's an uninvited guest to our comfort zones. It disrupts our sense of normalcy, challenging our feelings of being safe and secure in our world. It gives rise to unpredictable and uncontrollable emotions. When change is upon us we often swing from one perspective to its opposite, from holding on for security's sake to anticipation of new life yet worrying what will happen. When change strikes through adversity in our lives, we can believe bad things are happening to us. It can feel like everything is falling apart and often it is. For that is the inexorable process of change – the old structures we rely on crumbling, to be replaced by new energy and forms. Yet in truth the process of change is not happening to us but for us. The cells in our body are constantly being renewed; nature is eternally moving from dissolution to renewal; day is slowly turning towards night, night towards dawn. The cycles of life are constantly on the move. We know and accept this in the impersonal movements of life, such as the seasons. Yet when they occur in our personal lives, it can feel like they are creating chaos.

Change creates discomfort in our human system. Depending on the nature of the change, we can feel inspired by this, or challenged, especially where it forces us to let go where we are attached. Yet change is the most natural process; without it we would never mature: a child wouldn't learn to talk or walk; the adolescent wouldn't become an emotionally mature adult; an adult wouldn't reach towards their fullest potential. If we are maturing with support as a child, and consciously as an adult, we meet these growing edges. We go beyond them to embody a new sense of self. If we are maturing well, we discover how to take care of our self when our sense of security is threatened, our emotions are tumultuous, and peace of mind is compromised. This is the journey of evolution. Yet it's not always easy.

The Eris archetype represents the challenge to change and how we respond or react to it. She represents the challenge that comes from truth or honesty. She is a no-holds-barred catalyst for deeper authenticity. She dares us to go, and grow, beyond what is comfortable or familiar, to perceive, acknowledge and transmute what has been hidden. Such a process is impersonal in nature, although it often feels deeply personal. It is simply evolution in action, calling us where we are ready to go and grow, even though we may believe we are not. Being a dwarf planet that stretches beyond conventional planetary orbits, Eris delivers the frequencies of new consciousness to us. Her orbit, outside of even Pluto's, takes us way beyond current power structures on this planet. She invites us to embody deeper truth personally yet also to live from a new collective way of being that not only honours truth but lives it. As Eris was only discovered in 2005, we are in the tentative new beginnings of this quest.

The Golden Apple myth from the Greek culture demonstrates Eris's gift as catalyst. Rebelling against her exclusion from the wedding party, Eris's action, revealed the hidden dynamics at play within the Greek pantheon, particularly in the foremost goddesses. She was shaking up the Olympian status quo with a calling for more honesty. She works this way in our lives now. We can see the themes of her energy clearly in our collective circumstances since 2020, when she has been strongly aligned with outer planets, particularly Pluto. The theme of social exclusion in the myth is reflected in the global circumstances of lock-down. Revelations about the 'gods' (politicians) contempt for the rules they are imposing are rife, along with their double standards. This is raising issues within us both personally and collectively about honesty and authenticity. Issues that perhaps would not have arisen if we weren't facing such restrictive and tragic circumstances globally.

In Homer's Iliad, Eris is described as 'at first small and insignificant, but she soon raises her head up to heaven', indicating how something small, particularly when it challenges our comfort zones, can have a powerful impact in our lives. It also mirrors how the smallest shift of energy can be blown out of proportion by our perspective on it. In Eris's second major mythic theme, she resolved a conflict by working with Zeus and Helios to reverse the usual rhythm of nature. Perhaps you can see how this is taking place now, in the 2020's, as our human lives are deeply affected and limited by a natural force, a virus, one of the smallest forms of life on Earth. In the ensuing events, it's possible to see how something tiny can have huge impact on our lives. Perhaps this is nature's backlash against our violation of the natural world.

The hierarchical order of the natural world – with humanity supposedly as peak – is undoubtedly brought into question through the pandemic. One might even say a war against nature is taking place through reaction to it. Our own bodies have become the war zone. Despite all its obvious challenges and tragedy, there is evolutionary purpose in this experience. With the comfort of 'normal' disappearing, we have been shown we must change our ways. We can take nothing about life for granted. Now we know any disruption of the system is global. We can see the hand of Eris at play here, for her energy always disrupts a system that no longer serves its purpose. To some individuals that is a threat; to others it raises truly valid questions about our responsibilities, and a potentially radical evolution. Our animal bodies may always be under threat of illness or death, yet we are blessed with consciousness that can evolve. Doesn't such a state require us to make consciously different choices about how we live on this Earth?

During lockdown our usual ways of life were reversed. A slowdown happened that was measurable by scientists. Seismometers around the world registered a sharp decrease in the vibrations produced by human activity that was immediate. Air pollution decreased. Earth-observing satellites detected a significant decrease in the concentration of a common air pollutant, nitrogen dioxide, the atmospheric result of emissions from cars, trucks, buses, and power plants. Noise pollution decreased measurably, including that created by cruise ships, thus giving marine mammals a rest from our intrusive behaviour. The pandemic certainly brought trauma to many people's lives and livelihoods; it brought chaos globally. Yet without doubt, nature benefitted from the enforced restriction of our activity levels. Here in the UK, the weather during the first lockdown brought weeks of clear skies and warm sunshine. Many individuals enjoyed a reconnection with nature that they usually would not have had time for. It is also known through environmental projects, that when the interference of human beings is removed from nature and her natural processes, such as happened at the start of the pandemic, nature heals and renews itself. Tropical rainforest has been seen to thrive on land that had been previously cleared for grazing cattle; without any input from human beings, it returns to its natural state. Nature's intelligence works to restore balance when we desist from imposing our human will on the environment.

From her mythology, Eris has gained a label as a disruptive influence but sometimes we need trouble; it wakes us up. We need a catalyst. It compels us to enquire into what is deeply true. Is Eris's motivation in the myth of the Golden Apple to do harm or simply to unsettle the status quo and bust a few egos? Is the virus here to destroy human beings or to make us deeply question how we are behaving within the context of our global community and the unity of natural life? It might seem that nature (or even the hand of man using nature) has turned against us, yet in truth it is we who are continuously acting against nature. Now we are reaping the harvest of our irresponsibility towards all life. The chaos brought about by these circumstances, and our responses or reactions to them, heighten an evolutionary imperative. In the disruption of what has become crystallised, potentially we are kicked out of our apathy or helplessness into new ways of being. Research reveals we grow through crisis, despite our lack of welcoming it.

Cataclysmic events globally around the time of Eris's discovery further amplify her associated themes of systemic breakdown and chaos. For when a planetary body is first discovered, or viewed, the archetypal energy it brings to our consciousness becomes evident. Outer planets in particular draw our attention to global experience and our collective consciousness, along with the imperative to evolve. They represent the impersonal nature of change, for even when change affects us personally, there are always larger themes at play. Eris is not the only planetary player in these events, yet she is a major one.

Through the 2000's (she was discovered first in 2003 and actually seen in 2005) we experienced local events that brought impact on a massive scale globally: in 2001 9/11 happened and the rising threat of global terrorism arrived; in 2004 225,000 people perished across ten countries in the Pacific Tsunami; in 2005 Hurricane Katrina devastated New Orleans, killing almost 2000 people and causing $125billion damage;

144

2005 also saw the Kashmiri Earthquake that affected 3 countries, killed 73,000 people and made 3 million homeless; in 2008, in a cyclone in Burma and China 140,000 people died and 2.5 million were made homeless; in 2010 Haiti experienced a 7.0 earthquake that left 3 million homeless and 300,000 dead; then in 2011, the Japanese Tsunami wreaked yet more chaos on humanity and our environment. Seeing these events listed in this way is shocking yet without doubt has expanded our attention globally towards nature's potential for creating chaos, the evolutionary processes of Life and our Earth, the environmental crisis, and for many of us, honing our sense of responsibility for each other and our Earth. Such events highlight the fact that we are not in control, despite our desire to be. Like all of nature, we are subject to natural laws.

When a system breaks down, the natural reaction is to try to repair it, or to fight the change. We are seeing this now in reaction to the pandemic through increased control and the imposition of rules and laws framed through the old order that is breaking down. This is not the solution. The truth of Eris is to realise we cannot repair what's already rotten. We must discover a new response that demonstrates a greater alignment with truth, integrity, and co-creative responsibility. We must work with the natural laws of life. The ego's desire for order and control must be replaced with a higher order, one aligned with higher consciousness, cosmic law. Firstly, that requires us to create a unified field of response within our whole self, as an individual. The potential is that inner alignment translates to collective action and evolution. Presence is the key to this process; being present to what is felt as chaotic, challenging, even threatening to our very survival. The Eris archetype, in her role as disruptor of systems, provides the means for this.

A fight for, or against, the evolutionary imperative

In Greek mythology there are two versions of Eris, one of whom is described as the sister of Ares (aka Mars). Homer interchangeably uses the names Enyo and Eris to describe her as 'deadly Eris' who 'delights in bloodshed and the destruction of towns and accompanies Mars in battle'. Mars (Ares) is the God of War and like him, Eris loves to be in battle. In astrology Mars (Ares) rules the sign of Aries, where Eris spends much of her orbital time. Her presence in Aries for a lengthy period gives us real clues to her nature and her deeper relationships to Aries's (and her brother Ares) qualities. She can reveal to us where we are either for, or against, the evolutionary imperative, life's natural impulse towards development.

Aries is the first sign of the zodiac. It's the sign of 'I am', the ego or personal will, pure life force, as we see in spring's uprising energy. In human beings it expresses as the fight for survival, passion and motivation, confidence, and assertiveness, both the necessity to take care of our self and an immature need to be first. Our Aries energy indicates how we face competition and its extremes, from aggression to passive aggression, to withdrawal, and our conditioning around anger, assertiveness, compromise, or compliance. The God Ares (also known as Mars, ruler of zodiac sign Aries) delighted in both bloodlust and feats of great strength and courage, revealing to us the range of this energy, from passion for life and will to survive to outright aggression.

According to Homer and Hesiod, Eris spanned the same range of fierce expression as her brother, Ares. Yet Hesiod also has a different take on her energy, particularly as regards competition. In his Works and Days 11 – 24, Hesiod states that Eris was not just a bringer of strife, but she could also do good for mankind. He states, 'As for the one, a man would praise her when he came to understand her; but the other is blameworthy: and they are wholly different in nature. For one fosters evil war and battle, being cruel. But the other is far kinder to men. She stirs up even the shiftless to toil; for a man grows eager to work when he considers his neighbour, a rich man who hastens to plough and plant and put his house in good order; and neighbour vies with his neighbour as he hurries after wealth. This strife is wholesome for men.' This version of Eris is so utterly different from the Eris of the battlefield that they were sometimes considered two different goddesses. The battlefield Eris was deemed cruel, whereas the alternative Eris reflects competition as supportive to striving for improvement in life circumstances, through willpower and healthy struggle.

If we look deeper into these two versions of Eris, it seems one Eris focused her unhappiness outwardly in the enjoyment of battling others, whilst the other focused inwardly, inspiring a fight within, against lethargy and bad habits. Hesiod gives us clues to Eris's dual nature here: the instinctual urge to win, used violently, versus the instinctual urge to evolve, used as a catalyst to fuel our own growth. The evolutionary-orientated Eris represents how we might fully engage our creative self-expression with willpower, to take our growth into a higher frequency and our lives into better circumstances. Competition is used in a healthy way, as a spur to excellence.

Nature reveals to us that competition is an evolutionary imperative. Plants in a forest compete for light and thus, for life. Animals compete for food and shelter. Even plants compete for space, sometimes aggressively. As human beings, in animal bodies, we have similar needs. At times we must use our will to fight for survival, for the means to feed ourselves and our families, sometimes for a home. Yet we are different in that we also fight beyond the need for physical survival. We fight to protect our identity; for our beliefs and ideologies; for principles; for territory beyond what we need; for greed and not need. Some people fight for pleasure, or for satisfaction. Eris represents the fight aspect of our survival system, especially in Aries. She represents how we connect to our instinctual survival mechanism and how we use it. Like Inanna and Black Moon Lilith, she reflects our primary nature, or aspects of it, and just like Eve, Eris is innocent. Her action with the Golden Apple reveals her link into the Tree of Life – primal nature. She has no agenda beyond seeing what might happen. She does not know what will ensue when she throws the apple into the wedding party, she simply does it. Perhaps she has an instinctive knowing that it's a catalyst; it's what is needed?

There have always been catalysts to evolution. From meteors to global floods to widespread famine, it seems humanity needs a crisis to evolve. Our evolutionary process over eons, seems to have been a civilising process. The definition of civilisation is the process by which a society or place reaches an advanced stage of social and cultural development and organization. Yet it depends on what you consider civilised, and if it's merely a façade. History reveals that great civilisations have appeared, thrived, and then gone. If we look at the best of human progress, we can see great works of art and creativity, social, cultural, and technological advances. Yet we can also see desecration. Eris will challenge us on exactly how civilised we are, and what is its value.

As we approach what appears to be yet another global evolutionary crisis, it is vital to ask, in becoming more civilised, have we truly transformed human nature? Have we moved beyond the basest of our instincts? Have we made friends with them, acknowledging their right to exist, and their supportive nature within our human system, or have we simply split off from them in judgment and finger-pointing projections?

Have we made enemies of instinct and its actions in others, rather than owning it in ourselves? These are pertinent questions. For it is often the worst of human nature that disrupts what purports to be civilisation. There must be a reason for that. Surely there lies a clue and a key to our dilemma. Perhaps civilisation as we know it, is a fight against our own nature, rather than a transformation of it? It's an attempt to control the uncontrollable in our self, or Mother Nature, rather than living a balanced conscious relationship with all aspects of ourselves and forms of life. If we look at our world with honesty, right now we could easily say, civilised stands for corrupt.

One of the meanings of the word corrupt means 'to alter for the worse'. It stands in opposition to our beliefs about being civilised. Such a strong word has real meaning in a world where force and hostility are often exalted, especially when justified in the name of 'economic growth' or 'defence'. How more corrupt can a culture be? We don't have to scratch far beneath the surface to see aspects of human nature that are still barbarous yet are masked in sophistication. Nature is regarded as a resource for us to exploit, not caretake. Defence of what we believe we own has led to the development of phallic shaped missiles of war, along with similarly shaped spaceships that aggressively penetrate outer space, whilst our Earth suffers our disconnection from our bodies and Hers. The head has become split from the body in this realm, technological jargon covering the reality of what is truly being done. On the news we may hear of 'collateral damage' rather than the death of innocents. The use of the word 'targets', as with so many militaristic words, denies the human element. It's clear to see our instinctual nature has run amok in places it is not needed, whilst at the same time we have disconnected from its naturally healthy expression that can be lifesaving with right use.

It appears that Eris has come to remind us of the ill use of our competitive urges and the consequences of them. She is calling us to a new relationship with our animal nature, our connection to Earth and each other, not by denying the worst of our instinctual nature but through engaging it consciously and evolving it. The differing versions of Eris stand for the very worst of our human nature and our evolutionary potential. It is not without reason that she was discovered in 2005, when humanity faces the potential of environmental devastation, another mass extinction, or a profound evolutionary shift.

Catalyse or compromise?

In my book 'Sacred Pathways – Discovering Divine Feminine Archetypes in You' I shared the evolutionary potential of humanity from participation mystique to conscious individuation. How we have disconnected from the natural world, along with our instinctual knowing of oneness with life, into separation and dominance of it. We have become imbalanced through our denial of our animal body. Even in our reaching towards the Heavens, through religion or spirituality, we have not taken our humanness fully with us. Instead, many have labelled our human qualities as 'unreal' or 'illusionary', even as 'evil', either spiritualising our humanness through bypassing, or denouncing it. Yet it is very clear to me, both our humanity and our Earth are screaming for acknowledgement.

Eris is an awakener archetype. Her mandate is to cause unrest for the sake of evolution into more embodied consciousness. This happens through disruption in outer life that penetrates to the core of our human fears, our security consciousness. Such disruption of what we rely on, or consider stable, makes us extremely uncomfortable. It makes us vulnerable – but only to what is deeply true, or essential. Where we can accept discomfort as an agent of change there is potential to evolve. Yet evolution is not without its crises.

Eris acts through the fight mode of human survival instinct. That fight is motivated by threat, conflict, and competition, or by a desire to evolve beyond our current capacities. We use the energy of willpower, as motivation or force, to act to keep ourselves safe, to fight what is happening, to crumble in confusion, or to resolve and potentially evolve. Whatever our reaction, it's the Aries energy that is active in our reaction or response.

The zodiac sign of Aries, being the first sign of the zodiac, is both instinctive and primal, freedom loving and combative. It is where we act and react without forethought. It is where we defend a personal position. Remember, as Eris has been in Aries since 1922 and remains there until 2048, she is in this fiery first sign of the zodiac for almost every human being on the planet. As with any energy, the sign of Aries can act healthily or be out of balance. It can range from healthy self-confidence to overly aggressive to passive-aggressive, to manipulative to self-repressive whilst inwardly seething. Through her link with Aries (and her mythic brother Ares), Eris expresses similarly in us all. Our experience of her energies and her expression ranges through victim orientation to growth orientation. These are the two faces of Eris in us.

When we have encountered, accept, and engage Eris's play within us, we can be said to be mature in our understanding of crisis or chaos as the agent of change. Eris then acts to support us in defying our unhealthy habits, going beyond unconscious needs for approval, or playing by society's false rules. Her radical intelligence is awake in us and in that, is growing ever more conscious of denial and suppression of the deepest truths. She helps us explore the depths of self-honesty within us, which when it's alive, is always changing. Mature Eris understands the need to mitigate antagonistic reactions to a higher unity beyond reaction. She knows anger is an effective tool but a poor master, so a transforming Eris in us will challenge our use of it. She calls for personal will, the 'me first' of Aries to be in service to higher consciousness, to divine will, to growth for us all, an evolving humanity.

Eris is a Sacred Feminine warrior for soul purpose, the deepest truth. In her finest expression she honours chaos as potentially constructive, depending on how we react to it. Physically, she moves through the survival reaction within us as a healthy result of crisis. When she's awake in us, we recognise our instinctual reactions to physical threat as utterly natural, feeling it viscerally and responding or reacting appropriately. I experienced this whilst living in New Zealand through two years of strong earthquakes. I was fully aware of my body's survival mechanism being active. It felt like a layer of armouring within my body fascia, my senses on constant high alert. I did not allow fear to dictate my actions though, except when I was in imminent danger, and it was necessary. This is an evolving Eris at play – responding to an actual threat, not a psychological one.

This period of heightened instinctual reaction taught me about how our human survival mechanism works – how it's a healthy response to the threat of danger or death. It taught me about taking good care of my human system – instinctual, mental, and emotional. I learned how the mind could feed the heightened state of vigilance that comes with danger or hold it with awakened conscious response. I learnt to feel my fear but not to feed it. I discovered how to take better care of the health of my body, particularly its hormonal system. Although it was an extremely challenging period in my life, I learnt much about how my human survival system works, what is natural and what distorts a natural response. For the truth is, wisdom is, the recognition that our reactions have been corrupted, perhaps through the civilising process. Now we react to all kinds of threats, real and imagined.

Eris in us is not afraid of emotional reactions. She calls us to develop our response to them consciously, recognising them as signals of imbalance or misalignment. This is a maturing process. Maturity means we've learned to discern, that we have realised not everything in life is personal, or that where it feels personal, it is a catalyst for growth. Eris in us realises that ultimately, our reactions hold a gift of wisdom, an energy to be seen and embraced. As we take the lid off our reactivity, as we let go of controlling and judging it, it reveals the potential for a new relationship with self, leading to new values and ways of being. Reaction, although challenging, is a catalyst. It upsets the established order.

As we break our own unconscious rules about behaviour; those we have taken on without question from family and societal conditioning, we begin to realise that we can be unknowingly complicit in maintaining an unhealthy system. Freeing ourselves up from complying for peace, from compromising what we know to be true, we are more available to our self and our potential for creative fullness. As we take life less personally,

155

our energy is drawn towards its centre, we become grounded in authenticity and begin to discover deeper meaning in our own life stream. Eris in us then expresses through passion for our own way of looking at things, despite resistance or censure from the world around us. Einstein is a good example of this. 1905 is known as his miracle year. Despite considerable ridicule or misunderstanding from the scientific community, he came up with five theories that changed the face of physics! Eris was clearly alive in him.

However uncomfortable, a mature Eris in us understands and inhabits her right to exist in a world that doesn't welcome her, or her truth. She challenges the need to belong at the cost of pure authenticity. Authenticity then becomes a ground of being to operate from. She empowers standing firm within the challenge of conflict in relationship as a means of evolution. Even playfully active in bursting other individual's bubbles of illusion, or pretence, as she did with the Golden Apple. She may appear malicious or mischievous, but Aries is the sign of innocence. It doesn't think through its actions or reactions; it merely expresses or moves.

If a warrior (the Aries archetype) thinks before acting, it's likely he won't survive. His world is one of pure instinctual action and reaction. Such a way of being (as many with strong Aries energy may know) can be challenging, even shocking to others, especially those it affects. But this is an Eris gift. I received pure Eris reflection from a friend many years ago, when she said to me, "Cassandra, I love your honesty, but sometimes it's like being hit with a sledgehammer!". It utterly shocked me but was eye-opening. I welcomed it. Although I didn't know of Eris then, it was Eris in my friend meeting Eris in me! My friend's forthright statement supporting me to see my own sometimes brutal self-expression in truth. I didn't take my friend's statement personally; I used it to grow. When Eris is taken personally, we may experience her as destructive, despite her intention. Then she can express through us as reaction, rising in fury at provocation, or defending the ego and its stance, afraid to back down when we appear to be being made wrong.

The second face of Eris expresses her shadow aspects from a foundation of victim mentality. When our sense of self is weak, Eris energy can wreak havoc within and with others. The placement of Eris in Aries (for all human beings alive now in 2022) can symbolise a deep wounding to identity and self-trust. As such, being the fighter of the survival system, her energies can actively provoke competition, simply for the sake of a fight, or can turn inwards towards oneself. Such energies struggle to assert a sense of self in a healthy way. They play either through masks of compliance to social trends, particularity on social media, without any true foundation in self-knowledge and confidence, by bucking the system without any real foundation in truth, or by withdrawing. Eris as victim is the ego's immediate reaction to any kind of psychological threat, even a 'wrong look' provoking an aggressive reaction, albeit masked. The antagonistic or withdrawn victim stance comes from insecurity, lack of self-esteem, and feeling unsafe. Reaction may arise through the Eris signature of being ostracised as a troublemaker, or simply feeling like an outsider. With an Eris wounding, life and interactions with others are often taken too personally. This can result in a violent attack (of oneself or another) in defence of the victim wound.

The victim stance, rather than being overly aggressive in reaction, can also express through manipulation. Where Eris is not allowed out to play in constructive ways, she can turn inward to create wounding through self-hatred, the biting inner critic or super-ego. Externally we see the passive-aggressive stance of Eris that deliberately stirs up trouble simply for effect, without there being substance behind the behaviour. Misplaced anger simply creates chaos. It is controlling, potentially keeping others in a position that makes the angry one feel safe, or distortedly satisfied at creating obstacles for others. It's the underhand use of trauma that comes from oppression or being ostracised. It's over-reliance on validation-seeking in a negative way, so obvious in children's behaviour when they feel unloved. At its worst, it's a reaction to deep psychological, mental, or physical abuse. I experienced this in the manipulation of a violent husband, who justified his actions through my apparent behaviour or moods. Such behaviour is always based in powerlessness, despite its aggression. Even what seems to be indifference can be a mask of self-denial or hostility turned inward. When Eris is playing as victim, always the action or reaction is inappropriate to what comes before it. Yet even that is a catalyst. For Eris is always asking: what is the deeper truth here?

Honesty is key

Eris calls us to awaken unconscious behaviour patterns within the self, particularly when they operate through reaction. She is the requirement for honesty, the willingness to explore what's not working, or is painful, in our lives. She plays in so many subtle ways – through the shadows of female competitiveness, where we collude with patriarchal mindset to be the 'best', where we put on a mask of civilisation to play nicely but it is only skin deep, where we bite our tongue to fit in. Self-honesty is the starting point for transforming Eris energy within us from victim to catalyst for growth.

When we engage Eris consciously, she acts like a laser beam, pinpointing the truth. She's certainly not comfortable to be around, or to engage within our self, yet her honesty is ultimately refreshing when we seek to grow. We see growth-orientated Eris at play when we face and engage our shadow energy to fuel our evolution, to become healthier conscious human beings. We see her at play when we strive for growth. This is where a habit of aggressively expressing or holding anger, can transform to becoming a warrior for honesty, for truth. Eris has no need to incite or enjoy violence. She naturally uses her will to create change. She simply is who she is, seeing through the facades and behind the masks, caring deeply for truth.

The challenge of Eris when her archetype is strong in us, is we cannot pretend. Often people may feel uneasy around a strong Eris woman. There's an energetic resonance that speaks volumes. She's not a follower and she's not passive. She's purely herself.

Honesty in us knows that the nature of change, even when self-motivated, is disruptive. As our established behaviour patterns give way to the possibility of change, often we experience chaos. In our relationships, honesty potentially leads to strife. Yet without honesty how true is relationship anyway? Honesty is love, when it is delivered without censure; it is self-love and potentially the opening to love with others. When we are not honest, we are somehow diminished, yet we don't know why. It's because we are not fully inhabiting our self or our lives.

We cannot have a healthy relationship with our self without challenge and turmoil, without becoming a little, or very, messy. it is a healthy requirement of change that we can hold ourselves with love when we are in the uncertainty and confusion of changing. After all, change is the very fact of life, mirrored to us through the natural world. If we are awake, every day the flow of our changing thoughts, feelings and emotions will be disruptive at some level. Being alive without strife is naïve. Just as love without strife is an unrealistic expectation. If a relationship has no friction in it, it's dead. Friction is a necessary aspect of growth. Think of the pressure of a seed's shoot breaking through the earth in spring. Yet where friction leads to conflict without growth, or love, we are facing Eris's darker side. As Eris shows us, strife without love is war, rather than an impetus to evolve, to deepen.

Becoming an agent of social change

Eris's activity as an agent of social change becomes a primary expression when she is becoming integrated within an individual. Moreover, she often signifies the action of an individual to initiate social change becoming widespread. This expression of her strong evolutionary imperative is reflected by some of the aspects she was making (especially with fellow evolutionary planets Uranus & Pluto) long before her discovery. I've already mentioned the environmental shifts that took place around the time of her discovery. Just a few examples before that include the opening of the first rape crisis centres in the UK and USA in the 1970's, as Pluto was opposing Eris, and the #metoo statement (instigated by Tarana Burke in 2006) becoming a global movement as Uranus was conjunct Eris in 2017. Whether activated by violation of the natural world, or the plight of those most vulnerable, the disenfranchised in society, by the presence of dishonesty, or simply through an individual's passion and drive, Eris shocks us out of our blindness and comfort zones, towards enlightened action.

Once we are rooted in growing healthy relationship with our emotions and instinctual reactions, Eris is a platform from which to enter the world as a mover and shaker. Without that growing healthy self-honest relationship to our own reactions, there's always a risk of self-sabotage, for busting our own ego is an Eris gift.

Eris in the world seeks to address issues that are not considered important by the status quo, or that have been side-lined as unimportant. She finds the weak spot in any system very naturally, for she feels it instinctively. The honesty of Eris in us is so fiercely honed, that she is a threat to what deems to be civilised but is corrupt; the abuse of power that is rife in our current global paradigm. This is the main reason she is unwelcomed, an uninvited guest. For she will reveal the elephant in the room; she will speak the truths that others don't want to hear or be accountable for. Eris is a catalyst that opens the locked cupboards of secrets and lies. All for the sake of growth, yet also to simply see what happens. As Eris's capacity for revelation and creating trouble is rooted in the instinctual layers of our being, it is action more than words that is the mover and shaker. Like her action with the Golden Apple, she reveals what's underlying the games through what she does, rather than what she says. Her actions can instigate reaction, where those involved may unwittingly display their true intentions or underlying agenda.

Where Eris is active in us, the energy of 'Enough!' is strong. We get to see where we have zero-tolerance for bullshit. Eris is the courage to engage the masks and facades of polite society or the corporate maze. She's where our fierceness meets purpose. One key of activist Eris in us, is in engaging with strong personal feelings (not denying or suppressing them) but acting impersonally. This initiates the fight for a cause that has influence in more than our personal lives. It requires risk-taking, for we are breaking boundaries of what is deemed acceptable. We are going beyond the false ethics of a patriarchal world to create freedom for more than our personal self. This is freedom of being beyond what is generally considered to be civilised, anathema to man-made law where it does not serve. 'Erin Brockovich' (the woman and the movie) are a strong example of Eris in action. There are many more.

Eris moves to bring about true justice, where the 'system' is just paying lip-service to it. She calls us to come into alignment with what serves the whole. This is where the healthy use of will, or even force of will (consider those gluing themselves to the streets in recent Extinction Rebellion protests) can be used intentionally and purposefully to create disruption. Eris rules a way of life that comes from inner alignment, not a system of ethics, laws and rules imposed by those who seek to control rather than serve. As such, she is naturally controversial, taking us to our edges and beyond.

Disruption, despite its challenge to our human need for certainty, is always an aspect of a healthy system, whether through the actions of social justice warriors, a pandemic or natural disasters. Nature's storms and wildfires, albeit devastating, are a healthy aspect of rejuvenation. They remove the 'dead wood', that is no longer needed; they clear space for new growth or for specific species that fuel diversity. Our bodies have evolved to manage disruption to a healthy system. Stem cells, that give rise to different tissues and organs in an embryo, have the potential to also develop into different cell types in an adult. Some scientists now suggest that faulty stem cells may play a role in the development of cancer. Like Eris, they have two functions, as potential challengers to health and as catalysts for health. Similarly, the bodies T and B cells are natural born killers, circulating through the body to identify, deactivate, and get rid of potentially harmful substances or rogue cells.

Like disruption, discord (from 'dis' meaning 'apart' and 'cor' (genitive cordis) meaning 'heart') is usually taken to signify conflict. More accurately it relates to contrasting resonance, the differing frequencies we encounter in our daily interactions and how we respond or react to them. 'Apart heart' could be said to represent where we're not truly living from the heart. This often happens when our natural capacity for connection is stifled by conditioning (our beliefs, fears, and prejudices) and projection of difference as a threat. With an active Eris, we are challenged to be honest about this, to stretch beyond what's familiar and comfortable, to risk engagement in a new way. She is a natural bridge-builder through difference, particularly in relationships.

Eris's nature within relating is illuminated in that she was excluded from the wedding of Peleus and Thetis. For marriage and autonomy are uneasy companions. They are an evolutionary, somewhat experimental, element in partnership in our time. An individual with an active Eris may find intimate relating challenging, for the desire for truth is often felt to be anathema to intimacy. Yet in my experience, it feeds it. Eris teaches us to evolve from fear of honesty, through competitive or compromised relating, towards collaborative relationships where conflict is known to be a healthy motivator for growth. In conscious partnership, with a willing partner for evolution, Eris can integrate with other Sacred Feminine archetypes, thus creating rich and rewarding connections.

Living paradox as reality

At core, the Eris archetype reflects a basic discord between our animal nature along with its natural will to survive, our evolutionary consciousness and the fact of death. Eris calls us to be the conscious bridge for all of this, not just for our self but for us all. The truth, as Eris sees it, is we are both consciousness and form, both eternal and subject to the natural laws of change. New physics now demonstrates all matter is both energy and form, particle, and wave. Perhaps the truth of our dual nature is our basic conflict? To go beyond it into truth, we must embrace the impasse of opposites to come to the paradox of 'both/and'. We must navigate the inherent challenge of conflict between our self as a spark of divine consciousness, as ego and as instinct. This is Eris's realm, both in her lower frequency expression and her evolutionary state in us.

The scientific logical mind works through differentiation, boxing up different aspects of our being as separate, potentially complementary, or contradictory, but seldom unified. We do this to create knowledge, that potentially informs progress, and to create emotional security. For the chaos of an ever-changing nature, filled with contradiction, is a threat to stability, to the ego's desire to know what is happening. If we think we know, we feel safe. Yet science now knows that even the presence of an observer influences outcomes. Life clearly reveals to us that change and flux expressing as infinite possibilities are the only certainty. When we choose to live with the fact of uncertainty, we become more available to our free-flowing evolutionary potential.

The quest for civilisation, or for progress, is different to that of evolution perhaps? I would certainly say so. The history of civilisation (as it has been recorded) reveals not only a growth process but the control and domination of unacceptable elements of our nature. Does this work? Or has it simply led to a denial of our nature as one with Nature? Have our attempts to suppress our naturalness led to the chaos we are trying hard to avoid? In so many ways we fail to see that our violation of the natural world is a violation of ourselves, and vice versa. Perhaps Eris is the cosmic awakener to shock us into recognition that our betrayal of the natural world, comes from our denial of, or discomfort with, our own instinctual nature.

So how might we close the divide between being civilised and honouring our wild nature, our oneness with the natural world and its ever-changing rhythms? One clear way is through the fact of death. When civilisation avoids the fact of death, then we are immediately disconnected from the very basic truth of our human nature. How might we live, awake consciously to death's imminence – death as a fact and as the nature of change. How might we connect with that fact, not through fear but as truth? Eris, as representative of the deepest truth, brings us to awareness of cosmic law. All physical bodes are born, change and die, even stars. In this knowledge and in conscious alignment with it, would we not live differently? Would we not recognise the wonder of every moment of being alive in a body? Would we not dare to live more fully? Would we not recognise that we are both a unique aspect of life in expression and yet also one with it? Paradox.

Eris demonstrates our potential to grow from polarised consciousness into the Mystery in radical ways. The strange thing is, we already are that Mystery in form. Many philosophical systems and religions already point towards this. Buddhist interbeing states that the existence of light points to the existence of darkness; there cannot be one without the other. The yin-yang symbol of Chinese philosophy states similarly. It mirrors opposite qualities, or polarity, as contrast yet also complementary, rather than conflicting. One naturally contains the seed of the other.

These systems may support our denial of contradiction as a reality too, through judging the instinctual responses and reactions of our humanness. The gift of Eris, even in her war-like nature, is that she chose no side. She knew that the misery of conflict affected both sides equally. Whilst the other gods watched the battle from afar and did nothing to intervene, Eris stood at the centre of the conflict. Nowhere in her mythology does it state that she incited it. She witnessed it from the centre of the chaos. This is her most profound key.

When we can stand at the centre of our lives, holding paradox, even though that may mean 'I don't know…. until I do' we are actively engaging Eris's wisdom. The certainty is that change will happen, often instinctively, or change will find us. We are moved in the moment, without an agenda to be in control. Or we simply act. Whilst standing at the centre of the chaos, the tension of holding opposites requires that we evolve through the insecurity of not knowing, through the Mystery of life, rather than polarise into either/or, this/that division, creating conflict in our self. Seen in this light, with her origins in a growing patriarchy based on control of nature and of women, Eris begins to look like the scapegoat.

The root of the issue of change is not chaos - a fundamental aspect of existence - but the human ego's need to control. The need for control can lead to acting in arrogance, either unaware or wilfully ignoring the full dynamic of a situation. Similarly, discord, dissonance, competition, even conflict, are not of themselves problematic. What creates the problem is the established order of social mores that no longer serve. Or the tyranny of an ego believing itself to be separate from the natural order of life, with rational thinking that needs to separate to maintain the illusion of control. Eris in us invites us to go beyond the superficiality, and damage-inducing separative consciousness, to a deeper recognition of reality. She invites us into unity with the chaos of life. With this recognition, the Golden Apple myth could have had a different outcome perhaps. If the Goddesses had been truly self-connected and in harmony with each other, they might have laughed about the Golden Apple bouncing into the wedding feast. Perhaps they would have thrown it to each other shouting in celebration, 'To you my lovely, for are we not all fair?'

Eris reveals the paradox: competition can lead us to recognise unity. Such is the nature of life: appearing separate yet not.

Chapter 3

At the Crossroads – Witch
Queen Hekate

Stay or go?
How to know?
Is this choice
a glimmer of light
or taking flight?

This dance
of 'make a choice'
is a cross,
seemingly
a game
of gain or loss.
Who's the chooser?
Perhaps the loser?

Does it matter?
This way, that?
Who can say?
Yes/No is the Kiwi way.

Yet
sitting on the fence
creates defence.
Fear, doubt,
either/or
dance of choice
deluding me
whilst
Mystery beckons.

In confusion
Mystery

is non-revealing.

An opening
to who knows what?
Endless possibilities
infinitely appealing?

Stop!
Relax and wait.
Light appears.
Hekate's torch
begins to glow.

This is truth:
life is a choice field.
There's no escape.

Beyond should,
beyond could,
beyond what's right,
Hekate guides.
She holds the light,
She knows the play,
She knows the way.

On this cross
of choice,
Hekate's keys
jangle me.
Yet I'm at peace.
As I trust & wait
in liminal space.
Cassandra Eve

Archetype: The Goddess of the Crossroads; Witch Queen; Crone; Guide through the soul's dark night

Symbols: Two or three torches; keys; Hekate's wheel; a bronze dagger; a knife or sword; a rope; dogs, snakes, lions, horses, and bears; red mullet; a headdress of stars; black poplars and yew trees; herbs and herbal medicine

Message: Trust the resting place of the unseen and unknown. Be in liminal space.

Themes: a guardian of the unconscious and the Underworld; cutting through duality and the threads of the known; death and the dead; interdimensional doorways; the liminal space; crone wisdom; protector of the threshold; sanctuary & refuge; oracular wisdom; the witch archetype & magic; connection to gifts of the natural world.

What the Hekate archetype calls for: Deep trust in the processes of loss and the cycles of life. Trusting the unseen, the liminal space where all possibilities exist.

Also known as: syncretised with Isis, Artemis, Selene, and Ereshkigal.

One of the most well-known Feminine archetypal forms in ancient mythology is the Triple Goddess: Maiden, Mother and Crone. To ancient writers and storytellers in western culture, the Triple Goddess represented the rhythm of the Moon's cycles, the ability to shapeshift, the power of transformation, and the seasonal progression. She stood for the three primary phases of the Moon: New Moon, Full Moon, and Dark Moon. Hekate is one representation of this Sacred Feminine archetype whose roots lie in pre-history.

Hekate was known as both an unwed crone, linked with the dark phase of the Moon, and the entirety of the Triple Goddess energy. As Triple Goddess she is named Triformis (Three Formed) and Trimorphis (Three Morphed). The Greeks honoured her in this form by giving her dominion over the Heavens, Earth, and the Underworld. Hekate is more commonly seen to preside only over the Underworld and death; the secrets of regeneration; magic, ritual, and prophetic vision where she is known as Mistress of the Restless Dead, Mistress of the Crossroads. Hekate is associated with initiation ceremonies across the ancient world. These include the Mysteries of Eleusis and Selinus in Sicily. She was also worshipped in temples on the islands of Samothrace and Aegina, along with Argos on the Greek mainland. There was a major Hekate temple in the city of Lagina, now in modern Turkey, where a ceremony of the key was held annually.

Statues and representations of Hekate appear as three female figures conjoined; as one body with three female heads and a triple crown; or with three animal heads - cow, dog, dragon, goat, horse, serpent in any combination. Hekate's three faces represent her sovereignty over the three worlds: Heavens, Earth, and the Underworld. In the realm of nature, she was associated with Moon Goddesses Selene and Artemis, the huntress, whilst she presided over the Underworld. Similarly, she is linked, as the waning and dark Moon, with Artemis as the crescent Moon, and Selene representing the bright full Moon. As Moon Goddess Hekate stands for the power inherent in the darkest nights. These three phases are also reflected in the ancient Triple Goddess and the three phases of a woman's life told within the Persephone myth: Persephone as daughter and maiden, Ceres as mother, and Hekate as crone.

Whatever her changing form through the ages, Hekate travelled to and from the Underworld at will, so is a potent guide between worlds. She is a torch and key bearer, guide, companion, and protector.

Her-story

As with many of the Greek and Roman Goddesses, Hekate's origins are complex and mostly lost in pre-history. Her roots are many yet indistinct. At different times she was syncretized with Isis, Ereshkigal, Artemis, and Selene. The Greek name of Hekate may derive from an earlier Egyptian frog-headed midwife goddess called Heqet, Heqit, or Heket, who ruled over magic and fertility. She was associated with Egyptian Hathor, celebrated as a resurrection goddess, and loved by women. The Greek word hekatos, meaning "who works from afar," may be a reference to Hekate's magic powers, but may also reference her possible origins in Egypt. There are also links to Hekate-like archetypes in Bulgaria, Serbia, and Romania.

In ancient sources, Hekate first appears in Greek mythology as a goddess given great honour, with domains in Sky, Earth, and Sea. According to Hesiod's Theogony, composed 730–700 BCE, in which he describes the origins and genealogies of the Greek Gods, Hekate is the daughter of Perses and Asteria, making her the granddaughter of the Titans, Phoebe and Coeus. Hesiod describes Hekate in these glowing terms: *"Zeus, Cronus's son, honoured [Hekate] above all others. He gave her splendid gifts, to have a share of the earth and of the unfruitful sea. She received honour also in starry heaven and is honoured exceedingly by the deathless gods."*

On the other hand, Euripides (480-406BCE), mentions her mother is a different Titan, Leto, mother of Apollo and Artemis. These differing origins reflect how both time and history hide the deepest truths. It is a mirror for their innate mystery. It reveals how different archetypes hold the same root energy yet change appearance or expression through time and culture.

Although a powerful goddess, Hekate was not a major deity within the Greek pantheon. Like many of the pre-patriarchal goddesses, her roots and her ancient dark face as a Moon goddess were sanitised by the Greek culture, When Olympian God Zeus took power by killing his father, Ouranos (Uranus), he ousted the Titans. With Hekate (also a Titan) he was more accepting. He offered her the power he alone had, to grant or deny humanity anything she wished. He gave her dominion over the Heavens, Earth, and the Underworld. She was both a bestower of blessings and the guardian of birth, life, and death. This gift of power reflects the importance of Hekate within the pre-Olympian hierarchy. She was seen to act as a gateway to the Great Mother energy: She who births all and takes all forms back into Herself at death. Perhaps the change in her status under the Greeks shows Zeus's awe (or fear) of the potent nature of the Dark Goddess.

The Greeks portray Hekate as a torch-bearing Moon goddess who wears a headdress of stars, lighting the way for those who need it. She had few temples in the ancient world, but small household shrines dedicated to her were common. The ancient Greeks worshiped her in various ways, seeing her as a guardian and protector of households. It was common practice to place images of the Triple Goddess on city walls and gates, entrances to sacred sites, and the doorways of private homes, where it was believed she warded off evil spirits. A triple Hekate form - the 'Hekate Epipyrgidia' by the 5th-century BCE sculptor Alcamenes -

guarded the entrance to the Acropolis of Athens. Examples of triple-form Hekate statues can be found in the Vatican Museum and Antiquities Museum of Leiden. She is also seen commonly on Byzantine, Roman, Jewish, and Greek coins from 400BCE to 222CE, a lengthy period. This symbology (over 600 years) shows her wide-ranging presence as protectress. Her presence on coins, with the growth of money's perceived power amongst human beings, reveals how she was respected in their cultures.

Hekate sculptures at important sites, her presence on coins, and her appearance in text fragments known as the Chaldean Oracles, reveal her significance in the ancient world. The Chaldean Oracles were originally a single mystical poem received in trance by Julian the Chaldean, or his son Julian the Theurgist, in the 2nd century CE. In these writings Hekate is associated with the Anima Mundi, the World Soul. The Anima Mundi is purported to be a principle bringing the Universe to life, much as the soul animates a human being's body. This idea of the world as a living spiritual being was put forth in the writings of early philosophers. They referred to this spiritual essence of the world as the anima mundi, the 'Soul of the World', a divine essence that embraces and moves all life in the Universe. The Greeks were profoundly interested in and inspired by the wisdom traditions of other nations, particularly the Egyptian and Chaldean (otherwise known as Babylonian). They believed the wisdom of these cultures was rooted in ancient sources and wisdom traditions.

Oracles were in common use in both Chaldea and Greece, so the Chaldean Oracles were highly venerated by the Greeks as a true source of mystical knowledge. This adds stature to Hekate's role in their culture and maybe why Zeus honoured her with such breadth of power.

Even given this highly significant role within both ancient and Greek cultures, over time Hekate came to be associated only with the Underworld and its spirits. As patriarchal thinking took over, the denial of the innate sacredness of the natural world and women grew. The early days of Christianity compounded this. The church fathers created a doctrine where the world (including nature and human beings) was neither divine nor sacred, but only God was the source of creation. They placed humanity in exile from the divine, in a state of sin, thus creating a split between matter and spirit. As this belief took over, the Anima Mundi, and Hekate's association with it, was carried forward only by a few, mainly the Gnostics and many alchemists.

In the Greek culture, as patriarchy took hold, Hekate's role as guardian and protector was forgotten or more likely, denounced. She came to symbolise only the darker side of the human experience: the dark of the Moon, death, witchcraft, magic, dreams, fierce hounds, and devilish creatures that roam the darkness of night. She became a torch-bearing goddess of the night, accompanied by ghosts, her passing marked by the baying of dogs. Hekate's accoutrements as a guardian of the Underworld were serpents, keys, daggers, and torches. Her function was cutting the cords of the past and lighting the way for those in transition after death.

This link with the Underworld, rather than the three worlds Zeus gave Hekate power over, perhaps came about through the Homeric Hymn to Demeter (Ceres). In the myth of Persephone's abduction, Hekate is the only one to hear Persephone's cries. It was Hekate who suggested asking Sun God, Helios, what he had witnessed when Persephone disappeared. Eventually she becomes Persephone's guide between the Underworld and the human world, using her torches to light the journey. I went fully into this myth and the Demeter (Ceres) archetype in my book Sacred Pathways – Discovering Divine Feminine Archetypes in You.

This myth is an evolutionary story based on the essential tearing apart of the mother/daughter symbiotic relationship. The quintessential representation of Hekate, as a goddess holding a flaming torch in each hand, is derived from it. It's interesting to note that the myth relates Hekate asking Helios for insight, rather than relying on her own inner light of wisdom, represented by her torches. It's a shift away from the ancient wisdom she represents towards the solar light of patriarchy, represented by Helios. Yet still Hekate acted as guide for Persephone's return and emergence from the Underworld in each transition. In The Homeric Hymn to Demeter, Hekate is described as both preceding and following Persephone, suggesting she both prepares the way for her and follows her. As transition is a time when we are most at risk, Hekate's guardianship of Persephone's passage strengthens her continuing role as a protectress.

The Homeric Hymn probably dates to the first half of the 6th century BCE, but its origins are uncertain. As with many Sacred Feminine archetypes, how the change in Hekate's role takes place is uncertain. What is certain is that it did. The myth and Homeric Hymn related to the Eleusinian rites, demonstrating nature's cycles of birth, life, death and rebirth, and our human unity with that cycle. In these rites Demeter represents the force that sustains life (Mother); Hekate acts as a keeper of the Underworld, the vital force that both pushes the plants up from the ground to light and draws them back down at death; Persephone is the mediator between the two; the light-filled Earth world and the dark mysterious Underworld. Although the form of expression that the Eleusinian mysteries took remains a mystery to us, there is no doubt Eleusis was an important spiritual centre and that Hekate was intimately involved in these rites with Demeter and Persephone. At other Demeter temples, including those in Sicily and on Samothrace, Hekate is found as a guardian at the gates. Despite the patriarchal overlay, her role and importance for women continues.

Another myth of Greek origin may point in part towards Hekate's role change, her demotion from Triple Goddess to Guardian of the

Underworld. In this tale she incurred the wrath of Hera (Juno) by stealing a pot of rouge to give to her father Zeus's lover, Europa. Afraid of Hera's anger, Hekate fled into the house of a woman who had just given birth. At that time, contact with childbirth was considered to make you impure – an undeniable legacy of patriarchal control, keeping women away from their places of power - so Hekate was plunged into the river Acheron of the Underworld where she remained, banished. Hekate then became known as the Prytania, the 'Invincible Queen of the Dead.' As Prytania, her magic included purifications, penances, and enchantments. As souls entered the Underworld, passing the triple-headed Cerberus, and judged by the three Judges of the Dead, they came to Hekate's triple crossroads. Here she sends them on to the appropriate realm for their journey. Those who had lived mediocre lives went to the Asphodel Meadows; those deemed wicked went to Tartarus; the heroes and those of good deeds went to the Orchards of Elysium, the Greek equivalent of paradise.

Crossroads have a sinister reputation throughout history, often being depicted as places of terrible deeds such as kidnapping, hangings and murder. In ancient times, victims of violent crimes were often buried at crossroads so that Hekate would find them and despatch them speedily to her domain. Her presence as a funerary priestess was acknowledged at tombs and funerals, for she was active in liberating the souls of the newly dead. To the Greeks the night roads were the roads of fate, yet it seems Hekate's more creative role and powers were eventually forgotten by the Greeks as her role as a guardian of the Underworld overlaid them. She became the protectress of remote places, her triple nature suggesting her presence where three roads converged.

Over time Hekate's role as the Guardian at the Crossroads took on cult status. Triple-faced Goddess figures were frequently found at crossroads, or other boundary places, with offerings of ritual food left there by the ancient Greeks during special festivals, particularly at the dark of the Moon. Her cult followers often left offerings or scraps of food at this sacred place for dogs (or the poor) to scavenge. These offerings could take the form of small cakes, eggs, cheese, bread, and dog meat. They were lit with miniature torches. A dish of red mullet, which was usually prohibited from offerings to the other gods, was often offered too. It was common for Hekate to be offered the sacrifice of dogs, especially puppies. This came about through the belief that dogs would eat the dead who'd been left unburied. This links Hekate back to Egypt once more, to the Egyptian God Anubis, who guided souls to the Underworld. For protection and positive magic, herbs, myrrh, seeds, or fruit pips were also left at crossroads. The goddess was especially appealed to for support in magic and curses. She became known as a magician and seer, purported to send prophetic dreams to humans.

On her nocturnal wanderings, Hekate's animal familiars were her hounds. She was often accompanied by a pack of black baying hounds, or Cerberus, the three-headed dog of the Underworld. She was also a guardian of all wild animals, sometimes shown with three animal heads; dog, snake, and lion; or dog, horse, and bear. All these animals are considered sacred to her, but a dog is usually her primary animal familiar. They were considered harbingers of death, yet also to carry the dead across to the refuge of the Underworld. The Greek three-headed hound of the Underworld, Cerberus, may be an earlier form of Hekate and is certainly connected to her role.

At times Hekate was accompanied by her three sisters, the Erinyes, or Furies, who punished those who insulted, disobeyed, or violated a mother. Hermes is another familiar companion to Hekate, as he is the only other god who traverses all three realms. In some sources they are purported to be lovers. Circe and Medea, both accredited with magical and divinatory powers of shapeshifting, enchantment, and herbal medicine, are said to be their daughters. In another myth Hekate is married to Aeetes and these two daughters are with him. Circe is the first great witch in Greek mythology, with wide-ranging magical abilities – controlling the weather, love, magic, the ability to move unseen, shapeshifting, control of animals, and herbal lore. The most famous tale of Circe involves Odysseus, who was only able to escape her magic using an herb given him by Mercury. Medea is portrayed as either a villainess or tragic heroine, depending on who you read. She is described alternately as a daughter, or priestess of Hekate. Her reputation was to bring the dead back to life, continuing the thread of meaning symbolised by Hekate.

Hekate's meaning is deeply embedded in her symbols, that also demonstrate her powers. With her keys she unlocks the secrets of the Underworld and liminal spaces, the secrets of occult mysteries. Her rope represents the umbilical cord of renewal and rebirth; her sacred dagger relates to ritual power to cut delusion, to sever the past and whatever is ripe for death. She continued to serve a purpose as protector and guardian, despite her patriarchally induced reputation as a dark figure. Greek women called on Hekate as a protectress for their families from the wandering dead. Her image was set outside their homes to let these wanderers know that they honoured their queen and therefore not to haunt them.

According to church records the practice of leaving Hekate's suppers at the crossroads continued into the 11th century CE, maybe longer. Eventually Hekate's role became fully demonised as the patriarchal and dualistic views of 'good and evil' became entrenched in the collective. The Church actively projected fear about the nature of women and the mysteries of the Feminine onto Hekate. Midwives, healers, nature-based medicine women, those who bucked the system, and even those who simply refused to comply to the controls of a husband, father, or brother, were caught in these projections of 'evil'. Hekate's role as Guardian of the Three Worlds became lost in the evolving dualistic paradigm. Yet she is not lost. She remains waiting at the crossroads for those who seek her guidance, for those who are willing to enter her mysterious realm.

Hekate's place in the Universe – Astronomy & Astrology

The asteroid Hekate was officially discovered by J.C. Watson on 11 July 1868 in the main asteroid belt between Mars and Jupiter. Her asteroid number is 100 as she was the 100th asteroid discovered. Her orbit is 5.43 years.

Asteroid Hekate is in the same area of space as the Hygiea family, a group of dark, carbonaceous asteroids that also includes Artemis. Hekate is considered too light to naturally belong to this family, so is classed as an interloper. In her discovery chart, the planet of awakening, Uranus, is in exact conjunction with bright Sirius, the brightest star of them all, also known as the Dog Star. What a symbol for Hekate's torch! There is an interesting synchronicity with dogs there too. This star suggests the capacity to shine a bright light out of darkness, to illuminate the way.

Hekate by sign and aspect in an individual's astrology chart may reveal gifts of deep intuitive knowing; the capacity to hold space for transitions; knowledge of plants, sacred medicine, and magic. Intuition is a strong quality associated with this asteroid, as Hekate acts as a messenger between all the realms of intelligence, particularly the conscious and the unconscious mind. She points us in the required direction and teaches us to trust our own decisions.

As the Gatekeeper of the Underworld, Hekate operates as the one who bridges the light with the dark, the living with the dead, negotiating the unseen realms and showing the way when no one else could. Hekate makes her most obvious appearance in the charts of those who work through divination or mediumship, counsellors, psychotherapists, facilitators, shaman, and healers, particularly with natural medicine. If challenged by strong aspects, Hekate's darker side may be evident in an archetypal journey through the Underworld: the use and abuse of drugs; manipulative behaviour patterns; abusive relationships and power struggles with patriarchal authority. She is a strong Sacred Feminine archetype of the Mystery inherent in any transition, particularly for females, a guide through menarche, childbirth, and menopause. She works in conjunction with Persephone – as guide through the initiation of sexuality – as mentor and supporter on the bridges of life and death. As such, she is essential to being conscious in the natural rhythms of our full embodiment.

My journey with Hekate

My life has been a series of transitions, as if many lives are contained within this one life. From childhood into maturity, life would sweep away the existing forms. Or sometimes I was its agent, clearing the decks of my existing life and starting anew. Initially this was patterning rom my childhood, the legacy of being sent away to boarding school and earlier trauma. I'd be left at ground zero, vulnerable and uncertain about what was next. Somehow through it all, I survived and even thrived. Discovering a deeper truth in and of myself was always my guide. I did not know of Hekate, or her role in these experiences, until I was well into my forties. Apt timing for conscious connection with her role in the processes of choice and change, as I entered perimenopause, then menopause, the gateways towards being crone.

Moments of truth change our lives if we let them. I have always been able to let inner truth have its way with me eventually, even though vulnerable, afraid, or filled with apprehension. When it arises, the resonance of truth pierces me – often with utter beauty, sometimes with awe or dread, sometimes both – but I cannot deny it. To do so is to reject my deepest knowing, what I now know to be the Sacred Feminine in me.

Picture this: a cool and beautiful autumn morning in New Zealand. I am living in community, where my life has been passionately engaged for thirteen years, seven of them in New Zealand. I have just awoken and can see the Sun shining on stunning autumn colour through the open curtains. The scene is beautiful, yet somewhat surprisingly, I feel an unexpected deeper calling in my heart. It feels like a deep hunger yet also a blessing. As I gaze at this scene of summer passing in the southern hemisphere, my heart is alive in spring – late spring in England, my favourite time of year. I could viscerally feel nature's wild flourishing in May: lush green hedgerows filled with cow parsley and delicate wildflowers; fresh leaves unfurling as trees donned their new dresses; bluebell woods; early roses; soft daisy-covered lawns. I knew it was time to return to the land of my birth.

When I had moved to New Zealand, I knew it would not be forever. I had simply followed an invitation and fully enjoyed what flowed from it. After seven years of community life in the southern hemisphere, this emergence of spring in England filling my heart came as a complete surprise. My heart was overflowing with its calling, yet to my mind it made no sense. There was no reason behind it. I struggled with the knowing of this truth. Yet I saw clearly that when truth came along, there had never been a reason behind it - simply recognition. I knew I must heed it, otherwise my energy would be split. Knowing truth but not acting on it would cause me pain. I would be at war with myself.

I know now that Hekate was beginning to appear consciously in my life at that time. I was in menopause, being drawn and directed by my inner world in new ways. I was at a crossroads, not knowing where a move back to the UK would take me in my life. Eventually I grounded my inner knowing. I spoke of it with my spiritual teacher and the community. My commitment to truth became ground and came to life. Two months later, I left New Zealand.

I had felt when I left the community that somehow it would travel with me. It did, but not in its previous form. When I reached England, it was clear that part of my life was over. As with any life change, it was useless to hang on. I had reached a completion. I was at rebirth, standing alone, the keys to new life in my hands. A journey into the Underworld, Hekate's realm, followed. She walked with me all the way in and out again, as guide and protectress in deep grieving. Persephone came too. Eventually spring began to emerge within me.

It is only now, through a different transition in my life, that I realise what Hekate opened in me then. The real freedom to arrive, to fully engage what is here, then to fully let go in right timing, whilst resting in transitional space, with all those states sourced from a subtle awareness of completion. That freedom, when rooted in truth, opened deep knowing in me; that when love has been given and received, the purpose of relationship is fulfilled. Whether that remains for a season, a reason, or a lifetime, is not really in our hands. Moments of truth create the crossroads if we listen well. In my life, Hekate's appearance began to open the integration of Maiden-Mother-Crone in me. It is a state of Grace-filled being that expresses as evolving wholeness.

Hekate's Message: Trust the resting place of the unseen and unknown. Be in liminal space.

At the crossroads.

As Guardian of the Three Realms (Underworld, Earth, and Heavens) for the Greeks, Hekate has a natural capacity to see in many directions at once. She liberates us from the rational mind's duality of either/or, and opens the possibility of both/and. The mind's rationale is familiar to us, with its 'either/or' loop, or the direct conflict of opposing viewpoints. Dualism finds us firmly stuck in two separate worlds, with no way of crossing the divide except through compromise. It works from the world of facts so in truth has no place in our inner processes.

Hekate presents other options to the rational scientific way of processing. As with many dark Goddesses, she goes beyond what seem to be the only options, i.e., this way or that, my way, or your way, towards what serves a more expansive way of being. For example, in an individual choice, Hekate guides towards the unseen option; in partnership conflict, she calls towards what serves love or the relationship, rather than either partner. In holding the space beyond duality, Hekate encourages us to engage every facet of the question or challenge. We are encouraged to let go of a simple 'yes/no' solution, to allow previously unseen or unacknowledged dimensions of a question to emerge. This process can take time. It is subtle and requires us to listen deeply, to wait and allow different elements of a situation to cook, just like making a tasty soup.

The symbology of triple faced Hekate reveals the gifts of looking three ways. She represents an holistic expanded vision that bridges past, present and future. Yet it is a perspective that does not sit tightly in these three realms alone. It allows a communication with the unseen worlds, the between-worlds, where psychic gifts or knowing can lead the way. It goes above, beneath, and around particular perspectives, exploring all elements. It's beyond black and white thinking, or conscious and unconscious, and takes us into the grey areas where nothing is clear, yet anything is possible. Opening in this way stretches us beyond our usual patterns of response or reaction. Our sense of possibilities is always limited by the lens we are seeing through – what's familiar rather than what holds real promise. The gift of Hekate is to loosen up our thinking, our beliefs about what we think is possible, into what could be a potential. Her gift is to cultivate and encourage our feeling-intuiting responses to emerge. Her gift is to encourage trust in process orientation and the arrival of serendipitous insight therein.

We come to crossroads in many ways in our daily lives, in the small choices we make hour by hour. Yet inevitably there are times when crisis, moments of truth, situations in which we feel powerless, create a major fork in the road. Crossroads represent these transition times and have spiritual significance. Despite our desire to know, make decisions, manage change, and control outcomes in our lives, transitions hold the space of unknowability where past, present and future collide. Our dilemma is to choose well. Yet often this is the most difficult task. This point of a process raises self-doubt and fears, the 'what-ifs' of uncertainty. Sometimes we simply leap, we choose quickly to avoid the uncomfortable crucible of not knowing, or to avoid a certain projected outcome; other times we simply avoid or procrastinate, feeling confused or powerless. Choose or not, both these ways reflect duality if we have not allowed the fire of transition to make us fully ready.

Hekate goes beyond duality. She presents a different option to the need to choose, or not choose. Often what we think is a choice, is simply a projection of our limitations, of what we already know. Even though it may be dressed up differently, the need for immediacy often arises a sense of panic or discomfort. The compulsion to simply 'trust to luck' can come from the threads of the past, the already-known-already-experienced in our psyche, either as a comforting possibility, or a feared one. Hekate's magic, held in the symbology of crossroads, is the liminal space, where we go beyond the known, where the unnoticed possibility can present itself or begin to gestate. It's a state of being that takes us into the Mystery.

There's an interesting synchronicity, encoded in the mystery of what it is to be human, that symbolises this crossroads state of being. Our sex is determined by DNA comprised of X and Y chromosomes; X being the female chromosome. The appearance of X looks like a crossroads, yet also like crossed or open legs depending on how you look at it. It reflects the potential of crossroads activating a closure, or an opening up, in our psyche. The closing down to control our experience, the opening that may conceive, gestate, and birth new life. X is mystery, a female mystery. Its mystery is there in our genetic make-up. It is wisdom to recognise this.

Our genetic make-up brings in Hekate's association with the Anima Mundi, the World Soul. She holds our collective memory of the origins of creation, as does our DNA. In these mystical writings, both Hekate and Sophia (see Black Moon Lilith, Chapter 6) are designated as the Anima Mundi, the animating spirit in all living beings, including plant and animal life. She is the One that mediates between the divine and matter, calling the soul out of matter back to its Source.

A further link with Hekate is evident in the Chaldean Oracles' focus on syncretism – the attempt to reconcile or merge disparate, even opposing beliefs or ideas, to create a whole system of thought. Because of this attempt to unify, and therefore embody our divine nature, the Chaldean Oracles were held in the highest esteem by both the Greeks and the earliest Christian Church (that included both men and women). Albeit expressed differently, it was a connection into the old forms of the Triple Goddess through the Moon phases, which in Platonic philosophy is seen as the seat of the World Soul.

It is believed the Anima Mundi conveys the animating spirit of life from the pure source of the Sun via the Moon into the earthly realms. Shakespeare alludes to this numinous connection in his Faery Queen Titania, in 'A Midsummer Night's Dream.' Puck also refers to himself and all faeries as being ruled by 'Triple Hekate,' meaning the Moon, as opposed to the Sun. When viewed through the lens of archetype and myth, other Shakespearean female characters, such as the weird sisters with their gift of prophecy in Macbeth, can be linked to the Hekate archetype. They function as a sort of triple-formed hive mind. In Shakespeare's time, witches and fairies were strongly linked. Hermione and Perdita in 'The Winter's Tale', female characters in Twelfth Night, and many others express the Sacred Feminine journey, albeit hidden in the mores of Shakespeare's times. Even though the pure direct expression of the Sacred Feminine became lost over time in the fog of patriarchal thinking, the Goddess was visible to those who sought and honoured her. Her mystery is hidden yet always close at hand.

The space between

Our human body-being is a miracle. In our waking state and during daytime electronic signals are constantly passing through our system in clear and more subtle ways. Our body-being works as a super-sensitive highway conveying information from exterior to interior that the brain endeavours to categorise and make sense of. At best, this is a miraculous natural system. Yet inevitably it is also flawed. Hekate moves beyond our everyday states of consciousness. She lives in the transition times, in the half-light times of dawn and dusk, or during night-time darkness. At these in-between times what we see with our eyes is indistinct. Our other senses must become heightened. Even when they are, we cannot see clearly; we are aware of subtleties that make no sense to normal consciousness. These subtleties can activate our imagination, or the mind's delusions. To our mind, the shape of the curtains at night becomes a monster, that shadow is an abductor lurking, the eyes of a fox peering from the blackness become something more sinister. Everyday appearances become distorted by the mind's capacity for imagination, fantasy, and fear. Twilight and night-time are Hekate's realm of mystery, where our usual ways of perception, particularly through the senses, don't operate well. It is when we are in these transitions within, that her support and guidance is most needed. For she is guardian of the liminal spaces, where the Mystery resides.

The space between can be beguiling yet frightening to our normal states of consciousness. During periods of chaotic change, everything is indistinct, just like at twilight. Nothing is clear, subtly changing moment by moment, yet we know we're heading towards darkness. Many human beings find this state uncomfortable. It is neither one thing, nor another. Twilight mirrors the unknown changing rhythms within us. We can be afraid of these tides that take us beyond what we know. We can resist or deny them. We dance between attempts to control and the recognition that we can't, despite our best efforts.

The fact is: life is change. We have different ways to manage this fact. For instance, philosophy, religion, and spirituality act as a means of exploring what cannot be fully understood. They can provide a sense of security when life is chaotic. Religion, traditionally the seat of mystery and faith, directs the 'how' of worship, prescribes ethical and moral codes, and much more. Mystery is held within a set of commandments, rules, and laws, perhaps channelled from a divine source yet usually written by a male. Our need for security can be soothed through these guidelines, or our spiritual practices, yet ultimately, we must come back to the Mystery, along with practical elements of the processes of change. We must face the human aspects - our fears, doubts, old trauma - to embody our spirituality, to live in a conscious way. This is Sacred Feminine spirituality, embodiment, natural alignment with Mystery in the body, in the human realm.

Hekate, as a goddess of the inner worlds, reveals how we may penetrate and pierce the twilight zones and darkness, not to control life, but to willingly engage it as our own mysterious nature. She stands at the crossroads of all frequencies of consciousness, gifting us the possibility of multi-dimensional awakening, infused with inspiration, vision, magical manifestation. She stands for the Underworld's demand to constantly die to our past, or what we think we know. Hekate's spacious medicine, the medicine of liminal spaces, allows the uprising of potential beyond what we already know. She is our connection to oracular wisdom, knowing without needing to know how we know, trusting the Mystery revealing itself in this moment alone. She holds open the gateways of multi-dimensional consciousness, particularly between the conscious and unconscious mind.

In her expression as the Triple-Moon Goddess, particularly through transition times, Hekate is naturally with us. It is in these times that we consciously seek her crone wisdom. She is particularly present where we face transition in our womanhood, at the gateways of birth, menarche, pregnancy, birthing, menopause, and death. These are liminal times of both darkness and light, where every potential lurks, with its prospect of death and its gift of new life. We do not know the outcomes of these transition times. We don't know how we, or our lives, will be. We face such times now, the potential of birthing a new humanity. If we are wise, in these times of great change, we let go of projecting outcome, but rest in the arms of Hekate, allowing her torches to guide us through the passageways of change. She knows the interdimensional doorways we must pass through. Hekate in us is both protector and guide through the evolutionary birthing process.

In times of great transition, both personal and collective, we are required to stretch way beyond our known existence. Hekate guides us beyond the boxes of our stored knowledge if we allow her to. Rather than chasing mental projections towards incomplete conclusions, Hekate calls us to rest in the space between. She supports us in seeing when we're holding on, or leaping ahead, ill-prepared, not yet ripe for the task. When we are seeking the solid ground of 'I know', rather than resting in the grounding of her liminal spaces, Hekate gently, or sometimes fiercely, pulls us back into her void. We don't find her in a specific space. She is both everywhere and nowhere. For liminal space is full of potential. We know this, for we enter the void every night when we fall asleep. Yet in other circumstances, we fear it. We're not programmed to value this loose state of being. We are taught that we should know, that to fix or chase a solution that looks like security is to be on solid ground.

Liminal space is a constant and only certainty. Replace 'liminal space' with the words 'fluctuating possibilities' and you may well agree. If we are awake, we recognise this. Yet it is more challenging to live with this knowledge. Being human can be likened to liminal space. Potentially we are always in transition between who we have been up to now, and who we are becoming. This is our wondrous mystery; so inspiring when we rest in our true state of unknowability and potential. Nature is a primary mirror for this state of being, always in flux. It mirrors our own lives as a changing balance of stability and change. Whatever is stable in our lives - those we love, our homes, jobs, facets of our self – is stable only temporarily, yet whilst it is so, acts as an anchor. Much like the fertile earth acts as foundation for the natural world. Yet all is subject to flux, to transition, in nature, in our self. Recognising this, we can connect with the Hekate archetype within. She is an anchor. Other Sacred Feminine archetypes can be an anchor. Our partner or family can be an anchor, sisters can be an anchor, as can our connection to our divinity and to Earth. When in transition, it is good to know, what remains constant. Yet also to acknowledge, all is subject to change.

Consciously being in our witnessing consciousness can provide stability when in liminal space. It could be said that witness consciousness is a liminal state. We are awake to life's infinite variance, yet also intimately connected to the expansive steady rhythms of breath in body, and nature. Witness consciousness allows all experience to pass through. It recognises when we have become caught up in experience rather than fully feeling its passage through our presence. The process of transition invites us to consciously be in the open state of liminality. To live awake to the paradox of individual perspective and how limited that is. To fully feel our way through the process, whilst also rooting our self in knowing the ultimate mystery of life.

Similarly, in difficulties with others, we can consciously anchor our self in Hekate's place, beyond either 'this' or 'that' as defining a situation, open and resting beyond the duality of a polarised position. Simply bringing awareness to this expanded field of infinite possibility, dropping the agendas of right and wrong, feeling the feelings generated by uncertainty or experience, allows one to relax, to become spacious, and therefore open to the unexpected insight that resolves whatever needs resolution in natural timing. When in transition, rather than becoming tight with fear or anxiety, it is vital we become spacious. That we gift ourselves the open-hearted presence in which a new truth may be revealed. The presence of Hekate within us guarantees the arrival of wisdom. We merely need to wait without waiting, available to the new life coming in. Like the in-breath, it arrives quite naturally when we open to it.

Our naturally magical connection to life's mystery

Hekate holds the keys to the unseen worlds. She stands at the juncture of the mundane and mysterious. She unlocks the secrets of the Underworld and liminal spaces, the secrets of occult mysteries and much more. In an individual strongly aligned to the Hekate archetype, the inner worlds are often more appealing that the external. They are richer, pulling us inward towards their mystery and innate potential. When we are drawn to discover what lies behind our day-to-day experience, Hekate holds open a door. She's the Guardian at the Threshold. Expect to be surprised! For what we think lies in liminal space is often not what we discover. It is concealed from our everyday consciousness, accessible only in our full readiness. Crone space, Hekate's gift to us, is the recognition that there is always a deeper, finer state of being here, when we choose to tune in. This is natural law; new life is constantly arriving. The mundane, man's laws, have less relevance to a Hekate aligned individual than natural law. There is recognition of the limitation of the human mind and what it creates, irrelevant in the unknowable nature of the sacredness of the natural world and the divine.

As Witch-Queen, Hekate's role in what we would call 'magic' is well-known. In ancient times she was invoked at the dark of the Moon to bring knowledge of the other worlds: alchemical processes reflected by the Moon's tides, the transition zones between life phases, or life and death itself. She was invoked through rituals, spells, and enchantments, and sometimes for healing. Charms and amulets were common in the ancient world. Hekate appeared on many of them. She is a common reference in the Greek Magical Papyri, a body of papyri from Graeco-Roman Egypt, dating from 100s BCE to the 400s CE. These texts were written mostly in ancient Greek, originating either in Egypt or Greece, perhaps written by Egyptian priests. Each papyrus contains magical spells, formulae, hymns, and rituals. Scholars suggest the texts form just a fraction of the magical books that existed in antiquity.

As Christianity took over from the ancient gods and goddesses, these texts were considered 'underground literature'. They became the subject of book-burnings or were hidden within institutions such as the Vatican. In many cases the formulaic words and phrases used are strikingly like those found on defixiones, otherwise known as curse tablets, common in the Greek and Roman worlds from as early as the 500s BCE. Curse tablets were used as binding spells, written on small lead sheets, or sometimes in the shape of human figures, invoking Hekate's support for the purposes of romance, eroticism, competition, ill will, or protection. Defixiones have been found as widely as Athens, Asia Minor, Rome, Sicily, and Egypt. It's likely they evolved from an Egyptian practice of 'letters to the dead' written on papyrus or metal and buried with the deceased or thrown into water. This action gave access to the Underworld where the dead were considered to have powers far beyond those of the living. Their help was sought in many ways through this means, just as the support of a medium or psychic might be sought nowadays.

Hekate's demise from Triple Goddess occurred as patriarchal perspectives took over, as rationale overrode a respect for the mystery of life displayed through nature, the night sky, and women's natural role as creatrix. Her original role as guardian, guide and protector became distorted, along with many other goddess archetypes. What couldn't be easily explained, or controlled, was judged. Fear in the natural powers of life, nature and woman were actively promoted. What were previously honoured as gifts of the Mother Goddess, mysterious or miraculous, viewed with awe and respect, eventually were deemed to belong only to the religion of patriarchy. Nature, women's mysteries, and ancient practices were relegated to the realm of sin, magic, and sorcery. Those who respected the rhythms of nature and its cycles, the mysterious natural alchemy that life is, the use of plant medicine, intuition, or other super-natural gifts, learned to hide their aptitudes and their craft. What had been accepted as natural aspects of our oneness with life became relegated to the realm of sorcery. Our unity with nature, the mysterious abilities of certain individuals, nature's gifts to us through herbs and plant medicine, were lost, except to a few. The vestiges of what was considered normal, albeit held in awe, is held now only in some tribal cultures, shamanic or holistic practice. They are the remnant of what was perhaps once a global wisdom, a natural alignment with the magic and mystery of life itself.

What is magic? The dictionary definition states: an extraordinary power or influence seemingly from a supernatural source; the use of means (such as charms, spells, or sleight of hand) believed to have supernatural power over natural forces. Our current belief systems label magic as anything beyond the norms, from downright evil to fantastic. Yet to the ancients, magic may have been natural, albeit mysterious, a customary function of the mystery of life expressing through the natural world, the movement of the stars and at times through human beings. The need to understand, to dissect, explain away and categorise was not yet evident in humankind. What is now labelled witchcraft was medicine. Ancient cultures honoured their medicine men and women, their shamans, priests, and priestesses, as possessing extraordinary powers, aligned with the natural world in numinous ways.

Over eons, those gifted with a capacity for magic, or those who devoted themselves to the healing gifts of the natural world, became outsiders. With the advent of patriarchy, a change in the roles of women and the establishment of the Christian Church, those who possessed extra-ordinary abilities were named and denounced as witches, sorcerers, wizards, or necromancers. Considered to have no relationship with the 'God' of the Christian Church in the western world, these individuals were feared because they did not conform. What we might now term shamanic, a healing gift, differently abled, psychic, sensitive or intuitive, even mentally unstable, or mad, due to a capacity to see and act beyond the norm, or experience life differently, became unacceptable to a scientific or religiously orientated way of life. Considered lawless - yet actively aligned with natural law - these individuals lived outside the norms. They honoured and could align with nature consciously; they recognised that trying to control it was not only futile, but it was also abusive. As mainstream life became more and more disconnected from the divine within, those who honoured what Hekate stands for, became increasingly isolated.

As the control of the Christian Church grew, the active pursuit, vilification, and punishment of those outside it grew. Violent action against them was based in fear, the need to control the natural world, and the misguided belief in woman's nature as basically sinful, due to the perverted Adam and Eve story. The very mystery of the divine was deemed as belonging only within patriarchal religion and those who served it. The many women involved in early Christianity were ousted. Anything mysterious that was outside the sphere of scripture – or men's interpretation of it – was regarded as 'evil'. In the western world, over a long period, pagan religions and their sacred sites were taken over by Christianity. What had been commonly accepted ways of honouring the divine became intolerable to a growing 'civilised' western world. Persecution of those who practised a more holistic way of life or worship, became common.

The documentation of this shift over time is clear in historical texts. Its memory is held in the collective unconscious. As early as the sixth century BCE, the Old Testament books of Exodus and Leviticus (written by an unknown Jewish writer, perhaps a priest) assumed the existence of witches and deemed they be killed. Christian philosopher and theologian St. Augustine (354-430CE) argued that the 'error of pagans' was to not recognise God alone could suspend the laws of the natural Universe. This hounding of those outside the Christian religion came to its peak through the inquisitions of medieval times. Begun in 1208 by Pope Innocent III's attack on the Cathar religion, the persecution of anyone who dared to live by a different belief system continued into the late 1700's. During these times, witchcraft hysteria periodically took over in different countries through Europe and the Americas, with widespread witch trials, torture, and burnings from the 1400's. It was not only pagans, witches, healers, and herbalists who feared for their lives, Jewish people and Muslims were treated similarly. Religious persecution became a norm and continues today. This tool of state control became more and more established as what is called 'civilisation' grew.

Despite (or perhaps because of) its link with religious control, an estimated 75% to 85% of those accused of witchcraft in the early modern witch trials were women over the age of forty. Misogyny on the part of those persecuting witches is documented. The fact that most were older woman links to the Hekate archetype. Those who held crone wisdom were not honoured but denounced as 'witch' for not conforming to society's growing rules and control, or simply through malice. The last witch to be tried and executed in the UK was Janet Horne, in 1727, despite the growing Enlightenment Movement's opposition to witch-hunts throughout Europe from the 1680's. This movement promoted empirical reason, scepticism, and humanitarianism as evolved human qualities. These new values helped mitigate the superstitions of the earlier age. Yet such superstitions still exist; they are an unevolved aspect of human nature when faced with life's mysteries. As recently as 1944 medium Helen Duncan was convicted and jailed as a witch. Magic is still viewed by many as manipulative or malevolent action. And of course, it can be used in this way.

The archetype of witch has a shadow aspect which has been fixated upon by the patriarchal power structure, or more commonly, through fear of the unknown. The mystery of natural, esoteric, and occult practices has been labelled and reinforced as 'wicked' in western culture. Magic, and those who practice it, have been condemned by ignorance, fear, and through the activities of a few. In some ways our western culture has been drained of its riches through a closed-door policy on magic. This has robbed many individuals of the opportunity to grow their natural gifts. It has perpetuated fear. Fear that we may have allowed to restrict our lives and constrain our creative potential, reinforced by a deep-seated belief in 'sin'. Or simply through fear of judgment, what other people might think or say. The witch, the shaman, Hekate the Witch Queen, the Dark Feminine, are alarming to many because they align with a truth that is inherent in the dark. They bring the unacknowledged mystery of life to life, confounding our rationale, challenging the status quo.

Truth is often confrontational. It requires that we get to the core of something with courage and commitment. We can apply this quest for truth to anything in life. Considering 'magic' in this light, perhaps it is simply how we use our creative intent. As human beings we have free will on this Earth. We are given the opportunity to play at being creative. Will is one way we actualise this.

We are always giving out energy, through the volition of will, or unconsciously. We are always moving between the worlds of conscious awareness, intuition, thought, feeling, and instinct within ourselves. Our will takes those states further; it expresses and potentially manifests something from them. A simple pointer to understanding 'magic' is in being awake to our will, to our motivations, which lie behind our self-expression and actions. It's knowing whether our intention is purely for self, maliciously against someone or something, or for the greater good. It's in our alignment; either with the pure frequency of our deepest heart, or something other. Who's to say a bitchy comment towards another woman is not 'black magic'. It wouldn't be viewed in this way perhaps, but it begs the question. Who's to say that prayer is not magic, i.e., magical thinking. Or that affirmations are not. It all lies in the energy of intention behind the expression or action.

Fundamentally 'magic' is about how we use power, or energy. It's about how we use the gift of our natural creative capacity. When we're aligned with what might be called 'goodness', highest intention, then miracles can and do happen. The healing power of prayer could be considered magic. The wonder of coincidence or synchronicity could be seen that way too. It's a natural alignment. Such alignments can often be 'blow your mind' moments. They don't always appear in the ways we think they should. I had one such moment that might be considered magic many years ago. Watching a wildlife programme about the illegal trade in animals and animal products on TV, I saw a snake being skinned alive. My reaction was visceral and instantaneous. I simply shouted 'No!' with the full power of my heart. The TV blew a huge spark and went completely dead. Later the engineer could find nothing wrong; it worked perfectly. Magic? Who knows? What we consider to be magic is simply an alignment with a specific energetic frequency, or natural law. At times we align, at times not. At times that is conscious; other times it's not. Magic, i.e., alignment with natural law, can be used by individuals for their own ends or for the greater good. Ultimately, it's not the practice or technique itself that has the greatest impact, it's how it is used.

Although magic may be used through different techniques, it is not really a procedure or performance. Its truth is alignment with that which we already are, the power of the Universe, at whatever frequency we're operating on. In that alignment, I believe what goes around, comes back around. Our intention, for the greater good, or for self, will come back to us in some way. Magic is like that, whatever frequency, it knows its home and returns to it.

Hekate's devices

Although we wouldn't necessarily term it 'magic', there are equivalents to ancient magical tools today. Vision boards, prayers, affirmations, tarot cards, psychism and mediumship are all aspects of Hekate's toolkit. They are the current equivalent to oracles, magical formulae, defixiones, and amulets. They provide access to the liminal space that is Hekate's world, where all possibilities exist simultaneously. They speak to the right hemisphere of the brain where images and symbols open the realm of imagination, intuition, and insight.

Images from our dreams are another aspect of Hekate's world. They arise from the unconscious reframing of our experience in symbolic form. Sometimes they seem to emerge from the past, or they present intimations of the future. They exist in what seems to be a twilight world, levels of our mind that are not accessible normally. Dreams may express subtly, or shockingly as in a nightmare, erupting into consciousness like a blockbuster movie. Their symbology is open to multiple interpretations. The skill or gift, as with any predictive art, is in allowing them to reveal their gifts, or simply staying with the feeling of them. Although they may be framed by our own mind or another's as in a definitive way, I see them as a flowing symbology of our infinite possibilities, messages from the unconscious, or from other realms. They are links between liminal space and our everyday lives, revealing insight perhaps, or acting as the mind's way of cleansing itself.

In antiquity, the liminal space available when we use the tools of divination, is represented by a symbol known as Hekate's Wheel, also called the Stropholos of Hekate. The earliest depictions of this symbol are from the 1st century CE. Hekate's Wheel reveals how she is the guardian of the cycles of time itself, yet she exists beyond them, in the void. This symbol is described in the Chaldean Oracle as a labyrinthine serpent surrounding a central spiral. More commonly, it is seen shaped like a spinning wheel, featuring a central six-sided star surrounded by a circle, a triple-sided labyrinth, and an outer circle.

Within Hekate's wheel, the visual labyrinth and the three whirls represent interconnectedness to earth, sky, and sea. The six-sided star signifies the divine spark in our soul linking us to both divine and earthly planes. The labyrinth refers to the stages of life that every individual navigates; the three stages of life, death, and rebirth. Hekate's Wheel is a symbolic representation of Hekate as the Anima Mundi, who creates and resides within all life, including time and our fates. It shows she is always there at all transitions – birth to menarche to menopause and beyond; birth to maturity to aging to death. She is transition, our protection and sanctuary through its gateways. Yet she also represents what sits beyond them all – the void: timeless liminal space.

Although comparatively recent in Hekate's her-story, her wheel was used primarily to invoke the goddess and her powers of blessing and protection. It represents our journey through life, guided by her, to the centre of the wheel and thus reflects the journey to spiritual enlightenment. Hekate's Wheel honours both dark and light, the full spectrum of life, its seasons, and rhythms, also what lies beyond it: divine essence. It served as a symbol of the unity of the divine and human life, yet as often happens with human involvement, the purity of the symbol became distorted over time. Its original purpose as a sacred symbol became diminished; as a charm to attract lovers, spun as a devotional wheel (for its whirling hum induced altered states of consciousness) or used in divination. Eventually, Hekate's Wheel became associated with witchcraft. Nowadays it may be used by practitioners of Wicca as a symbol of religious identification.

Hekate's liminal space is also known through nature and marked by the cross-quarter days of the Celtic calendar. These are times when nature is changing her dress, a time of transition from one season to another. One phase is coming to closure, the next opening. Traditionally the cross-quarter days are fire festivals. Hekate's torch burns brightest at these times and is symbolised by the fires lit to mark these transitions.

Samhain (Halloween/All Saints Day) is the end and beginning of the Celtic year, also known as the 'Witches' New Year'. The harvest is in (but not yet consumed) and the seeds of some crops are planted. The veils between the worlds are thin at Samhain. It is Hekate's primary phase as a guardian of the Underworld, the time of the crone, when communication with those who have passed, or the unseen worlds, is more available. The seeds planted at Samhain lay dormant until Imbolc, in early February, when they begin to stir. Persephone is returning from the Underworld, guided by Hekate. The Crone renews life as the archetypal maiden once more. Her return is celebrated as the gift of new life, and with more seed sowing as the earth warms. At Beltane, more commonly known as May Day, plants are actively growing, the earth is greening, revealing its fertile nature. Then at Lughnasad, or Lammas, marked on August 1st, the fruits of nature are celebrated, as the harvest begins. These points in the calendar are also celebrated in different ways in cultures other than the Celtic. The relevance of the crossroads is held in their marking out of the year.

Through all these phases, Hekate's torch is available to guide us, if we tune in to the light as we pass through her void. In ancient times, fire was seen as a gift from the gods. It represented their divine light. Hekate's torch is a gift to deliver the illumination of spirit into the darkest places. Her torch also represents our inner light of knowing, that which is always there and glows from the darkness, but which necessitates we become quiet and still to hear it. It illuminates all things, both the riches and horrors of the inner world, our imagined fears, and our brightest potentials.

Within my own experience, her world can lead us into chaos and confusion, other dimensional realities, even madness. Her far-seeing possibilities can shatter the human mind, the 'norms' of reality. Her world of dreams and visions can beguile. Sometimes, when catapulted into her realm, we must say 'Stop, this is too much'. I had a period in my life when in that liminal space between sleep and waking, I was making love with a man I knew. It was ecstasy, a bodily rather than a dream experience, and yet there was no connection in physical life. Eventually I fell into a daytime state where I no longer knew what was real. I became lost in this enthralling, blissful experience. I knew I was losing all capacity to function in daily life. Saying 'Stop', taught me I have the power, and the right, to say 'Thank you but no more' to some altered states. That was just one purpose of the whole experience; there were many others.

The word 'lunacy' is related to the experience of going too far beyond what the psyche can hold in its present stage of development. Its roots lie in the Latin word 'lunaticus', meaning 'Moon-struck' – another link into Hekate's Dark Moon states of being. I needed her wisdom when wooed by the Moon-struck ecstasy of interdimensional experience. I needed her torch to recognise I was lost, her dagger to cut the intoxicating bliss of the experience. A while later I spoke to the man involved in this alternate reality; he had no conscious knowing of it. This experience was one of Hekate's symbolic keys for me. A step in beginning to acknowledge and understand the weaving of our diverse states of consciousness, to know what was truly relevant to my evolution, to know how to engage her wisdom. Hekate's keys open the doors to all realms and especially the Underworld. We need her wisdom to discern exactly which to walk through and which to close. Her torch shines a light into dark corners yet also illuminates our bright insight. Her dagger is the tool that helps us cut through any illusions, to know when altered states of being have served their purpose.

Many ancient cultures used daggers in ritual and sacrifice. Hekate's dagger is the tool that cuts through duality and the threads of the known. It cuts delusion with the sharp edge of truth. It requires maturity to know exactly when to express truth and how. Its misuse can be like a blunt knife, wounding unnecessarily, whereas a clean cut may hurt but breaks what has served its purpose with precision. The capacity to understand right timing for a necessary cut is a gift of Hekate's crone wisdom. It applies equally well with a psychological process as to a physical one. Witches and wisewomen were often intimately involved in human birth. A knife was a necessary implement to cut the umbilical cord. To support birth and life, as well as its more obvious use as a tool of death.

In ancient literature witches cut herbs with a bronze sickle dagger. The link to the sickle phase of the Moon is evident here, as was the right phase for the cutting. The witch stands at the centre of our true nature, one with all life. So, this ancient understanding of all facets and rhythms of life is natural. She both cuts and binds, creates, and breaks. She stirs the pot, and waits to see what happens, yet she also knows. Not in exact ways, or factual ways, but in her knowingness. This is alive in us today if we choose to listen. The possibility is always to deepen our inherent unity with everything natural. Hekate's devices are merely tools that mirror our innate capacities. For truly, we are the magic.

Our inherent unity with wild nature

The Hekate archetype represents the innate capacity in every woman to be a healer, seer, witch or medium, to cross the realms of physicality and consciously connect with the flowing frequencies of liminal space. Every possibility exists in liminal space, therefore the opportunity to access the very fabric of life is alive. Commonly known as 'the field', liminal space is the very fabric of existence; it is what we exist in and at the deepest levels, what we truly are, but cannot see. We are always interacting with it, subtly influencing its manifestation. New physics is now exploring this quantum realm, the fact that energy can express simultaneously as both particle and wave, form, and energy. They are accessing the potential of knowledge held by shamans since ancient times – that we are intricately woven into the web of life itself. Yet many are missing that vital element of understanding – that the mere presence of a witness to experiments influences the results. That the observer, their beliefs, perspective, even perhaps their karma, is an innate and intricate aspect of the experiment.

Hekate within us can reveal how the world works, simply by our being in the mystery of liminal space and discovering through direct experience in the moment. Mystics through the ages have discovered the divine in this way, through meditation, prayer, and ritual, through allowing their usual sense of self to dissolve into space, consciousness, potentially bliss. Such experience defies rationale; it defies explanation, often being too expansive to even allow expression. For instance, I have directly experienced the stars in the night sky as being within my body. Yet in that occurrence what is 'my body'? It felt like they were in my woman's womb, yet how can that possibly be? Clearly, I was awake to a different body. Yet what is that 'body', and can I define it? No, I can't. Yet I know without doubt, the truth of the experience. It is as real as my sitting here typing these words now.

Some scientists are researching mystical experiences such as this. It seems the divide between science and spirituality is being crossed in some ways. Yet we will never do it through rational mind. Perhaps, in realising the limits of patriarchal separative thinking, we may turn back towards the knowledge of the ancients, to give it due value, to integrate it within our technological world. Perhaps having individuated, we are returning to unity consciously. It is a mystery indeed. Perhaps we are not meant to solve it, but simply be in it.

Hekate is naturally attuned to the medicine needed, for any of our ills of body, mind, and soul, perhaps even collectively. She is the medicine woman within, carrying a gift in the use of herbs, potions and healing tools that work in the subtle and physical realms. In some cultures, she would be known as a shaman. One who has the capacity to move between the worlds, bridging visible and invisible, forms and energy. This may be for the purpose of healing and regeneration, to access wisdom that serves a certain individual or the tribe, or simply to acknowledge or celebrate our divine nature. Intuitive and psychic wisdom is a gift we all carry but which is accessible to only a few perhaps. It certainly requires our willingness to accept its existence and to trust it. In my experience, when we do, we are shown time and time again its practical relevance to our lives. Intuition has even saved my life on one occasion. Such is the gift of the medicine woman, should we choose to listen.

The inner gifts of intuition, and access to vibrational frequencies of healing, is a valuable aspect of medicine in both ancient cultures and our current holistic world. Tribal cultures access their medicine wisdom in many ways. They use natural substances to open alternate realities, to journey and uncover wisdom needed for physical healing, to resolve conflicts, to discover expanded vision for the tribe, even to find food.

221

Similarly, they use herbs, plants, and other natural substances, for physical healing. In ancient times the medicine woman or healer of the village, often a crone, would work similarly, also acting as midwife to birthing mothers. Hekate is present at the edge between where the veils between life and death are thin. As such, her gifts often reveal this knife-edge between potential for health and the end of life. Natural substances such as herbs can also be poisons, psychoactive substances that are mind-altering and enlightening, potentially fatal. They can open portals to other dimensions and the occult knowledge stored there. They must be used wisely.

Subtle medicine is also the realm of the ancient Triple Goddess in Hekate's form. Like the differing vibrational phases of the Moon, subtle medicine works through frequency to align imbalance in mind, body, and soul. Homeopathy is a medicine that uses the vibration of a substance to effect change or healing. It defies rationale, for nothing of the original substance is in it, except its energy. Healers, through opening and letting go into liminal space, become the channel for healing. Shamans, through inter-dimensional travelling, reclaim and release trapped energies, facilitating cleansing and soul restoration. Working with energy is natural medicine, available to us through the multi-dimensional field that we are part of. It requires such individuals to step over the edges of rational mind, to tune in, listen, and engage the infinite possibilities of healing and balance. It takes courage and trust to do so. It requires we break through the status quo into realms we have no words or framework for.

Edge-dwellers naturally receive negative labels in a 'civilised' culture. They work with potentially dangerous natural substances, or the mysteries of energetic frequency, within dark shadowy realms as well as daylight. A system bent on control does not allow space for the irrational, inexplicable realms of the natural. A system rooted in fear will not countenance such freedoms, especially from women. Over time, as patriarchal culture tightened its grip, medicine was taken from the hands of the elders, the shamans, witches, wisewomen and healers. Our capacity for the natural knowing of intuition, connection to altered states, alignment with nature's energies and gifts, honouring of the liminal beyond structured religion, and thus our capacity to naturally heal body-mind-soul, was replaced by the fix-it culture of control. Split from the vast expanse of our true nature, belief in our powerlessness became a strangely natural state of being.

As many human beings have become denatured, the loss of connection to the natural world and our Earth is perhaps unsurprising. In cutting off from our roots, we have lost alignment with our wild self too. We temper, even destroy, our own wildness. The way of the wisewoman is in the wild of life; it belongs to the wilderness yet can reach into the mundane. This capacity to travel between worlds can seem strange to the mainstream culture, even frightening, because the wild edge, and the edge-dweller are uncontrollable by usual means. Yet these edges are not beyond our alignment if we dare go there. To do so, we must rewild our self. We must know and acknowledge our place in the Great Mystery; we must become humble. Edge-dwellers know and accept this, so can access the messages and gifts available.

Transmutational medicine comes from deep in the Mystery. Hekate's world and work is to bridge the liminal with the world of form, creating alchemy. Dreams, imagination, synchronicities, intuition are part of her wild medicine. Wanderers in that world, those who allow the unconscious to speak – the artists, dreamers, midwives, witches, and healers - have mostly been denied full value in our collective culture. They exist on the fringes. Their gift is to call us, invite us, remind us of our own naturally wild edges.

The wild edges of our soul are naturally shamanic in that to reach them we must journey through the unconscious to the deeper worlds within. A witch, using plant medicine, or her own inner key that unlocks liminal space, travels deep into the unseen wild places of the soul too. Hekate, when known as the Witch Queen, combines Sacred Feminine energy with shamanic gifts and those of the witch. At the crossroads, she has access to both the formless and form. It is this capacity that frightens those who wish to control it. This wild garden on the edges of sacred and mundane is full of spirits – etheric and nature-all. It is the domain of paradox: poisons that heal, the serpent that bites yet protects the sacred temples, the dagger that delivers life and takes it. It is the dwellers on the edge, those who dare to explore and trust the unseen worlds, that can deliver this subtle medicine.

Although this knowledge and its usage has been constrained by patriarchy - by labelling it malevolent – the holistic world is alive and growing in our collective culture. It lives through the healers, psychics, environmentalists, artists, pioneers, musicians, and anyone who bucks the system in conscious ways. The word 'sorceress' has come to mean a woman using magic for ill means, yet there is clearly a link to the word 'source'. Like Hekate, demoted from Anima Mundi to Triple Goddess to Witch Queen, our innate capacity to work in alignment with Source, the very fabric of existence, may seem lacking collectively. Yet all is not lost, for Source is our very Being. That is the truth. Hekate is a guide back into our true nature, liminal space full of potential, one with Source. She is guardian and guide, protectress and wise friend on the wild edges of life. She is our sanctuary when the ways of our current world become too much.

Sanctuary through the dark night of the soul

As a queen of transition and wisewoman, Hekate rules over the processes of regeneration, holding the hand of Maiden-becoming-

225

Queen Persephone. With her lighted torches she guides souls to their appropriate worlds, either the orchards of Elysium (the heavens) the Asphodil Meadows (a place of neutrality where ordinary or mediocre mortal souls are sent to live), or Tartarus (a place of torment for the wicked). This role is an allegory for our own processes of change. For we may be thrust temporarily into any of these states before we find our way onto the ground of new life.

In myths it is said Hekate glows with phosphorescent light. This links her with the glow of death that happens as forms release their light during death and decay. What were Hekate's sacred groves of alder, poplar and yew trees eventually became cemeteries. Black poplars and yew trees are particularly sacred to her. The yew's roots are said to grow into the mouths of the dead and release their souls for rebirth. It also absorbs the odour of putrefaction and the phosphorescence of bodies decaying. This composting process is Hekate's realm, for its heat of transformation generates fertile soil for new life, just as a composting heap eventually feeds a generation of new plants.

Hekate is our guardian and protector through all transitions and temporary states. As guardian of the Underworld her energy is akin to autumn and winter. Both are essential to spring. She is there through disappointment, failure, censure, and grief. She is there when the black dogs of depression strike. She holds open the door to new possibility when the harvest of our experience is not what we've envisioned. She holds us gently at the crossroads until we know what step to take, or we move naturally into new ways of being.

Darkness is Hekate's home; here she is vibrantly present. Yet the between-worlds are where she guides and protects the transitional space. She is not bound by fear and doubt, by loss, or fear of loss. She knows how the liminal space offers sanctuary and refuge when we allow it to. Her role is to guard and guide us when we don't know where we are, or what to do, until through her wisdom of quiet and waiting, we do know. Like the comfort of a dark black night when we are cosied up in bed, or warm by the fire whilst the wind howls and rain lashes against the window, Hekate provides refuge that ultimately leads to renewal. Just as she is guide to the maiden Persephone in her journeys to and from the Underworld, Hekate awaits our call on her when we are challenged by life's upheavals.

Hekate's capacity to live on the edge between the civilized and the wild is a light in the darkness of unknowing. Her torch sheds light where before there was none. Its warm glow is a comfort whilst her keys jangle us awake with the possibility of new delights. The primary key to finding her lies in our commitment to simply enter the darkness willingly, not knowing where it will take us. We must be willing to undergo psychological death. We cannot control new life's conception, gestation, and birth, much as we might like to. Incubation of new life involves a deep descent – into silence, towards the still solitude of winter, towards inactivity and unknowing, rest and regeneration. Hekate's gifts lie in allowing it all. As we let go, we discover sanctuary may be found in the darkness.

What is sanctuary? At its roots the word comes from the Latin 'sanctus', meaning holy. It is also related to the Latin 'sanctuarium', meaning a container, perhaps for holy relics or cherished individuals. In its modern usage, sanctuary is more usually taken to mean a place of safety, refuge, or protection. Hekate provides all this and more. She is the container, or holding space, in which we grow, often despite our self, or our resistance to being in the dark. Recognising our perspective on darkness is essential to this journey. For the dark holds both our fears and our unseen potential. In Hekate's liminal space life is fluid. Fluidity can be overwhelming. Without our known sense of self, our sense of normality, we may feel out of control. But this is necessary. We cannot embody new life whilst hanging on to what was. Like a woman making the transition to mother, we must die to who we were. In that dying 'woman' becomes an integral aspect of 'mother'. She is not lost; she is absorbed.

When in a dark night of the soul, the fear in us is we are losing our self completely. This fear must be embraced, for our knowing contains truth. Yet what is going is not being lost, it is being transmuted. It is a paradox.

Energy cannot die; it merely changes form. Hekate's role in what seems like death is guardian and protector. Just as with Persephone, she will guide us into spring. She is a sanctuary. As a crone, she is unbound by disappointment or loss. She has seen it all, felt it all. Her losses have grown soul strength, self-knowing, intimacy with the journey to wholeness. She knows that death grows life, that darkness is not opposed to light but its companion.

We have been taught to fear death, and of course fear is natural to our survival consciousness. Yet some fear is unnatural; it has been learned. The dark, the void, the unknown, have all been projected as a potentially 'bad' place. We have been conditioned to resist aging and death, and to see the processes of decay as repulsive. The mysteries of the wisewoman, the old hag, the witch, Hekate, have been distorted. They are seen as ugly through a projection of patriarchal fears about the dark realms of Divine Feminine power. They are not welcomed in any way. The power and true mystery of sexuality, conception, birth, life, and death flowing through women's bodies has been denied, even actively vilified. The primal messiness of our menstrual blood, of birth, and of death, have been excluded from 'civilised' culture. How can they be denied? They are gateways to life. Every woman knows this and the war within herself, with others, or both, as her vital experience, her living existence in all its expressions, is being denied, or condemned. If we are to claim a full life, we must penetrate these distorted projections to reach our brightest luminosity and wisdom, to honour our dark chaos.

The dark face of the goddess is essential to creation. Just as composting is essential to healthy soil. The dark transitions we make are exquisitely fertile if we trust them. Resting in the void, we come to know that the ending of life as we know it is eventually to receive the impulse that opens the gateway to new life. Whilst in this composting process, it is essential we regularly turn over the soil of our life. Without conscious exploration into our process of change, we become stagnant. It is true that life's timing is not necessarily ours. Paradoxically we must learn how to be both active and inactive at the same time. Hekate in us understands, is immersed in, these processes of decay and regeneration with us. She holds the knowing that energy does not die but transforms. That the caterpillar becomes the butterfly through the death of its old form, incubation, then the struggles of birth. She is there in all transitions and at all thresholds. Her presence at the crossroads is vitally alive in us.

Hekate within us guides us in the subtleties of knowing the threshold we stand at, in small and life-changing ways. She is the wisdom that recognises: what am I leaving, where am I being called to enter? She holds us in our wholeness when we are in pieces. She knows the resistance to not knowing where we are, or where we're going. She knows that gifts are found in that space of unknowing, in the waiting and seeing, in the allowing. A threshold is not a simple edge; it is a subtle fluid borderline between two different ways of being. Being a gateway into the unknowable, it generates a complexity of thoughts and feelings. It is vital to take our time at thresholds; to feel the differing impulses, to listen without judging the numerous voices, to wait whilst a deepening presence makes itself known there. That deepening presence is lit by Hekate's torches.

In Hekate's protection, we find our rest. Like a grandmother, she naturally knows the need to guide and protect the more vulnerable aspects of new life. She is also a death doula. She will hold us tenderly like one passing over; she will swaddle us like a new-born baby, until we are ready to be fully new. The knowing of readiness is a tender knowing. The western perspective is constantly focused on time, on what 'should be happening'. In Hekate's realm we must wait for a sign at the crossroads, resting in the unknowing of her vast spaciousness. The balance of readiness is not really in our hands. Like a bud opening in spring, we are subject to more than just our inner impulse. Yet we must be as aware also of getting stuck in the void through depression or resistance, as the risk of stepping out too early for our vulnerability. It's a fragile state of being. This is where we can consciously call on Hekate for her guidance and wisdom, even as we rest in her sanctuary. For she is both maturity (crone) and potential (maiden) at the same time. Mother sits naturally in her being, the bridge between both. Looking three ways at the crossroads, she is both maturity and wisdom, the capacity to nurture what is here right now, and new potential.

Experiencing Hekate's realm can be fierce, yet when we allow it and open, ultimately it is comforting. She lies in the wholeness of our experience, in the paradox of what we feel and the Mystery that lies beyond it. Her symbology greets us in our dreams, imagination, and synchronicities. She always invites us deeper. If we are called to wholeness and healing, we must listen and persist. Hekate calls us into the void, for she knows it is only through the death into liminal space that wholeness is found. We don't have to wait for physical death to receive her guidance. She is us, as guide, guardian, keeper of the keys, as sanctuary. It is in her sanctuary that we discover her temple. That temple is our Feminine way of being and knowing; open, available, free-flowing in liminal space.

Chapter 4

Renewal in The Underworld – Persephone, Queen of the Dead

Everything I touch
is light
emerging from dark.
Anything I touch
reveals darkness
turning to light.
Light that pierces shadow,
shadow that pierces I,
no opposites here,
no divisive shaft
of separation,
only dark light turning,
wholeness,
surface to depth,
depth to life,
death into life,
burning my heart,
burnishing my soul
to gold.

Cassandra Eve

236

Archetype: Queen of the Underworld.

Symbols: narcissus; crocus; an ear of grain; pomegranate; bats; rivers and springs

Message: Go deeper, my darling. There you will discover the ripe fruit of rebirth. I am here in the Underworld, waiting to feed you with its seeds of renewal.

Persephone themes: the journey of maturing; guidance through the shadow realms; a descent and return; sexual initiation; abduction & abuse; the harvest of crisis

What the Persephone archetype calls for: integrating extremes of experience; facing the dark side of life; allowing an Underworld journey to mature you.

Also known as: Proserpina (Roman).

We have briefly encountered Persephone and her myth already in the chapter about Hekate. Now we approach her directly to discover her gifts of evolution held in the Underworld. Persephone is the maiden phase of women's lives and rules our emergence as woman, then as queen. Her journey reflects our own transitional process between innocence and knowing, virginity and sexual initiation, light and dark; it's a psychological and physical birthing process. Persephone's calling is to maturity as Queen of the Underworld, the abode of the dead. Through her initiation Persephone, along with Hekate, became guide to souls who pass through the world of the dead. She reveals to us the initiatory journey of the shadow realms, our return to the light with wisdom and the assurance of new life.

The mythology of Ceres and her daughter Persephone relates how Persephone was abducted by Pluto, Lord of the Underworld (or in some versions of the myth, chose to go willingly). Eventually she found her way back to the earthly realm and to her mother. Yet both were forever changed. The myth is an evolutionary tale that relates a personal journey of rebirth, yet also the collective theme of cultural change, where patriarchal rule was growing. In more ancient tales from Mycenaean, Cretan and Neolithic cultures, there is a similar myth with a different unfolding to the Greek version. It reflects the deep connection of these earlier cultures to the natural processes of life and death, to nature's cycles and the Great Mother Goddess who took care of it all.

Persephone's story of being initiated into the Underworld by Pluto weaves into that of many other goddess archetypes, each with a similar theme yet taken at a different stage of a women's life cycle. This journey is reflected in a different way in Chapter 1 about Inanna and her sister Ereshkigal. Persephone's journey demonstrates the evolutionary demand to grow consciously from girl to woman that we cannot avoid, then our further maturing into the Queen archetype. Her myth reveals how initiation can occur through crisis, particularly the transition between girl and woman that includes sexuality and partnership. Persephone's journey is the primary shift from innocent girl to full-bodied woman, and maturity into acceptance of the dark realms of the psyche and intimacy. She is our guide from naivety to wisdom, into the revelation of our innate power as Sacred Feminine, even in the darkest places.

Her-story

The myth of Ceres and her daughter Persephone is relatively well known in our western world. It comes from Homer's 'Hymn to Demeter' (Demeter is Persephone's mother, known as Ceres to the Romans and in astrology) written around the 6th century BCE. Its echoes reach into our own times with its themes of abduction and rape, powerlessness, and redemption. Yet behind the obvious mythic theme lie many layered allegories for women's menstrual cycle and evolution from maiden to mother to crone, the processes of life and death in all human lives, and within all civilizations.

Prior to the Olympian Gods, Ceres was known and celebrated as a face of the Great Mother Goddess. Her meaning within the cultures of that earlier time reflected the cycles and abundance of nature. The Greek myth arises in a period when the stable Mediterranean civilizations were being over-run by invaders from the north. The destruction and desecration of the goddess temples that occurred at that time was just one aspect of a patriarchal takeover that took place over a thousand or more years. Homer's tale of Persephone's abduction symbolized what was happening in the culture, as women's roles in life were increasingly denied and controlled. It related a seemingly personal yet mythic story that portrayed collective circumstances. It suggested the potential of deeper understanding of the processes of evolution, as it also alluded, in literary form, to the Eleusinian Mysteries. These sacred rites had become established in Greek culture from 1450 BCE. They continued for two thousand years as an initiation in spiritual illumination, offering initiates the power to transcend the fear of death. Little is known about the form of these Mysteries, yet they were clearly a potent transformative experience, held in great respect by the Greek culture at that time.

The myth goes like this: Persephone wandered the Earth with her mother Ceres. Everywhere they went flowers bloomed, nature thrived, and crops grew abundantly. Yet as they wandered, they also encountered the lost and bewildered spirits of the dead. As Persephone grew, these encounters began to distress her. She felt sad for these souls and asked her mother what could be done to help them. Ceres told Persephone that these souls were part of her natural realm but that she was too busy feeding the living to take care of them. Persephone was deeply moved that there was no-one to receive, counsel and guide these souls through the Underworld.

Ceres loved her daughter Persephone beyond any other. They enjoyed nothing more than to wander together in the garden of the Gods, sharing the beauty of nature. They were at one with each other, needing no other. Although Persephone was well into puberty, Ceres was turning away all males. Nowadays we might say they had a co-dependent mother-daughter relationship. In the myth, Ceres's brothers, Zeus, and Pluto, saw they must do something about this situation. They had heard Persephone's calling to lost souls. They hatched a plot.

One day whilst in the garden with her maiden friends, Persephone spied in the distance a beautiful new flower birthed by Gaia. It was a deliciously fragranced narcissus, never seen before. Persephone wandered off from her mother and friends to look at this new flower. This was the moment everything changed. For suddenly the earth cracked open. Pluto, Lord of the Underworld, appeared from this fissure, driving his black chariot with six jet-black stallions. Here we find two versions to the myth; one tells us that Pluto abducted Persephone, another that she went willingly with him into the Underworld. However, the event happened, Persephone did shriek with fright before the earth closed over, leaving only a bunch of withered narcissi to witness her transition. Hekate, Crone Goddess, resting in her cave, heard her cry and noted it.

Meanwhile Ceres, feeling something was amiss, called out to her daughter. Hearing no response, she began to search frantically for Persephone. Fruitlessly Ceres searched the garden, then the entire Earth, looking for her daughter. Wandering amongst mortals, disguised as an elderly woman, she roamed, and she grieved. Persephone was nowhere to be seen. As Ceres grieved, the Earth became dry and barren, crops withered, animals began to die.

Eventually Hekate, hearing of Ceres's plight, came to her and shared what she had heard on the day of Persephone's disappearance. Together they travelled to the Sun God Helios for they knew he would have witnessed the events in the garden on his daily travels across the sky. Helios revealed the plot hatched by Persephone's father Zeus and his brother Pluto. Together they had schemed to break Ceres and Persephone's bond and for Pluto to take Persephone as his queen. Ceres was furious. Nonetheless she pleaded with Zeus that she be reunited with her daughter. He would not hear her, or interfere in his brother's realm, so Ceres totally withdrew her fertility from the Earth. She stayed in her grieving. All the Olympians came down to encourage Ceres to let go of her grief but to no avail. Realizing that there were no animals being sacrificed to the Gods, Zeus eventually agreed to intervene in the situation. He sent Mercury, the messenger god who could travel through all realms, to reclaim Persephone from the Underworld.

Meanwhile in the Underworld Pluto and Persephone were getting to know each other well. Persephone sat on her throne as Queen of the Underworld with Pluto by her side. Happy as she now was, still she pined for her mother and their time in the garden. As Mercury arrived in the Underworld, Pluto knew this, and that Persephone may soon leave him. Afraid she would not return from visiting her mother, he persuaded her to eat some pomegranate seeds, the fruit of the dead. In this act he ensured she would come back as his queen.

Persephone was reunited with her mother Ceres. In their joy, the Earth's fertility returned. The crops grew, the animals flourished, the people ate and sacrifice to the gods resumed. Yet all was changed between Ceres and her daughter who had now become a woman. Having eaten the pomegranate seeds in the Underworld Persephone had to return to Pluto's realm as his queen. So, following the harvest each year, Persephone is reunited with Pluto. Nature dies back, the fruits fade and the leaves drop; just like Persephone, nature returns below ground.

Through Ceres and Persephone's experience evolution was accomplished. The natural cycle was fulfilled. Ceres had come through her winter of grief and received a profound learning experience.

Persephone had made the transition from maiden to woman to queen. In honour of Persephone's return each year, Ceres shared her mysteries as a gift to the people. They became known through the rites of the Eleusinian Mysteries in her temple at Eleusis. These rites helped to diminish the fear of loss and death in the initiates who came. The cycle of birth-life-death-rebirth was acknowledged and celebrated in its entirety and its purpose. The illumination of spirit was known as the constant beyond, yet within these cycles.

Through her own initiation into Pluto's realm, Persephone, unlike other wives and consorts of the gods, held power in her own right within the Underworld. She was queen within her realm. She had no challenge with infidelity from Pluto apart from a claim from his former lover Minthe declaring she could win him back anytime. Persephone soon countered that by turning Minthe into a mint plant. Despite this momentary act of malice, Persephone is portrayed as a benign figure, a guide and supporter. She is Queen of the Underworld, a helper of heroes and mortals, as well as souls, featuring in the Greek heroic tales of both Odysseus and Heracles as a support in their quests.

Given the familiar tale of Persephone's initiation into the Underworld, she features in other myths in somewhat surprising ways. Another tale links her with the God of agriculture, wine, theatre, festivity and sexual ecstasy, Dionysus. One version relates how Zeus, her father, came to her as a snake and made love to her. She gave birth to Dionysus from this coupling. Another myth states Dionysus was born from Zeus's thigh and then was nursed by Persephone, with whom he rested between bouts of orgiastic? merry-making and sex.

The cult of Dionysus dates to the ancient Mycenaean and Cretan cultures and involved anything from simple agricultural rites, celebrations and theatre to the secret cults involving ecstatic dancing, ritual sacrifice, mind-altering substances, and sex. These activities were gateways into Persephone's world, where through altered states participants could connect with the dead and souls in transition, as well as travel across normal psychological and psychic boundaries into states of euphoria and bliss. Like Persephone, Dionysus is a god of transition, acting as a mediator between worlds. His celebration of the gifts of the Earth, through wine or natural narcotics, through full indulgence in sexuality, lead to altered states of being, from sexual ecstasy to spiritual revelation, to despair.

Three well known historical figures were members of Dionysian cults: Roman Mark Anthony, Alexander the Great and the gladiator Spartacus. There was also a group named 'the maenads' or 'wild women', female followers of Dionysus, who were thoroughly disapproved of in the growing patriarchal culture. In the Roman culture these rites were known as the Bacchanalia after their equivalent god, Bacchus. These lines from Euripides tragedy 'The Bacchae' written in 405BCE describe the growing patriarchal view: 'but I hear about the disgusting things going on, here in the city Women leaving home, to go to Silly Bacchic rituals, Cavorting there in the mountain shadows'. Clearly the growing patriarchy wasn't happy with women 'cavorting', asserting their right to freedom, or their potential for sexual ecstasy through these cults. Persephone's gift through Dionysus was to open further gates of sexual initiation and maturity. To allow women to claim not only the fullness of woman in themselves, but the majesty of their queendom as a fully active and free sexual being. The patriarchal desire for control was to soon stamp this out.

Persephone's Place in the Universe – Astronomy & Astrology

Persephone is an asteroid in the main asteroid belt lying between Mars and Jupiter. It was discovered by German astronomer Max Wolf on 23 February 1895 in Heidelberg.

In an astrological birth-chart Persephone reveals a place of initiation into maturity. This might be where we get shocked or abducted into an Underworld journey, where we are forced to navigate a crisis, or to confront situations we would rather not. Persephone in the birth-chart can point towards traumatic experience, the death of someone close at an early age, a sexual initiation such as losing virginity, or an experience involving the misuse of power, abuse, or violence. Aspects will reveal the necessity and timing for healing, the potential for renewal, and deeper maturity. She reveals our relationship to our core power, our capacity to go through and transmute experience, to realise its harvest. She shows us where we may become a queen of the shadow realms in the psyche, with the power of renewal that may bring us to the spring of new life. In that, she will call us to periodic retreat, a dive inward, to rest and recharge, and to find the food and fuel of wisdom in the Underworld.

Persephone's gifts can include psychic and therapeutic sensitivity, the capacity to act as guide and mediator for others, born from our initiations in the Underworld. She is the queen of natural rhythms and the interface between dark and light, understanding the need to remain in the Underworld for a period, yet also the perfect timing of renewal.

My journey with Persephone

Persephone's realm first opened to me at age eleven. At that young age I was already accustomed to big life changes through my family's regular house moves. The nature of my father's work meant we rarely stayed in one place for more than a couple of years. When I reached the age of eleven, having passed my Eleven Plus examination, I was sent to boarding school. My parents wanted stability for my education. No thought was given to the emotional repercussions of this split from family life, or the fact that very soon there was a family rooting in one place. I simply had to face the transition from family life to aloneness.

There's no doubt the experience of being separated from my family grew me, yet it also compounded my sense of alienation from life at home. As the eldest child, with the arrival of my twin siblings when I was almost three, I'd had to grow up fast. The maiden hardly had a chance to be a child, very soon she was given the role of mother's helper. With the increasing isolation that boarding school caused, I felt the separation and lack of care keenly. It was an initiation into the shadows of life, the fact that ultimately, we are alone. To be thrust into such darkness, and grief for the family life I was missing, felt unfair at such a young age, cruel even. Yet even then, seeds were being sown for a deeper Underworld journey once I was mature enough to face it.

Persephone's presence on the edges of my life, erupted fully at the age of eighteen. Just having returned home to live full-time after seven years at boarding school, I was enjoying a sense of freedom from the rigid routines of school, anticipation at what the transition from maiden to woman would bring. Within a few months of leaving school, my mother became ill with cancer; six months later, she died. Thrust completely into the Underworld, our family dissolved. We could not get beyond the loss, for it was not shared together. Persephone took my hand and pulled me fully into her realm. Grief overwhelmed me. The maiden in me was becoming a woman. Mother, the nurturing space-holder for family, was gone. Subconsciously I decided I would create my own family. One that would not reject me or leave me alone with loss.

Initially I found solace with my boyfriend's family. For a while my future mother-in-law's kindness and care, and my boyfriend's love of me, held me close. I felt safe and loved. Within a few years I'd married and become a mother. I danced between Persephone and Ceres. Had I healed fully? I would say not, but I had found a certain rhythm that speaks of growing maturity. Through my marriage, Persephone pulled me back into her Underworld regularly. My quest in that place became: Who am I? What do I really want? Ceres flowered in me too, with motherhood. I loved being a mother; it came very naturally to me. But it was not enough. I was caught between worlds for a while - growing woman and natural mother but not yet the queen of my life.

When my son was two, I left his father. The queen in me began to blossom. I loved my life, my creativity bloomed, my home was my haven. Spring had arrived. Although I didn't yet know of her, with hindsight Persephone kept her promise of renewal. Yet life is never static. Within a year or two, she called me again. This time it was through the form of Pluto, a man of power. A man who abused his power and whom I allowed to pull me completely into his dark realm. I could not resist, for despite his behavior, there was profound love. Through this relationship, Persephone was teaching me, dark and light co-exist; embrace them both, for they will grow you. The queen archetype had been born in me, but her power in relating was weak.

Six years on, back and forth from love to the Underworld, darkness to light, winter pain to spring's renewal, I finally integrated. I ate the pomegranate seeds in my relationship. I embraced the reality; I digested the experience. I knew I must leave. My inner queen was alive and thriving. She knew what to do. My time as victim was over. Persephone was mature within me and appeared in my life too. I began to train as a volunteer for a Rape Crisis & Incest Line. My dance as maiden-woman-mother-queen was integrating. The seeds brought new life. I was in spring, blossoming in maturity, bringing the gifts of my experience to life in support of women.

The dance continues... maiden-mother-queen-crone, maturing in a woman's body on the Earth. The difference now is, I am ripe. I know the dance well. The phases flow naturally one into another, for I know how to be in this dance. I know Persephone: I allow her presence in me to fill the darkness when it comes. I eat her seeds of renewal and emerge.

Persephone's message: Go deeper, my darling. There you will discover the ripe fruit of rebirth. I am here in the Underworld, waiting to feed you with its seeds of renewal.

An initiation into maturity

In the opening scenes of Persephone and Ceres's myth we find mother and daughter in co-dependency. Neither wants to leave the other. They are in the garden of the gods, in a state of innocence and bliss. Persephone is portrayed as Kore, meaning maiden. She has no name. This immediately points us towards her innocent state of being and her immersion in her mother. She is undifferentiated, having no independent state of being. They are always together, even when Kore is with her maiden friends. Ceres has no partner. She is at peace in the garden of the gods with her daughter. Yet life is change, despite our desire for it not to be. Ceres, as Earth Mother, naturally knows this, yet she is also resisting it. As males show interest in her daughter, she turns them away. Naturally she is trying to keep her daughter safe, but she cannot. It is beyond time for Kore to mature.

In her undifferentiated self, Kore does not know who she is; she's passive and malleable in her innocence. She is naïve, therefore easily influenced, or seduced. This maiden state of Kore, the undeveloped aspect of the Persephone archetype, may be within us whatever our age. As we go through life experiences, it's active where we choose not to mature, to not know or see; it's where we live from passivity or compliance, are adaptive and accommodating to others because we have little or no will of our own. It's also where in a mother's attempts to keep her daughter safe, no matter her age, growth is stifled.

Just like us, the only way Kore will mature is through experience. Zeus and Pluto know this and decide to intervene, just as life experience arrives to grow us. Nothing is spoken of Kore's descent, or of how she becomes Persephone Queen of the Underworld, other than the mention of Pluto taking her. Perhaps it was her own calling that took her willingly into Pluto's realm, perhaps it was his. The truth is the maiden Kore had to cut loose from co-dependence with her mother. In the myth she was apparently drawn by the new narcissus flower appearing, put forth by Gaia, just as we are drawn by the promise of new life, a whim or desire. Desire moves us. Innocence births curiosity that overcomes fear. In innocence we do not know the risks or dangers that await us.

Just as a seedling does not know the potential of frost, grazing animals, the heavy tread of a human foot, or a lack of rain. Kore did not know what was to come, she merely followed her delight. Yet life knew she had reached a readiness to break away from her childhood. Pluto was the catalyst. His role and his domain reveal core themes of Persephone's journey and her developing gifts. Her transition to the Underworld involves a psychological death; the death of the girl that brings forth woman then potentially the queen.

Psychological death takes place in our lives in diverse ways. It occurs through loss; the early death of a parent, losing a beloved grandparent or even a pet; a parental divorce or disruptive home move, a first flirtation, or sexual encounter. We are gently taken, or more often thrust into a new world, one we have no experience of, one that opens our emotional realm in vulnerability. This occurs either as a natural transition of maturity, or we are thrust, ripped away from our former state of being. Either we begin to take steps on our own behalf, or life reveals the necessity to take these steps through crisis. The key is we are ready for transition to a new state of maturity, yet we don't know we are. It is a natural process, much as death is an aspect of life.

In Persephone's tale transition occurs as she is ready to move on from maidenhood. In our own lives it can and does take place at any stage of childhood or maturity. It might be the final shift away from a dominating or dependent mother figure; it can be the compelling insight that reveals 'this is done', or an unexpected loss that forces us to change. It can occur through a humiliation or a failure that makes us explore our deeper motivations or values. Like the flow of nature's seasons, we are regularly offered the opportunity, compelled even, to walk through the Underworld towards maturity.

Crisis initiates a descent

Crisis is the supreme catalyst for transformation and growth. When Pluto appeared Kore's life changed irrevocably (whether she chose to go with him or not). As do our lives when we are plunged into her realm.

Pluto, as Lord of the Underworld, can appear in many forms, physically as another individual, or as an experience that pulls us into his realm, the

Underworld of shadows. The common thread is an initiation; an irrevocable change that is usually beyond our control. Whatever the circumstances of the initiation, our old securities are removed. If we try to run back to them, or hold on, we discover they are no longer there. Or they no longer fit, for they are empty of life, lacking the resources to meet this initiation.

When change is upon us, it is tempting to step back its edge. If we do so, we escalate insecurity and feelings of confusion, or we create suffering, through resisting the change calling us. During such times we may feel at odds with our self. Our attempts to cling on to what was stable before are futile. We are on our own, even when surrounded by supportive others. It's only in stepping up to the maturing process that we fully claim our own growth. That may include a temporary collapse of our strengths, asking for help, relying on the support of others. Yet Persephone reveals ultimately, we are on our own, as she was. Discovering our strength and solace in her within us, we claim the initiation. We mature.

A psychological death does not necessarily mean we lose everything externally. It is our relationship to those forms that changes, as with the Persephone and Ceres connection. We renew our relationships from the inside out. We are called to relate in utterly new ways. With death, even psychologically, there is no going back. Persephone reveals that new types of relating are imminent, as with her connection to Pluto. For a time, we may not know our self, as innocence is disrupted or destroyed, as we tentatively walk the edge of new life. Yet within us, Persephone lives as our guide through crisis, whatever its form. Her descent reveals that we too must descend and go through the initiation of experience to realise maturity. We are being offered the opportunity to grow, to ripen, to emerge fresh and new, just like spring. The Underworld darkness hides a gift. We cannot avoid the transition.

Crisis forces us to transform, to pull up new resources and strengths from the psyche that have been growing there but of which we have no knowledge until we need them. It's like a seed taking root to produce a new flower. We may not know it is there until its shoots appear. Our new strengths root in us similarly, in the unseen realms of the psyche. We may not know our developing qualities and resources until we have cleared old ground. Just as Persephone's return above-ground with her gift of spring, renewal is guaranteed at some point. How we face and embrace our time at the roots is key.

Persephone's passivity is a key factor for us all when facing crisis. As we descend, we must first accept what is happening. Without acceptance we do not descend fully but stay on the surface, fighting or running from what is. Acceptance is the first initiation key to maturity, to the renewal of the next phase. Acceptance does not necessarily mean 'it's all ok', but acceptance as the fact of the challenge of change and our passage through the Underworld. Acceptance as acknowledging the facts, and our feelings about the facts, not as an escape through spiritual bypassing.

It seems Persephone's fate has been decided by one with greater power, Pluto. Yet whether she chose to go willingly or not, the fact is she was in the Underworld, a new realm where she did not know how to be. In being there fully, she was facing the initiation into power. This is the paradox of her journey and ours. We may not choose to enter the gates of the Underworld, the shadows of life. We may be taken there unwillingly. Yet we cannot know its gifts until we fully enter that realm. To fully know the blessings of light, we must also know darkness. To know our fullness of woman, we must accept the death of the girl. Only then may she re-emerge in different form, held within the growing woman. The state of victim and empowerment are natural partners. Persephone is here to show us that and to guide us through her dark realm into maturity.

Opening the gate of Woman

Persephone is the archetype of puberty and the transition to full maturity as Woman, then Queen. At the start of the myth, we see how an irrevocable change was both needed and imminent. The tale relates how Kore drifts off to look at the new flower, just as a teenager allows her innocent curiosity or budding desire to be both guide and catalyst into the next phase of her maturing. The sweetly scented narcissus flower indicates a sexual aspect of Kore's journey, as does her age. Sexuality is a flowering, or it can be. It's a catalyst for growth, a natural driving force of maturity. This new flower is reflecting the potential of Kore's flowering into Persephone, the maiden's sexual initiation.

The process of how we mature sexually is a mystery. The act that facilitates it is clear. The loss or gift of our virginity precipitates the sudden shift from being maiden to child-woman. It is a gateway like no other, akin to both a death and a birth. The girl dies; the girl-woman is born. It portends the opening of emotional, irrational, and psychic gateways that may leave a girl-woman both celebrating and confused, even traumatized, depending on the circumstances. Kore's descent, and our own, is a death and rebirth process. When virginity is lost or given, the compulsion to return to childhood may be strong, yet the girl is transforming into a woman. The emergence of sexuality is not simply a physical or sexual initiation; it takes place on every level of being. Its process is truly mysterious. It takes us deep into the secret places of how it might be to be a woman. We are entering Venus's complex realm of attraction, connection, and creation. Not only is a woman being born, the potential of becoming a mother is opening.

Sexual initiation, depending on its context, either opens the promise of woman blossoming, or the potential to fall into the potential victim aspect of Kore's journey. Sometimes it's both: joy and wonder at this intimate act, and insecurity, walk hand in hand, sometimes alongside guilt, remorse, or anger. This rite of passage is largely ignored in our western cultures, as is the onset of menstruation. More conscious women are holding space for that to change now as we reconnect with each other in intimate ways and claim our legacy from the Sacred Feminine. Yet sexuality is often still imbued with the advice not to go there just yet, with moral judgments, with shame and ridicule (especially from male peers) or the demand not to get pregnant. Just to navigate puberty with its storm of hormonal changes would be enough, without the often-conflicting psychological demands and drives within oneself and from others.

Where sexual initiation is abuse or a rape, a maiden is catapulted violently into Persephone's Underworld. This creates trauma on many levels of body-being – a split off from the naturalness and true power of female sexuality ensues. Trauma influences all aspects of life, not just sexuality. It drives the compulsion to deny ourselves the development of our sexuality through fear, or to act it out in the attempt to win love or approval., or to heal. The simple innocence of childhood is gone, replaced by the complexity of trauma and the need to heal. The victim aspect of Kore can become rooted in a girl's psyche well before puberty.

There are many of us whose sexual initiation involved abduction by a Lord of the Underworld figure, perhaps at a very early age. These abusive experiences fall under Persephone's care. She is the one who can guide us through the Underworld and into healing integration, often through the support of a caring professional or organization. Persephone calls us to find the courage to go through the gateways of the Underworld towards rebirth. It is not an easy journey. It may take a lifetime of descent and ascent between pain and hope, darkness, and renewal, yet its potential is fulfilment. Trauma can be transmuted. It can yield a return to wholeness that encompasses all aspects of being a woman, including the wonder of sexual connection.

Right timing is one of Persephone's keys. When the gift of recall hits us, or the knowing that something's 'not right' emerges, Persephone is appearing as a guide. Crone Hekate (see Chapter 1) arises with her. Both emerge as guides within; we can ask for their help. They may even appear as supporters or mentors in life. Our task - not always an easy one - is to allow them into our vulnerable places.

Choice as an initiator.

The two mythic versions to Persephone's tale point us towards a key element of our journey from Maiden to Woman. Was Kore abducted? Or did she choose to go willingly with Pluto into his dark realms? Either way involves a death. Yet the act of choosing to face this transition precipitates the ease of our journey with power or powerlessness.

We may not actively choose the way a sexual initiation occurs, yet we have choice at some point - to face the facts and feelings of the experience if we're aware of them. For some women there is no knowledge of what took place, and therefore no choice. Experience lies so deep in the Underworld of the psyche that it may not emerge for years. For many reasons, we may choose to bury it., or it simply gets blocked from consciousness. It's as if we must exist for a time with a hidden wound, feeling at odds with our self and those close to us, but unsure why. In my own experience there's often a sense of something hidden, but we cannot reach it through volition. Memory has a failsafe mechanism that protects us. Trauma can lie buried until we have developed the maturity to speak about an experience we know of, to face what we need to, or support is available. We have no control over the timing of revelation. The soul and psyche know when it's time, or if we're ready.

A clue to buried trauma lies in our choices as a woman. The thread of this appears in Persephone's differing myths. Did she resist the Lord of the Underworld and was she dragged screaming into her new realm? Was she drawn by her calling to guide lost souls? Or was she mysteriously drawn to this 'demon lover'? Or perhaps a combination of both? It is said in some sources that Pluto was obsessed with her. Perhaps his obsession was matched by her curiosity and innocence? Or perhaps she was compelled by forces beyond herself, as we sometimes are?

I recognize this calling to go where perhaps I shouldn't in my life, do you? Life, a quality within myself, has always pulled me towards what might be considered risky or even dangerous. The point of choice at these times is the edge of growth. It is also the means for developing maturity and wisdom – the journey from child-woman into fully being a woman. Destructive relationships are a sign of buried trauma. If we are not maturing consciously (because we're not yet ready) our relationship choices (or lack of making a choice) will reflect this. As will the rejection of intimacy. Not as a matter for judgment but from the understanding that we repeat, and keep repeating, the unconscious patterns arising from trauma, until we bring it to healing.

A key aspect of Persephone's gift of acceptance is to recognize that we're not ready to choose differently until we are. We are not mature enough. We are still child-woman, no matter our physical age. Trauma, sometimes a seemingly minor occurrence to the rational mind, is unfinished business. It calls for redemption. Yet we might need to wait before we take a dive into the psyche to fully transform soul or ancestral patterning. We may need to dwell in the dark awhile, to rest and wait whilst we care for the ghosts of our past.

The Persephone initiation may occur at any age, particularly after a period of sexual abstinence. We are healing for our sisters too, the sexual distortions and abuse in the collective psyche. The need to break away from the outmoded beliefs about our sexuality is compelling, in fact it's essential. As is the need to transmute the ghosts of our past.

Movements like #metoo, ongoing revelations about child abuse and pornography, or any type of power imbalance show the depth and transformative potential available for us in these times. We are all called to face the Underworld. Some women may face the Persephone initiation through extremes at an early age; others may do it more gently, or later in life. There are no rules on this journey. Without doubt our sexual initiation, whether gentle or more violent, is an event that opens a door of maturity in the psyche. Once our virginity is given, claimed, or taken, we cannot go back. The innocent maiden in us is gone, only to emerge again with the integration of crone. Our task at this stage must be a growing conscious journey into being Woman.

Lost in the Underworld? Or taking the journey?

Persephone is the queen who moves with ease between worlds, although she spends most time in the Underworld. When we enter her realm of initiation through crisis, she is waiting to guide us, not only through shock and trauma but walking with us into rebirth. She is guide both to souls and to our psychological death processes. She prepares us for rebirth with her caring compassionate hands. Yet we must be willing to make the journey. If not, the risk is we get stuck in the dark phases of our own maturing and healing processes. We are a victim of them rather than empowered through them.

There are many ways we become lost in the Underworld. The belief in our self as a victim is one of them. It's a tricky aspect of our psychology. In truth, we can be the victim of the actions of others, particularly when we are young, innocent, or simply naïve. Yet the victim belief can also act as a handy hook on which to keep hanging our experience, one that places us in a disempowered position. It's a perspective that invalidates our potential for healing. It's a story we relate about our self that keeps us locked in the past. Victim is an archetype that's also encouraged through collective beliefs and the media. To fully mature we are called to move beyond the victim perspective. To make a choice beyond this insidious 'catch-all' within our human mindset. We cannot change what has happened, but we must take full responsibility for how we respond or react to experience. This is key to the themes of power and powerlessness.

Power or powerlessness can be a choice. Projection of what we don't want to face onto others is an active component in our projective blame-based society. It keeps us powerless. When we may make the government, a partner, parents, anyone, to blame for what's happening in our lives, we forego the opportunity to grow. We may not be able to change the status quo fully, but we can take responsibility for our part in it. We can change the ways we see experience, respond, or react to it, and how we apportion blame rather than act on our own behalf. We can actively be the change we want to experience.

Can evolution happen without our active participation? I would suggest not. The recognition of this empowering truth is what moves us beyond 'victim' into conscious co-creativity with life. Its denial keeps us in victim mode and a prisoner of the Underworld of our own psyche. Besides its association with crisis and trauma, the Persephone myth reflects how we must regularly take a good look into the Underworld, perhaps facing something ugly that we have tried to avoid or blame on another. This is not to deny the truth of victimhood and its trauma, where there has clearly been abuse of power, sexual or otherwise. It is to recognise, embrace and transform the violations of our self, the traumatic elements of our experiences, with the support of a wise Persephone friend or facilitator. Terrifying as that may be, taking the journey is to claim the self-determining power of choice that may have been violently or manipulatively taken from us in abusive acts.

Claiming our fullness of maturity is a human birth right. To take that journey requires us to reclaim all the places we would rather avoid. To be fully oneself we cannot pick and choose in terms of our past. We live in a world of dark and light. We must fully digest it all. In refusing to even taste the fruit of our experience, we remain victim to it. Whatever our crisis, eating the fruit of our experience is essential if we are to evolve. It is the food of growth and renewal. Its seeds contain the promise of spring. Persephone's eating of the pomegranate seeds is an allegory for our acceptance of the fact of darkness and light, and our power of renewal and rebirth.

The harvest of crisis is a new Spring. As with our physical digestive systems, sometimes the processing of the psyche takes time. The Persephone themes of an Underworld transition may subtly haunt us for a lifetime: the spectre of sexual abuse, mental illness, drug, or alcohol misuse. Yet Persephone's gift is to reveal there is always hope, no matter how dark the process. That we can go through and beyond even deep trauma. For spring always follows winter.

To discover spring's renewal, we must be willing to face where we are haunted by the ghosts of the past; where we have been dominated or exploited, where we have turned anger inward through fear of its destructive power. The Persephone archetype does not rage against her life circumstances, she takes them inward and down. It is even suggested she goes readily into the realm of spirits, the Underworld. This certainly is her gift to us – to support us in facing our demons without a fight but with commitment. The fruit of experience contains the power of our life-force, often locked away. The choice is always one of two: to turn inward destructively towards our self; or to digest our experience fully. When we turn inward destructively, we not only remain a victim, but we also actively continue abuse. When we embrace our pain and anger, albeit a difficult vulnerable process, we eventually discover that seeds of new life can take root within us.

Getting lost in Persephone's realm comes from our subscription to the belief in the victim archetype. It may also involve an encounter with alcohol, drugs, or other dependencies, such as destructive relationships, perhaps as an attempt to escape pain. We become obsessed or possessed either by our past: running our lives from the same old stories or running towards a false saviour. Persephone's link with the Dionysian cults demonstrates the two sides of this process: how the right use of ritual, medicinal plants, and sexuality can be avenues for altered states and potential transformation.

In ancient times the Dionysian rites were held sacred and included ritual to enact the life-death-rebirth process, to connect initiates to that power within themselves. Such rites have the capacity to take us beyond our self. They open the gateways of release and rebirth. In our cultures now we have mostly lost this link with the power of ritual, the sacred use of plant medicines, or the healing paths of sexuality. Our understanding of the innate power of ritual has become institutionalized or demeaned to purely social expression. Our use of alcohol, narcotics or sexuality can strengthen our illusions when we lose the sacred connection, rather than opening the gateways for rebirth. We may be taken into the heights of ecstasy and temporarily released, yet just as easily plunged into despair. We become possessed by the ghosts of what we are called to move beyond or become addicted to the temporary relief of a false support.

The Persephone archetype, through her myth, shows us what is possible when we engage the dark side of life, particularly that experienced in relationships. We cannot avoid the shadows, even in a blessed life. If we avoid life's power of change even temporarily, eventually it finds us, sometimes more forcefully or insidiously than if we go there willingly. Persephone is a guide through unconsciousness into rebirth. The way Kore becomes Persephone, the way Persephone becomes a queen is a clear pointer to how this happens. Kore's acceptance of 'what is', fully digesting the experience, transforms her. Similarly, embracing the maiden-victim within our self opens the maturing process of becoming a woman, then Queen. Eating the seeds is engaging our creative power for rebirth. When we don't, we are held captive by our victimhood. We remain powerless, in the dark, unconscious of the blossoming that is calling.

Becoming Queen

The Persephone archetype reveals to us that as transformation is engaged willingly, its effects are magnified hugely. When we take her hand, spring is certain, rebirth inevitable. Our return to light is guaranteed, yet our return to darkness also, for that is the natural cycle. The pomegranate seeds offered by Pluto to his new bride are her release yet ensure her return. For at this point in the myth, Persephone is faced with a choice: does she stay powerless, a victim of circumstance, or does she fully own her experience and become Queen of the Underworld?

Persephone was wise. She took the seeds offered to her by Pluto; she ate them. Planted in the dark within her, just like sperm meeting an egg, this act opened a point of conception. Her willingness to eat the fruit of her experience birthed her evolution, both the return to her mother and her commitment to Pluto. She was still a daughter, but now a woman also, on her way to Queen. The pomegranate seeds were planted within to gestate her birth. She became a queen, known as Queen of the Underworld. Yet her realm is not only the darkness; it's the promise of spring's renewal.

The pomegranate has a hard shell but is a lush juicy fruit in its centre, filled with seeds. Its exterior belies its inner promise. Artwork and records from the time of these myths show women with pomegranates in their hands. This fruit was clearly of potent relevance in their lives. It features extensively in almost all the religions, in particular Judaism and Christianity. It is also seen in religious art, particularly in the hands of the Virgin Mary, or the infant Jesus. This depiction in the art of its time, combined with other cultural clues, has led some historians to believe that pomegranate seeds had a connection with pregnancy and birth, or its prevention.

There are clear links to the cycles of birth, death, and resurrection in other customs too. In the Greek culture it is traditional to break a pomegranate on the ground on New Year's Day, or on a home move. Interestingly, oestrone, a compound identical to oestrogen, is found in high levels in pomegranate seeds. They are used still in India and East Africa as a contraceptive. Studies with animals show the seeds reduce fertility by ninety per cent. Pomegranate juice is also known to increase testosterone levels, one of the main hormones behind sex drive.

The ancients related to nature and its gifts of plant medicine in ways we do not now. We do not truly know what the pomegranate represents in ancient art or culture but its importance, particularly to women's lives, is evident. One reference from the Song of Solomon in the Christian Bible reveals more. This song is an allegory for the love between a man and woman in which the pomegranate is portrayed, ripe with sexual overtones and imagery. In this ancient Song of Solomon, the lover's body is closely associated with fruit. 'Your thighs shelter a paradise of pomegranates with rare spices' (Song of Solomon 4.13). The obvious lushness of this ripe juicy red fruit, filled with seeds, has a clear symbolic connection to the vulva. Both are deemed delicious. When in love desire drives us to consume one another passionately. It is this linking of the pomegranate to passion that gives us the final key to Persephone's gifts.

Death becomes life

Persephone's transition from Maiden to Woman to the emerging Queen is complete in her eating of the pomegranate seeds. She makes a choice to return to Pluto, yet she also is claiming her own sexual ripening, passion, and creative power for renewal. Death becomes life, winter becomes spring. Persephone's journey reveals to us that without fully claiming the pain and darkness of trauma, we are unable to claim the fulfilment of our sexual potential. We do not have the capacity for embodied passion as our life-force is locked up in trauma, fear, self-doubt, or anger.

To embody passion is to know our fullness as a woman and to express it as a queen. It is to fully engage in the joy of being alive, the power and bliss of lovemaking. Fullness requires we actively engage our wholeness

270

in a total commitment to the experience of this moment, whatever it holds. Losing self is the key to passion. When we make love, we lose ourselves fully in the experience. Similarly, when we give completely to our experience, whether it's 'good' or 'bad' we disappear into what we truly are - consciousness. In losing our self, consciousness naturally opens the gates for healing transformation, for we are in an expanded state. The flow of consciousness takes us into renewal. We naturally open and can merge with all aspects of our being, encompassing locked-up trauma in our body with love.

In an open state, healing is natural, renewal can be instant. Yet Persephone's wisdom also knows transformation can be a process in time. She is willing to rest in the Underworld, open and willing to encounter the shadows, to digest the seeds of experience with patience. She knows the wheel turns, both in consciousness and in time. She trusts that, like in a pregnancy, sometimes we must wait for birth.

Persephone is present and alive in us when we accept that life is painful, but we choose to bear it, to abide, to surrender to what is. This capacity to wait in the dark realms is one of Persephone's gifts; it births compassion. Compassion is our tender allowing of what is to cut us even deeper, to allow our pain, to soften into it rather than resist. Compassion is our opening into self-love. Just as Persephone felt for the lost souls wandering the Earth, we feel for the lost or trapped aspects of our own soul.

Paradoxically the root of passion lies in our compassion. In engaging compassion for our self and our experience, the victim belief in ourselves can open. We begin to understand the link between compassion and passion. Compassion occurs when we soften, open, allow. It happens when we go to the roots of our pain with tenderness. In allowing what is to open and gently begin to dissolve, we open and touch the depths of new life within us, the possibility of passion's birth, mirrored by spring's uprising life-force.

Full aliveness comes from traversing our dead zones. It's our willingness to live or to let go fully, to give our all to life as it is. When we participate fully in the changing dance of life, we appreciate that pain and passion come from the same place, that pain is but one turn of the wheel from joy, that spring occurs as winter's freeze begins to melt. We deeply understand that the nature of life is change and we allow ourselves to flow with it. We understand the paradox that we are both powerless and powerful in the face of change.

Persephone's transition from an innocent maiden to a powerfully wise queen holds the promise of hope when we're faced with an Underworld journey. She signifies a capacity to be fully awake and alive in the light of springtime and the depths of a dark winter. She is the promise of renewal that is life's commitment to our earthly processes of evolution. As such Persephone, Queen of the Underworld, represents a female archetype of mediator, medium, mystic, shaman, or psychotherapist. She knows the dark realm well and how to move through it into the light. She can navigate the many realms of life and death; she can guide the lost soul aspects of our nature to release and rebirth.

At times journeying with Persephone may feel extreme. Yet she supports us to face the intensity of experience we would usually want to avoid. In maturity we begin to realise that avoidance denies us the riches of our own soul. Her queendom is the inner world of the psyche and the soul, the capacity to live amidst darkness but not absorb it, to live in the light yet not lose her depth, to retain her knowing of the spirit realms whilst navigating everyday life. She is at home with the mysterious and irrational elements of life, holding the flexibility to live fully in both light and dark worlds and to engage both well.

The Queen of revitalization

The Persephone archetype in us is moving back and forth constantly between our experience as child and woman, and the less tangible worlds of the psyche and soul. She's a mediator, living in and integrating both worlds. When we allow her in us to do the work, we discover how the dark side of life is a place of great fertility and renewal.

In the Greek myths, it is to Persephone that Venus sends Psyche for the box of beauty. Whenever the Greek goddesses feared their beauty needed revitalizing, they turned to Persephone for the box of beauty. One would think its guardian would be Venus herself, as she is Goddess of Love. Yet Persephone's beauty is deeply rooted in the cycle of loss and return, the whole of life experience. Psyche's myth (shared in my book Sacred Pathways) tells us the box of beauty appears to contain nothing but sleep. Yet it is the sleep of integration and renewal from which we awaken reborn. That rebirth heralds the power of renewal, with the gifts of deep self-understanding and knowing that only arrive through such a transition, fully being at home in oneself wherever we are. Persephone in us holds a depth of understanding that can hold space for another deep dive into the shadows or, for that journey in others. The kind of understanding that knows the wheel of life is always turning dark to light and light to dark.

Persephone's gift of rebirth requires the understanding of timing; the qualities of introspection, listening deeply, receptivity to the impulse of the ingested seeds towards new life. I experience this in my writing process. I cannot make it happen. There are times I must wait for new expression to emerge. I feel it gestating in me. In Persephone's way of being, the next life phase, the harvest of a process, arrives through time in the dark. Unlike Ceres who searches endlessly above ground for her daughter's return, Persephone simply waits in the Underworld. The next phase arrives naturally; she eats the seeds and is released to visit her mother. The gifts of receptivity, listening and waiting lead to 'right timing'. She arrives in spring. Or does spring arrive with her? In truth they arrive together.

Persephone represents the importance of introspection, knowing oneself fully, yet more so knowing and trusting the process of the seasons, the rhythms of natural timing for oneself. She gently but persistently enables the transmutation of past trauma and empowers us to take responsibility for life. She is our guide in uniting the light and the dark aspects of the self that lead to true empowerment, hand in hand with Crone Hekate. Her gift in us is integrating extremes of experience so we can be fully present here on Earth. The Persephone archetype within holds the infinite promise of renewal. Our journey is to trust. She knows the way even though we may not see it. Like spring's consistent return Persephone holds the certainty of the Feminine cycle.

Chapter 5

Into the Deep –

Mother of the Sea, Sedna

The call of the deep is upon me.
Like the whale
I breathe
and slowly
serenely
sink
beneath my heartbeat
into the deep.

There,
beyond form,
I rest.
There,
profundity of stillness
is my formless form.
I disappear
in an ocean of emptiness
knowing no thing.

Silence
Blackness
Peace
caressing
the wounds of soul

Then, like the whale
I rise.
Waves of being
flow to the surface,
rhythmically
pounding the shore
of my life.
They echo
the song of profundity
to those who can hear.

The deep is your home,
they cry.
Your ebony
womb
of wordless wonder
your chasm of Grace
your formless space.

Do not forget
the voice of the silence.
Remember, remember
the call of the deep.

Cassandra Eve

Archetype: Mother of the Sea

Symbols: The ocean; ocean creatures; fingers; ice; an eye; deep shadow; the Underworld.

Message: Our reactions are natural guides. Ride their waves deep into the psyche and beyond it, into transcendent consciousness.

Sedna themes: The rhythms of the ocean; human instinct; The Handless Maiden story; abandonment & betrayal, clinging to an old life or form of self-identity.

What the Sedna archetype calls for: embracing our instinctual reactions as teachers; soothing via self-care, touch, singing, ritual & offerings, facilitating reconnection to self.

Sedna is Mother of the Sea and marine animals in Inuit mythology, also known as Mistress of the Sea. Although in some references Sedna is known as a goddess, the Inuit people have no Divine Mother and Father figures, or creator gods. Their spirituality is based on humanity's union with the natural world, shamanism, and animism. In their culture, Sedna is seen as half-woman, half-fish, representing that aspect of humanity that is intimately connected with the ocean and marine life. She symbolises a link to our earliest form of existence: our presence as a foetus in the watery womb of our mother. Or even earlier, in nature's first processes of creation, the first forms of life emerging from the ocean to move on land.

Sedna has many names in different Inuit groups across Greenland, Canada and the Arctic Circle ranging from Sassuma Arnaa, 'Mother of the Deep', to Arnapkapfaaluk, 'Big Bad Woman'. These names indicate how she is respected as both a benign and fearful presence within Inuit culture. As Sedna caretakes the vital food sources of the Eskimo peoples, they rely on her beneficence to provide seals, walrus, and other ocean creatures for food and clothing. To them, she is a beneficent Mother, a presence in the Underworld, and a protector of the ocean.

Much like the ocean, the Inuit believe that Sedna's moods are changeable, even dangerous. They depend on her, so believe they must regularly placate her. When ocean storms rage, they say that Sedna's sea creatures become entangled in her hair, so she will not release her bounty to the hunters. The Inuit believe Sedna's storms are an expression of her rage at humanity's lack of respect for the ocean realms. So, they soothe her with offerings, prayers, songs, or a visit from the shaman. They also honour Sedna with some of the liver of the first-killed sea mammal of the season, in appreciation for her abundance.

The mythology of Sedna describes how she came to hold the role of 'Mother of the Sea' within the Inuit culture. It also represents, to our western mindset, archetypal themes of abandonment or betrayal lying deep in the psyche and locked in the body. Sedna reveals the play of instinct and reaction in us, how early wounding to our sense of self will always rise to the surface, to be seen, acknowledged, and potentially healed. She represents our capacity for transcendence too; opening our understanding that all experience, no matter how it looks or feels, is always held in the ocean of consciousness.

Her-story

The mythology of Inuit culture is passed down orally and therefore fluid in its telling. There are many versions of Sedna's myth, for the tale varies from one Arctic region to the next. Yet all versions have a common theme: how a young woman becomes the mother of all sea creatures. As mother, Sedna has dominion over all ocean life. She controls the availability of seal, walrus, fish, whale, and other sea creatures to the Inuit hunters. One of the early versions of her story is a creation myth, relating how different races populated different parts of the world.

One day, during a violent blizzard, a handsome young man enters an Inuit family igloo. He is welcomed and sleeps in the igloo with the whole family. They do not notice he is wearing a necklace with two large canine teeth.

When the family wake up the next morning, the young man is gone. As the father goes out to tend to his dogs, he notices animal tracks outside the igloo. He returns to the igloo and says to his wife, "We were deceived. That young man must have been my lead dog disguised as a human".

Some while later the father discovers his daughter has become pregnant. He remembers the visitor to their igloo and so is ashamed of what kind of creature she might give birth to. He makes his daughter lie in his kayak and paddles to a small island. Here he abandons her. Sedna is left alone on the island, pregnant, without care. Yet some versions of the myth state she receives tender pieces of meat from her father's lead dog, who swims out to provide for her.

After nine months Sedna gives birth to six young. Three are clearly Inuit babies, the other three have large ears and snout-like noses. They are not Inuit. The young mother sews some sealskins into a large bag in which she places the three alien children. She pushes them off the island toward the south, calling out, 'Sarutiktapsinik sanavagumarkpusi' (You shall be good at making weapons). Some Inuit people say that European and other peoples are descended from those three alien children.

An alternate version of this story relates how Sedna's father paddles in a skin boat to take his daughter to the island. On their way a storm threatens to capsize the boat so he decides he must throw his daughter overboard. When Sedna tries to climb back into the boat, her father cuts off her fingers. These fingers become seals. She tries again to get into the boat, and he cuts off her hands. As her hands fall into the sea, they become walrus. As Sedna tries once more to save herself, her father cuts off her forearms. These transform into whales. With no way of holding onto the boat now, the young girl sinks into the depths of the ocean. She changes to half-woman and half-fish and becomes known as Sedna, Mother of the Sea, the caretaker of all sea creatures.

In yet another version of this Inuit myth, Sedna is a giant with an enormous hunger. She is always angry, so attacks her parents constantly, demanding more and more food. Tired of her stormy behavior her father takes Sedna out to sea and throws her over the side of his kayak. As she clings to the sides of the kayak in desperation, he chops off her fingers. She sinks to the Underworld, her fingers becoming the seals, walruses, and whales hunted by the Inuit. Here in the deep, her anger cooled by the waters, she comes to rest as Mother of the Sea.

In Inuit culture, it is Sedna who decides how many creatures can be killed for food. When she is unhappy with the people's treatment of her realm or her creatures, she punishes them with storms, lack of food, sickness, and starvation. The Inuit believe that if a shaman travels to her domain, the Underworld, and performs a ritual in which her hair is combed, or offerings are made, she becomes calm. Sedna then releases her creatures to the hunters and the people are fed.

Sedna's place in the Universe – Astronomy & Astrology

Sedna is a minor planet, lying beyond the Kuiper Belt on the far edges of our solar system. It is one of the most distant space bodies ever found, discovered in 2003 by Michael Brown, David Rabinowitz, and Chad Trujillo at the Palomar Observatory. Sedna was so named, after the Inuit Mother of the Sea, as it is a far distant cold planet. It is 75% the size of Pluto, egg-shaped and a striking red colour, like Mars.

Sedna is so far out it takes 11,406 years to complete one elliptical orbit around the Sun. As such, she represents the outer limits of our consciousness, where we must stretch to encompass a vast new reality, way beyond that of our current consciousness. One way to understand the energetic signature of a new planet is to explore the links with previous cycles and events here on Earth. Astrologer Alan Clay links the last close pass of Sedna to our planet to the end of the last Ice Age. At this time human culture began to shift from a nomadic hunter-gatherer lifestyle to settled communities. This formed the earliest basis for our current socio-political structures and way of life. Sedna approaches her closest point to Earth again in the 2070s and may well herald a similar evolutionary shift. What that means collectively, remains to be seen.

In an individual's astrological birth-chart Sedna reveals where that individual may have experienced coldness, abandonment, or betrayal, especially by a parental-type figure. Her placement may indicate trauma, suffering, or illness, where an individual is clinging to an old form of life, or where anger is held. With healthy aspects she also indicates a capacity to sacrifice, incredible tenacity or devotion, and the ability to ride the storms of life. Her position can point towards extremes of experience and/or behaviour, from visionary and dedicated, to clinging and stubborn.

In her evolved form as Mother of the Sea, Sedna represents transcendent consciousness, that which is always available to us. She indicates a capacity to willingly surrender through and beyond traumatic experience, to rest in our beingness. When we come to an understanding of Sedna's energies, we recognise how in our human realm, we are but one aspect of a whole planetary system, and that our Source is both within and beyond that. Sedna reveals the paradox that we have an animal body and act from instinct, yet also are an aspect of divine consciousness.

My journey with Sedna

Byron Bay in Australia is a place where the wild waves of the Pacific Ocean pour ceaselessly onto the land. It's a surfer's paradise and a wave watchers dream. Yet the waves hold a strength one needs to be wary of.

They're as ready to pull an ocean adventurer under, as carry them to the shore.

I was on an eight-day retreat close to Byron Bay. Midway through the retreat, our group took an early morning walk along the coastline above Broken Head beach. The path brought us to 'Three Sisters Rock', a site where the Bundjalung Aboriginal peoples myth relates that three sisters were drowned. One sister got swept out by a strong current. Her two sisters drowned whilst trying to save her. The sisters are immortalised in the rocky outcrop here. It is said that Aboriginal parents tell their children this story to stop them from swimming in strong currents off the headland.

As the day was getting hot our group stopped at Three Sisters Rock for a respite from walking. Feeling very raw, open, and fragile in my retreat process, I valued the opportunity to sit close to the rocks, near the ocean and away from the main group. The sight of the huge waves rolling in was compelling. As I relaxed into their rhythm, rising, and falling back into the deep, one particularly large wave spoke within me. "Fall into me" it said. I willingly let go into its huge rolling presence.

Falling, falling, dropping deep inside myself, I was one with the wave, aware of nature and my inner world utterly in tune with each other. I was the air carrying the birds; I felt myself falling through earth and ocean; an explosion of fire took place in my hands; my legs opened wide as though birthing and my body dissolved in bliss. The elements were unified in me as the waves continued to roll and carry me into the deep, where all movement became stillness yet continued to flow, rising and falling from shallows to deep, from deep to surface, and beyond.

I didn't know of Sedna then, but her transcendent unity, one with nature, had claimed me.

Message: Our reactions are natural guides. Ride their waves deep into the psyche and beyond it, into transcendent consciousness.

The mirror of nature's ever-changing moods

Sedna is an important figure in Inuit mythology as the provider of nourishment from the ocean. Yet her moods, like the ocean, are ever changeable. She rests in the deep, yet seemingly on a whim, she can become stormy, threatening the essential supply of food to the Inuit people. Their need to placate her then becomes crucial to their survival. No wonder she is equally feared and cherished. Like many Dark Goddess archetypes, she calls us to sit on the edge of uncertainty, the thin line between life and death.

Nothing is certain about nature or human life, except movement and change. Nature moves from extremes of chaos to calm, mirrored particularly through the waters of our oceans. Sedna's stormy moods, reflect the extremes we must face through the natural world we are dependent on. Her symbology, representing both the psyche and the ocean of consciousness, reveals our inner flow from peace to chaos too. The Inuit know that to rely on Sedna's bounty is to learn to navigate life's rough edges: storms to stillness, chaos to rest, bounty to lack, knowing everything changes. The nature of the ocean allows one to be held as in a warm bath, to be tossed from high to low, or thrashed against rocks in a moment. Its waves both caress and destroy. When entering the ocean, we must be awake to these changing moods and their potential. It's the same in our psyche. When entering the deepest inner realms of self, our understanding of nature's changing moods and rhythms helps guide us through the intensity of challenging times, or our visceral reactions to it.

Sedna, as Mother of the Sea, lies deep in our psyche and, as her planetary body reveals, way out in transcendent consciousness. Her nourishment is for both body, soul and beyond into the furthermost reaches of our consciousness. When we enter her realm, we must be awake to the potentials held in all her realms. Bounty and storms emerge from the dark inner waters within our psyche. They feed or challenge our connection to the deep stillness and peace that is also available beyond all storms. What we know as 'the small still space within' – in truth, the vast expanse of our consciousness - sustains us through the ups and downs of life. It is a gateway to transcendent consciousness. Yet our inner darkness also holds the potential of emotional uprisings, or death and dissolution to what is ripe for change. In our lives we may avoid entering this deep dark world, we may cling to life as it is, yet sometimes we are thrust there through experience, much like Sedna. We cannot avoid the depths, much as we might try to.

In the depths of the ocean nothing is clear; there is no definition, much like our inner world in times of change or trauma. In some of Sedna's myths, she is portrayed with just one eye that sees all things in her domain. We need this eye as we descend into the dark mystery of her realm within us.

Nothing is as it seems in the deep. When it's boiling on the surface of the ocean, with huge crashing waves, down in its depths there is a soothing yet powerful gentler rhythm. Our inner world is similar. When called to the deep, we must remember this. That there is gentled transcendent stillness beyond our chaos. That we know these waters, for we emerged from them. We may not want to, but we can rest here in the dark for a while. To recognise this can be soothing; there is no need to resist or fight. We can play shaman to our own process. Our animal instinct knows how to breathe here, even whilst the rational mind struggles. Our consciousness knows our capacity to be submerged here and to go beyond. Sedna's myth shows us this: for as she loses fingers, hands and arms, new life is born. Her mythology, like that of many dark goddesses, reveals to us a rite of passage through the Underworld. That loss in one form leads to life in another.

The Handless Maiden

A major aspect of the Sedna myth is the loss of her fingers, hands, and arms. Without them she is powerless as a human being. The fairy tale 'The Handless Maiden', from the Brothers Grimm, has a similar thread. The story is about a maiden whose father sells her to the devil in exchange for wealth and comfort. It tells how a miller who has fallen on hard times, makes a deal with the devil to exchange what stands behind his mill for vast riches. The miller thinks the devil wants his apple tree. He doesn't realise his daughter is standing beside the tree. When the devil comes for the maiden, her father chops off her hands. She cries on the stumps so the devil can't touch her and so he rejects her as useless and disappears.

The maiden now wonders alone in a forest in search of healing. Here we encounter several versions of the tale in which she is either given a pair of silver hands by the king she marries, or her hands grow back. She transcends her suffering. What might this story reveal to us? What does it mean to be handless? And what does it tell us about Sedna?

The maiden represents an innocent aspect of the psyche in a woman or a man. It is the sweet feeling aspect of our humanness. It also symbolises the soul, with its purity and goodness. Here on Earth, we move through innocence in order that we mature. Myth and fairy tales can act as guides for our journey and many, such as The Handless Maiden, are ultimately a tale of redemption. For that to take place, we cannot avoid our wounding.

The maiden's severed hands point to a deep wound to the feeling function of soul that must be healed. Our hands reach out, touch, feel, connect, receive, soothe, and heal, as well as act and feed. After the maiden loses her hands, she cannot feel, touch, or hold anyone. She's powerless to receive or relate; she's lost the capacity to connect on a deeply instinctual level.

At the start of the tale the masculine aspect of the psyche, represented by the maiden's father, is also powerless, so he trades his inner feminine (represented by his daughter) for an easy life. In this myth, the father also represents the status quo, the collective attitude, or the patriarchal perspective. It sacrifices the innocent aspects of the feminine (feelings and soul) for material comfort, gain and wealth, not recognising or honouring the value of the maiden – the soul. In present times, our collective culture operates similarly. There is an obvious schism between mind, feeling, instinct and soul in many human beings. The material world, comfort and security are given priority over soulful creativity and true heartfelt abundance, our capacity to be fully alive and embodied. The Handless Maiden story represents this loss of soul and the capacity to feel deeply. Her wandering in the forest reflects the potential for the soul's restoration. Her story provides a map for wholeness.

There are many rites of passage stories in mythology. They relate a descent and return that brings a wounded soul to new life. Sedna's tale is one of these stories, yet it has no obvious resolution in her own life. Sedna moves into another realm entirely. Like her planetary body, her myth goes beyond the merely human realm; it embraces the animal and the otherworldly, instinctual, and transcendent frequencies of consciousness. It takes us deep within and to the furthermost reaches of consciousness. Sedna's story reveals deeper meaning behind her seeming death: that there is wholeness and a potential for new life in riding the waves of our human storms, even the most painful, such as abandonment or betrayal. Sedna show us humanness unified in the great ocean of consciousness, even as we feel broken.

Sometimes we have no option but to enter the inner realms we would rather not encounter. When life falls apart, it is wise to drop into the deep. Like a swimmer diving beneath the swirling maelstrom of a wave, there is a calmer flow under the surface. The wisdom of Sedna's tale reveals that we must go with the rolling waves of experience, rather than fighting them. For there is power in powerlessness when we willingly allow our self to be taken.

We live on a life/death/life edge always. Sedna shows us the inevitability of surrender. That ultimately, we must surrender to death at some point. We do not know where the wave will take us. We must allow ourselves to be taken. Perhaps into a challenging wild place, filled with storms, perhaps into deep peace and stillness, transcendent consciousness. Maybe into both.

In surrender we may feel out of our depth, yet Sedna reveals there are ways of being with our deeply dark times. There are ways to live through and soothe our storms. As we let go, we are taken beyond our need to find solutions on the surface of life. A return to feeling and instinct is our guide in these places, not the rational mind. When we allow our self to surrender, Sedna reveals both our oneness with the wild aspects of nature, the natural cycles that we have become disconnected from, and our true nature as a consciousness beyond all this. We learn to accept our wildness, our animal self, as a potent guide to that which we cannot yet understand rationally. We discover we are inextricably connected to all life and yet are also beyond it, as expansive consciousness. That our growth will naturally arise from consciousness, as new life, in right timing.

A landscape of abandonment

Sedna represents the archetypal abandoned or betrayed maiden aspect of the psyche. Like the girl in The Handless Maiden, she is innocent, unsupported by her father, the one who is there to guide and protect her. Sedna's father's abandonment of her is a betrayal of her unknowing nature. Without the input of a loving, caring mother either, she is alone. As such, she represents immature aspects of self that fail to grow beyond a traumatic experience. These aspects remain lost or stuck in the psyche. Living in a desolate landscape of aloneness, they lack the fundamental trust in life and others that is necessary for healthy maturing.

Father, as archetype, is a symbol for the strength that holds a child until innocence has developed maturity, establishing its own strengths through being protected, then guided, through life's experiences and challenges. In Sedna's myths, whichever one we look at, her father is either challenged by her behaviour, or by events. He does not have the strength of presence, or simply cannot be bothered, to respond consciously, or to care about what happens to her. He's looking for the easy option, an escape from his responsibility as father. His solution is to simply get rid of his troublesome daughter.

There is no question that fathers play an important role in their daughters' lives. An involved father is crucial for psychological and behavioural development, and the well-being of his children generally.

For a female, the father-daughter relationship sets up the template for intimate relationship, as well as the development of her inner masculine. Qualities such as strength, the setting of healthy boundaries, trust, support to stretch and grow, and the security of unconditional love are vital to healthy development of maturity. Research shows that when fathers are actively present in a loving relationship, daughters have greater self-confidence and self-respect. They can protect themselves better than those whose fathers are absent. When father as protector is absent, insecurity in oneself and in the world, debilitates a healthy response to the challenges that inevitably face us as we mature.

Sedna appears in different forms in different myths, whether she is an innocent girl, or a voracious giant, the father's role as guide, protector and strength of presence is lacking. Much as the father in The Handless Maiden facing the devil, Sedna's father does not embody the strength and maturity to fully face the circumstances that arise. Whatever the myth, he fails his task in numerous ways; not noticing that the handsome young man has large canine teeth; acting out of shame at Sedna's pregnancy and abandoning her; tipping her out of the boat for his own survival when the storm arises.

Sedna's father acts in a similar manner in the myth where she is portrayed as a giant with an enormous hunger. Sedna is always angry, so attacks her parents constantly, demanding more and more food. This suggests the tantrums of a toddler, a point when innocence is moving into selfhood. Who doesn't recognise the incessant 'I want' demand of the dissatisfied child who is discovering their power, yet has not learnt the right use of its will? The role of a father here is to establish boundaries, for the child does not have the capacity yet to do so for itself. The giant figure is like instinct running riot. Again, the father in the myth cannot hold the true authority that holds his offspring in clarity of presence and tough love.

When instinct runs amok in us, as Sedna displays both as the giant and the victim, it is calling for security. It is calling to be held in safe arms even whilst fighting them. Both archetypes stem from insecurity looking for boundaries. The instinctual layers of our being act in reaction to a perceived threat or lack, real or not. They are the self-preservation elements of our nature. Sedna's greed in this myth overlays her deep hunger for love, care, and clear boundaries. She's calling to be held, to know the 'No' that comes from authority and creates the reassurance of security.

If we have not learnt and matured through being held in the strength and integrity of a healthy, mature masculine energy (however that appears in our lives), we don't develop those strengths within us. We don't learn how to support our self in facing challenge, or to take responsibility for our self and our experience. Being held with strength and presence as we grow, guided to take on what we're ready for, supports the growth of self-trust and maturity. We know we are loved because our development is held with care. We build healthy self-respect and right boundaries through being guided and held in what we are ready for. If we have not been well-equipped with these learned skills, we may repeatedly abandon and betray our self, simply causing trouble for our self and others, or reacting inappropriately, because we don't know how not to. None of this is wrong, simply an expression of immaturity, a wound in the psyche. 'Father' supports us in learning how to access and implement clarity, strength, and boundaries, whilst 'Mother' teaches us to deeply feel the emotions and energy behind our reactions. 'Father' shows us how to be in the world, with all its challenges, to stay true to our values, to support and protect our self appropriately. 'Mother' demonstrates how to fully accept, nurture, and love our self.

If we've never known the strength and support of one who guides and protects us, how may we grow to stand strong when we need to? How may we know what is appropriate, respectful, healthy, if we have not been held in those qualities whilst developing? Abandonment leads to self-rejection. It's a learned pattern based in lack of self-worth and love. Life may bring us experience after experience that triggers old wounds of neglect. But we cannot heal our instinctual shadows through trying to fix them, or even through the usual therapeutic means. We must get into the body, descend into the deep layers of our survival system. Sedna's story gives us clues as to what takes place. For in her myth, she must let go of the boat and fall into the ocean.

In deep primal waters

What would you do in Sedna's position, being tipped out of a boat into the ocean? Sedna's natural reaction is to fight. She's terrified; she tries to hang on; she fights for her life. In similar circumstances, we would do likewise. Survival is not a choice. The instinctual reaction of the body's survival mechanism is to save life. It's an aspect of our animal body, an effective natural programme that we have no conscious control over. It's entirely appropriate when there is a threat to life. It's orientated to staying alive.

It's normal for the survival mechanism in us to become active when the body is in danger. Our bodies are made to react to threat. The autonomic system is key to our survival, the sympathetic and parasympathetic systems creating a balancing act between activation and deactivation of responsiveness, according to perceived threat. That balance is key to our ongoing survival and well-being on all levels. Lifestyle changes over time have distorted the responses of these systems though. Survival is now attached to factors other than a threat to our physical safety. Stress in our lives means that the survival mechanism is often turned on, simply through busyness, worry, or pressure of time. Instinct has adapted to perceive threat where there truly is none, at least not to physical survival.

Adapted reactions to psychological threat are now a major factor in most individual's lives. They not only limit physical well-being, but they also create huge stresses in our psyche. In any situation where security is pressured, we may argue, defend, withdraw, resist, or go numb as a means for some sense of control. These safety mechanisms are the psychological equivalent to fight, flight and freeze, our animal response to danger. Most of us are no longer facing the threat of being eaten alive as we wander in nature, nonetheless the current equivalent, perhaps in the office or home, may trigger a similar reaction in us. The threat of losing a job, partnership conflict, or the stress of simply earning enough to live, means many people run on adrenalin constantly. When we're in this heightened state, feeling our sense of control and our need for safety is under threat, heightened response takes over. The hormonal system activates. The body puts itself on high alert.

It's natural to fight for what we love. It's a healthy choice to try to preserve what has value in our lives. Sometimes this is exactly what is needed. The arising of an impassioned response or reaction can transform a situation that has lost its life. It can bring what was dead or dull to its next level of growth. Sometimes our reactionary attempts to resuscitate what has lost its life are futile though. Life moves on, people change, relationships either thrive or die as the individuals in them grow together or apart. Sometimes it's necessary to simply give up, or give in. Sometimes, like Sedna, who could no longer hang on, as her fingers, hands, and then arms were hacked off, we reach a point where even the choice to let go is taken. We can't do anything other than surrender, abandon our effort and let go fully. We realise that fighting the inevitable makes no difference. Like Sedna, we must plunge into the unknown; we must fall into the ocean of consciousness.

Letting go is never the final act in a series, although it may appear so. It is not a failure; it is a catalyst. In surrender, we move deeper into our self. This may be from exhaustion, or a sense of relief, and bring us the peace of transcendence, or it may be a shut down: cutting off, isolating, becoming cold. Either way, we recognise our current powerlessness in the situation. We realise it's futile to fight.

Shut down can be a form of protection from our fear of what is to come, or from the pain of what's occurred. Sometimes this is necessary; maybe we need a breathing space, a pause to gather our resources. For psychological health, it's necessary that shutting down is only a temporary measure though. We may believe it keeps us safe, but in truth it disconnects, not only from others, but from our self and our available resources. Locking our self (or our issues) away limits our life-force. We are actively foregoing the capacity towards self-support, or any movement towards new life. Closure may seem to be passively accepting whatever comes along, expressing as apathy. Or it may be resisting or struggling against circumstances, even in subtle ways. To believe that closure is a protection is to delude oneself. Nothing can move on in closure. Neither are we able to receive.

When we're faced with deep psychological challenges, letting go may seem to be a helpless option. Yet when we make a choice to fully accept whatever is happening in all its elements – the facts of what's happening, our feelings and reactions about it, our fight, the need to struggle or resist, grief, lack of control, the whole package – surrender is a catalyst. In the conscious choice to fully let go, at whatever point we can allow that, we open. We enter the expansive ocean where new possibilities may arise in right timing. If we choose to hang on, resisting the calling to let go the old life we are fighting or grieving for, we become stuck. We don't transmute or transcend. Our lack of acceptance pushes away the balm of love that's always available in the ocean of consciousness. We actively forego the renewal that can only be received when we are open.

Sedna's abandonment by her father is a core wounding. As is the brutal severance of her hands and arms. Such experience in our own lives disconnects the very aspects of our self that can help us heal. Our hands can touch and feel. They represent how we reach out, receive, and connect. To do so, they must be moving between their different states of openness and closure. They must be connected and responsive to our needs and desires. When we're abandoned or betrayed by those who are there to hold psychic space for our growth, the connective aspect of self is cut, sometimes before it's fully formed. This engenders lack of trust in life, in others and our own potential capacity. We become utterly alone, numb, living in cold, dark isolation, much like Sedna in the deep of the ocean. We are thrust into deep primal waters, lacking the resources to help ourselves.

In losing our connective feeling and healing aspect of self, we lose our potential for life and growth. We lose the capacity of receiving, touching, reaching out, holding, and caressing, connecting to love and the possibility of joy. We lose our aliveness. Sometimes we must simply endure this state until we reach a point of change. We must rest in the deep, in the dark, in the unknown, in the cold. Sometimes it's the only choice we have, for we cannot force trauma to heal. That simply deepens the wounding. We must gently trust that new capacities of consciousness beyond those we've lost, are waiting for us there. Sedna did not know that what she lost - her fingers, hands, and arms - would become the creatures of the ocean. Similarly, we do not know what new life awaits us as we let go into the transcendent ocean of all possibility.

A temporary detour

Sedna's fall into the ocean seems to be a tragic end to her story. She fails in her attempts to cling to her father's boat. She descends into the icy cold depths of the ocean. Yet there is considerably more to this tale than initially appears.

The dark depths of the ocean may represent how we cut off from feeling when overwhelmed. This is a natural fail-safe, especially when young, that protects the developing psyche from becoming flooded with material it hasn't the capacity to process. Sedna shows us the natural need to withdraw, to descend into the deep, after a shock or trauma. It's a temporary protection that allows the psyche to rest and digest until the time is ripe for re-emergence.

When betrayal or abandonment occurs, particularly through our caretakers, our sense of security is disrupted. We lose our trust in those who are there to love and care for us. Or we turn the wounding in on our self, feeling unlovable. We may even lose faith in life itself. As we mature, it's natural to cover over this sense of lack, or insecurity, contracting away from painful or challenging experience, yet also finding ways to live with it. We adapt. We contract inwards, away from others, away from life's power of renewal. As we do so, our natural vitality and power of renewal becomes more and more limited. The light has dimmed or gone out in us. It's like the Sun disappearing behind dark heavy clouds.

In a natural maturing process from child to adult, if aspects of our nature are numb, if we are core-wounded, we cannot move towards wholeness. Unacknowledged trauma affects us both subtly and in more obvious ways. We might try to stay closed off from life's ever-present possibility of renewal, yet it's constantly knocking on our door, inviting us out to play. Whatever our experience, however traumatic, change is inevitable. Like nature's seasons, like the flow from the darkness of night to the light of daytime, we are made to flow through our experience, not hold onto it. Whatever we try to avoid, inevitably finds us. Whatever we're trying to hide, eventually makes itself known. Yet we also must choose to befriend it.

Nature is our great teacher in the maturing processes of life. A tree may take years to grow its roots deep enough in the earth to blossom. Similarly, in our own lives, trauma may be held deep in our psyche until we have developed the inner resources to take care of it. A certain level of maturity naturally arises in us through navigating the normal ups and downs of life as an adult. Disappointments, being forced to change direction, or let go due to life's challenges, are a natural aspect of becoming an adult. It's impossible to go through life without feeling failure, let-down, tired, even exhausted at times. We realise we cannot always be happy or fulfilled. Such experience teaches us resilience, flexibility, when to stick with something and when to back off. Life is full of temporary detours away from fulfilment.

Accepting and navigating these states as a natural aspect of life, even when we don't like them, ensures we mature. These day-to-day experiences hold the potential for us to develop deeper roots in self-trust, the wisdom to understand that life is full of change. The potential is we discover that we can care for our self, and that others do, even when we feel unsettled. We may begin to discover we are lovable and loved. We may even discover our soulfulness, that we are held in the ocean of consciousness, even in our wounding.

Abandonment is a deep wounding that may takes years of experience to accept as part of our wholeness. Yet as our inner self stabilises, we potentially become accomplished in facing our deeper wounding. We might need to acknowledge where we been failed by our caretakers, have been forsaken, have failed our self, or simply are not ready to heal deeply yet. If we judge our emotions, or we belittle our self for what we feel so deeply, our woundedness is compounded. As with a physical wound, scar tissue builds up in layers around the original pain. It can take time, gentle care, and loving acceptance to open, trust and receive love again. We must approach our deepest wounding with transcendent consciousness. Not to rise above it, but to realise it is one wave of experience within an ocean of waves. That waves rise and fall naturally within the ocean. They are there, we feel them, then they fall back into the ocean. They rise again, maybe a little higher with a deeper trough, we feel them and then they're gone. They are always part of the ocean, never separate from it, as are we. Everything, even deep pain, is one with the ocean of consciousness.

Whatever the pain of our experiences or self-judgments, our grieving, our loss of vitality, our disconnect from others, it is only a temporary detour from our true state of being. It's a transient experience that is there to teach and mature us. It may seem we are lost, that our pain is all-consuming, as we are called to embrace the totality of our life's experience. Yet inevitably, in a life well-lived, we reach a point where we forego powerlessness and claim the intensity of every experience in order that we mature. We make a choice to live fully, rather than remain a victim.

The path to wholeness always calls us to encompass our pain and trauma. The truth is, we may never heal it, yet to be whole does not require healing. It's simply to be fully present with what is – our pain, disconnection, betrayal, grief, or rage. At times we may rest in the dark with whatever is uppermost. At times, like Sedna, we may rise through storms. The depths of the ocean are a symbol for how this takes place. For beneath the ocean floor, lies fire.

Reaching the core

Many of us lack the fullness of our life-power nowadays. The epidemic of stress many are experiencing displays the ongoing distortion of our life-force. Energy is caught up in so many ways: worry, anxiety, fear, and frustration, trying to manage and control the many factors of our existence. Becoming driven, irritated, experiencing ill-health or its companion depression, all indicate that at some level we're cutting off the ever-present gift of new energy available to us in every breath. We're not alone in this. It's a collective epidemic that cannot be simply fixed. It requires a reorientation, an awakened awareness of how we must consciously access and transmute our energetic habits. Thankfully many of us are taking this route. Slowing down is an essential aspect of this awakening. When we learn to pause, to venture into any energetic chaos, subtle closure, or deeper wall of numbness in the psyche, the wonderful potential is we discover life itself, always available. For the fire of life lies at the core of all experience, just as fire, the molten magma of this planet, lies at the centre of our Earth.

Magma is usually made up of four parts: a hot liquid base, called the melt; minerals crystallized by the melt; solid rocks incorporated into the melt from the edges of the magma zone; and dissolved gases. It's much like our human psyche, containing different energetic formations of mental-emotional energy: the molten fire of anger and rage, emotional experiences held in suspension, more solid resistance, and ever-changing mental landscapes. These energies in the psyche are constantly calling us. Their forms may change as we move through different experiences but the needs behind them, do not. We may build scar tissue over some of our trauma, nonetheless the core wounding remains.

This core wounding clearly appears in one of the Inuit myths, where Sedna is portrayed as a giant with an enormous hunger whose demands cannot be fulfilled despite its raging. This giant is symbolic of the psyche's craving to be filled, the instinctual demand in us to be safe, comfortable, and secure. Even when we have enough for survival, repressed instinctual and feeling aspects of our psyche can still be ravenous. They constantly call us to address the needs that have not been met. These needs can be quietly present, afraid to express, or they can be eruptive. Anger is one of their common forms. It's a healthy emotion, a pointer to an unmet need or desire in us. Yet anger is often misconstrued as a force to be condemned.

The fire of anger holds clues to deep layers of the psyche, for what triggers its outpouring is often not its true cause. Anger shows us when a boundary has been crossed, when our value has been ignored or rejected, a need hasn't been met, or abuse occurs. All human beings need to experience respect, healthy caring connection, and love. One could say that's a basic human right. Anger acts as an internal alarm when we feel afraid, or out of control. It's a signpost to the need and potential for change.

If anger is simply a messenger, why does it receive so much censure in our supposedly civilised culture?

Like volcanic eruptions that arise without warning, anger tends to express without our permission, often surprising us with its ferocity. There is much said now about the therapeutic potential of expressing our anger, yet it's largely unacceptable in the collective culture of Northern and Western Europe. Many of us would tend to avoid an angry encounter. Perhaps it has been judged and condemned simply because we allow it to take us over when it does. We're out of control with it because we've lost touch with its roots as a healthy expression of self-disconnection or misalignment. Always it's a pointer to where there is inner conflict.

Anger's reputation as destructive is part of our resistance to it. Yet it takes over simply because it's been held down. In healthy self-awareness and expression, we recognise anger's function. Its power to destroy is symbolic of the inner need of change that we haven't been aware of. Or that we're aware of but haven't acted on. Like Sedna's storms, anger may reflect feelings of powerlessness. It's a protective mechanism that shows where we are out of line with our self, but we may not know what to do. We are compromised in some way. Anger can be a cry for help. Ill-expressed perhaps, but entreating response.

Vulnerability often sits at the roots of anger. It may express as a cry for help, a shouting match, or a protest that reveals what's truly going on in the deep of the psyche. It is a mechanism to express what we feel we cannot say in other ways. Just like a storm, it has the power to make us stop and look.

Sedna's tale, her ocean existence, mirrors our human rhythms, the constant ebb and flow between calm and storms, the dark depths of life and our power of renewal. Sedna is not powerless, although she appears so. There is valuable learning in her extremes. From her woundedness she births children; the creatures of the sea that provide food, warmth, and clothing for her people. She shows us that our temporary swings between apathy and assertion, self-abandonment and empowered authenticity, powerlessness, and reaction, have meaning and purpose. States such as numbness or apathy are our psyche's way of self-protection until we have developed the maturity to enter them consciously. They are forms of nature's compassion that allows us to develop the resources we need, in time, through experience. Her storms are the ways we release the detritus of life. They thrust things to the surface. Whether we have been failed by those who are there to care for us, or whether we have seemingly failed ourselves, Sedna reveals to us that the potential of new life is always present, even in the lingering dark shadows of the deep.

Reactions as a natural guide

The need to control our reactions is probably familiar to us all. Certainly, if we're awake, they draw our attention in some way. Sometimes we approach them with curiosity, at other times, to suppress or judge them. It depends on the circumstances, the reactions of others, how comfortable we are in our self-expression and emotional connection. But what if we got to know our reactions as a guide? What if we view them as being a revelation, showing us something brewing in the subconscious that's ripe for change? What if reactions are a way-shower?

Sedna's creation myth gives us clues to what we may discover about instinct, reaction, and action. For this myth is different. In most of her myths, Sedna is portrayed in a powerless or passive role, even as the giant. Yet, in her creation myth, after giving birth, she arrives at a point of choice. This is her place of power. She looks at her babies; three are clearly Inuit babies, the other three have large ears and snout-like noses. Her instinctual knowing is that these babies are not for her to care for; they are alien children. She pushes them off the island in a sewn sealskin. She lets them go. It's a decisive act.

Having faced her trials, this myth reveals a point where Sedna discerns what belongs to her and what doesn't. Her instinct knows what is right for her, and more appropriately, what isn't. Through her challenging experience of being judged and abandoned, she is developing the capacity for self-knowing, self-trust and action. This is natural magic at work in her.

What a human being considers difficult, is often evolution's way of growing us. What we think we need and what we really need are sometimes different, simply for the purpose of growth. In this myth Sedna has now developed the capacity to say, 'That's for me; that's not for me'. She doesn't need to think about it. It's obvious. She doesn't question it. She simply acts. This is how instinct works. It simply happens. Suddenly we do something differently; we respond in a new way. The natural processes of growth within us have been gestating a new way of being in the deep, in the transcendent ocean of consciousness from which all new life emerges. When we make a new choice, we see gestation expressing. We are made new.

Reaction operates at a primal level. It's not a thought-through response or action; it simply happens. Destructive as emotional storms may be, sometimes they arise to show us something we didn't realise, or that we have lost our way. They might reveal that we have abandoned, betrayed, or compromised our self. If we don't judge our reactions, they reveal an aspect of life that is off balance. They might show us an underlying need or desire. If we're in tune to our reactions, we can consciously look and listen deeper to our unmet needs. The underlying meaning may be subtle, yet if we learn to accept our reactions, fierce or subtle, there is always something to discover.

Mostly, reactions are obvious, but feedback from our self can also be subtle. We can be reacting without being fully aware of it. A delicate yet telling contraction, where we pull in energetically, is a reaction. Our body language can reveal this, as can the sensational reality of the energy body. Like the ebb and flow of the gentle ocean waves moving the sand on the shore, the ways we withdraw give us clues to potentially larger issues. Contraction is an instinctual response to subtly resist discomfort or threat. It bears investigation, not in mental analysis but simply in noticing with curiosity. Curiosity about a contraction can lead us deep. We can notice how the ground beneath our feet is becoming unstable. Whilst emotional storms are nature's great cleansers and destroyers that clear the decks, more subtle contractions are gentle waves leading us into self-awareness. Both are guides.

The power of Sedna's bountiful gift to us lies in the rhythms of her calm gentle waves and her storms, in knowing what is needed when, in attuning to our inner rhythms. Storms are wild. They may be a cry for help. When Sedna storms, she is calling the shaman to pay attention, to listen, to ease her rage. For us, Sedna's gift is to reveal reactions are not wrong, they are guides into the deep. We are wise to listen. To enjoy both our storms and our calmer waters as the presence of Sedna, Mother of the Sea, within us and our woman instinct in her ocean of transcendent consciousness.

Befriending our instinctual nature

The Sedna wounds of betrayal and abandonment, whether in our self or another, need approaching with tenderness and care. These primal energies in us are often incredibly raw and reactive. If we dive in with good intention but without sensitivity, these vulnerable places can disappear in further contraction, like sea creatures diving deep. It is wise to take cues from the Inuit shaman in our approach to these delicate areas of our psyche.

A shaman or shamanka is one who is connected consciously to the sacred in nature and the unseen energetic frequencies of all life. They act as a bridge between the divine, our humanness, and instinct, and act as a way-shower for our innate connection to the Earth. A shaman or shamanka is a bridge between different realms: life and death, the Heavens, Earth, and Underworld. They understand animal instinct, its primal urges, and its needs, and they see its gifts as a guide. A shaman or shamanka doesn't work from logic, or even from traditional healing or therapeutic practices. They may take the opposite tack to what we think is needed. They embody the energies required to meet the wounding precisely where it is needed and can be most effective, generally by entering worlds other than the physical. With Sedna, the Inuit shamans know the need to befriend the instinctual nature, as a natural precursor to healing.

The actions of the Inuit shamans, with respect to Sedna's energy themes, guide us towards healthy connections within our self. When Sedna's storms rage, they befriend and soothe her. The shamans comb her tangled hair, disentangling her wild ocean creatures and the knots caused by wave action. As the shaman grooms her (much as animals groom each other) Sedna feels a loving, caring connection. This helps her primal energies to settle and calm.

Many indigenous cultures believe hair holds psychic energy. It acts as an antenna picking up subtle energies from our environment. It's a conductor of our own thoughts and impressions as well as those external to us. Our hair protects the Crown Chakra and as such is an interface between subtle energies and human intelligence. Some tribal cultures feel there is a connection between having long hair and intuition. Combing the hair suggests sorting out the strands of what we've picked up intuitively or psychically from the oceanic realms of our human experience.

Those of us who are sensitive often become overwhelmed by sensory input, along with more subtle psychic energies. We pick up what's in the environments we move through and therefore need to discharge energy consciously through spiritual and health practices. Hair combing suggests taking care of our self. It can hurt at first as we tease out the knots. Yet once those tangles are eased out, hair combing can be a soothing comforting activity. Much like stroking a cat or a dog, it is pleasurable and relaxes the autonomic nervous system. Hair-combing works both physically and psychically to calm and connect us. As we relax, there's an opportunity to listen, tune in to what's lying under the surface, if we choose to.

Any self-care activity such as massage, can help us to relax and connect with the deeper instinctual layers of our body-being. Nurture is essential to our well-being, for our primal needs require feeding. Touch, listening, loving self-talk and encouragement, acknowledging our need for care helps calm incipient storms brewing in the instinctual layers of the psyche. In creating the space to listen and tune in, to actively love ourselves, we recognise where we're out of balance, pushing too hard, not supporting our self. Our unsettledness, even deeper layers of our psyche, begin to feel acknowledged through our loving actions. They uncoil their tension; they open and transmute.

In taking care of our physical self, we honour our animal nature's need for care. Like mammals in groups grooming each other, nurturing self-care brings the collective aspects of our individual nature back into harmony. We become more attuned to our primal nature, our nature-all self, our gut feeling, the knowing that something is not quite right or feels off. We may not know what we need to do, but in the nurturing pause where we tend to our needs, an awakening of possibilities occurs on subtle levels. At some point that awakening rises in consciousness; we simply know what is needed. Deeper layers of our primal psyche, much like animals, do not use words to communicate. Communication takes place in other more subtle, or sometimes more obvious, ways. We might move instinctively to address a wrong, our body or health may display an imbalance, helping us bring our life to greater balance. It is in our self-caring that new inner connections open between the deep and the surface, the stillness and the storm, the gentle waves, and the wilder ones. It is how instinct, our animal self, and consciousness may intentionally meet.

When Sedna makes storms, a further approach by the shamans, is to sing and make offerings to her. Ritual is an ancient way of reconnection both to our roots and our divinity, honouring our primal connection to ocean and earth, appreciating our body's origins and oneness with all life. Making an offering to oneself of that which brings pleasure, or self-respect, or self-appreciation, is deeply healing. To offer a gift to oneself is to acknowledge, honour and love our self. To make an offering to the earth or ocean is to acknowledge our unity and origins, our unique place within the great scheme of life. Ritual can provide a framework for deeper connection to oneself as consciousness, as Source. To create space for daily meditation, physical practices such as yoga, chanting, connection to nature, not only soothes the soul, but establishes a grounding in our true nature.

Much is being discovered now about the frequency of sound and healing. The human voice is a profound instrument of expression for love and healing. Research demonstrates that singing lowers cortisol and releases both endorphins and oxytocin, lowering stress, boosting the immune system, promoting health and wellbeing. It stimulates the vagus nerve and helps with pain management. Singing as part of a group, also lifts confidence, improving social bonding and cohesion, generating a sense of community. Singing is an honouring of this gift of expression. It can touch the soul. It may open the heart, bringing delight and joy. It soothes and comforts too. The mother's singing of a lullaby to her child creates a psychic container of love that lulls the child into sleep, knowing it is held, loved, cherished, comforted, and protected.

Another tale from the Inuit people, Skeleton Woman, has threads of connection to Sedna that celebrate the gift of song as life-giving. This tale always makes me weep. It is so beautiful.

In Skeleton Woman we encounter a girl who is thrown off a cliff by her father for doing something of which he disapproves. What that was no-one remembers. As the girl sinks into the depths of the ocean, her flesh is eaten away by fish until all that remains are her bones.

One day a fisherman's hook happens to snag in Skeleton Woman's ribs. As he hauls on his line and sees her terrible state, he is terrified; yet try as he might, he cannot escape her. Tangled in his line, Skeleton Woman's bones follow his boat to shore, then jangle up the beach behind him as he flees. Eventually they both arrive in his igloo; the fisherman in shock; Skeleton Woman's bones simply all in a heap.

As he relaxes, the fisherman starts to look at Skeleton Woman in the soft light of his icy home. His fear dissipates; his heart begins to open at her plight. Softly he begins to sort out her bones, one from another, putting them in the right order that a woman's body should be. As he untangles her skeleton, he sings softly.

As the fisherman sings, eventually Skeleton Woman's bones are all in the right place. His actions to untangle her and soothe them both, have brought peace to his heart and a tear to his eye. His work complete, he falls asleep. Meanwhile, through his love, Skeleton Woman is changing; she is coming to life. As her bones begin to tingle, she drinks of the fisherman's one tear of compassion and drums on his heart for fullness of flesh. As she drums, her bones fill out with flesh. Her body warms: her heart begins to beat. She becomes whole. The tale ends with them both in a warm huddle; the natural huddle for a man and woman to be in.

In this tale, as with the shaman's song to Sedna, singing brings comfort to the inner tangling and jangling of Skeleton Woman's disjointed energy. It caresses what's uncomfortable, disjointed, irritated. It allows the chaotic energy in her to come to rest, just as they are, held in love, held in the ocean of consciousness they are part of.

With both Sedna and Skeleton Woman, the shaman or fisherman (who we might recognise is also a shaman in his actions) delivers to the psyche and body that which she cannot bring to herself. Being handless, Sedna cannot soothe herself; she cannot sort out her own hair or remove her attached and entangled children. The sea creatures represent psychic or emotional energies floating in the ocean of consciousness. Skeleton woman cannot rise from the deep, or untangle her bones, without help. Both the shaman and fisherman are connectors and healers. They represent a transcendent state of consciousness available to us from within, or through another, that holds, supports, calms, soothes, and ultimately allays reaction arising from the wounds of betrayal. The ocean of consciousness contains all possibilities, when we are in the deep wound of trauma, or immersed in a transcendent state, we often need help to discern exactly what we need. This is the shamanic function, to discover the ways and means to integrate that which is disembodied.

Just like gentle ocean waves connect us primally to our time in the womb, our deepest instinctual needs can be met very simply. When we are soothed, it's not only relaxing and connective for our body-mind, but we also become reconnected to the knowing that we are always held in the ocean of consciousness. We can recognise we are both human, with all its fragility and challenges, and transcendent. As Sedna simply is herself, the one with extremes, held in the ocean, so can we be. For all aspects of nature are held and play their vital role within the ocean of consciousness. We are always, in all ways, held by the Mother of the Sea.

Life is constant paradox. To begin to heal the deepest wounds, the fiercest rage, we need the gentlest touch. We need to connect on a primal level, letting go the complex agenda to fix, heal or resolve what we judge to be wrong with us, or what pains us, into the simple touch of loving care. The chaos of storms; both our own and those of the natural world, are a regular aspect of life. Sedna calls us to acknowledge our self as one with nature, not set apart from its rhythms but flowing with them. For me, this is the missing link in both our personal and collective relationship to body and Earth, to our psychic health and to our environment.

Unity consciousness

In Sedna's creation myths, she creates Inuit children and part human-animal children. She also births the sea creatures that dwell in the ocean. Like many of the Dark Feminine archetypes, in her creation, as Mother of the Sea, she calls us back to Earth, to acknowledge the animal aspects of our being. Not as negative energies that need healing or resolving, but as valuable aspects of our whole nature. Aspects that in their rightful place within consciousness act as guides to our human lives. Her children, the ocean animals, if we're awake, are not different creatures with which we have no connection, they are aspects of our self as oneness. For the energetic frequencies of human, human-animal, and the ocean creatures, many of whom are ocean guardians, are within our consciousness. They have much to teach us.

Sedna storms when we forget this unity, when we forget her, when we forget our role as one with, yet also caretakers of, her realm. Her ocean gives up bounty as it also gives us storms. When we forget to honour her bounty, she reminds us. When we forget to honour our own bounty, she reminds us. Whatever our experience, we are one with the transcendent ocean of consciousness. Sedna is here to remind us, anything else is merely a temporary deviation in human experience.

Chapter 6

Original Resistance –Black Moon

Lilith

She's the dark one,
terrible one,
defiant, name calling,
bludgeoning
thwarting of love
one.
I know her well,
self-punishing,
loathing,
door closing
one.
Her dark light
dread-full, raw,
distorted,
feeding on
death of life.
Her knife
opens doors of night,
delicatessen's delight
as inwards unravel
on the blood soaked
map of life.
She takes no prisoners,
all is food
for her bite.
No point to fight
or call for light.

Yet wait,
do you know
her calls to
open the heart,
the belly,
always the mind
to every facet
of beautiful,

terrible life
compels
and commands
to love with no limit
or cause.
To love every form
with her utter
contempt
for the norm.
To shatter your heart
with the pain
of it all.

For she is Life,
The whole of life.
Original Woman.
Mother of
every facet
of wonderfully
glorious,
unbearable
Life.
She is wholeness
in you
of you
through you.
Mystery in form.
Only in
her dark-light
may you know
your brilliance,
your genius,
your infinite
Bright
Cassandra Eve

Archetype: Original Woman

Symbols: Tree of Life, the serpent in the Garden of Eden, bird goddess, wings, bat, owl, claw feet, wild cat, amulets

Message: Be yourself, the whole of yourself, unapologetically, unashamedly! Demand to be known as equal but different, free to choose, determine and express what is true.

Black Moon Lilith themes: the demand for equality and sexual freedom; defiance of the status quo; good girl/bad girl, rejection, exile, alone; shame and its partner rage; impersonal lunar consciousness; mysterious, otherworldly energies; sovereignty; genius & brilliance

What Black Moon Lilith calls for: Standing for truth, no compromise

Black Moon Lilith is perhaps the most intriguing of all the Dark Feminine archetypes. She entices us towards her mystery; a mystery that expresses through a sometimes terrible, sometimes magical, dance of darkness and light. As with all the dark goddesses her calling lies in unacknowledged, unclaimed aspects of self. She holds both the dilemma and gift of our inner darkness, those aspects of our self that are essential to full embodiment. As the second focal point of the moon's elliptical orbit around our planet Earth (which is the first) Lilith's aetheric presence is intimately connected to our embodiment process. We cannot ignore her, for she lies close to Earth. Try as we might to suppress or reject her edgy presence, her void constantly pulls us into the ambiguity of being alive on Earth, with its dark-light polarities.

Lilith appears in layers of myth from ancient history. In the Sumerian culture she was the handmaiden of Inanna, Queen of Heaven and Earth, a priestess figure who called the men into the temple for the sacred rite of sexuality. In Jewish myth, she was the first wife of Adam, created equal to him yet refusing to lay under him, claiming the equality in which she was created. As such, she is Original Woman, whole unto herself. Labelled as a troublemaker in a growing patriarchal world, Lilith was denounced as dangerous, and demonized through history as a succubus and child-killer. She represents that aspect of the Sacred Feminine in woman that stands her ground, who acts in defiance of the status quo, especially when it's founded on patriarchal rules. In the psyche she represents the duality of defiance yet shame, often found in us as women. Rejected and exiled for demanding the equality that is rightfully ours, for simply being female, and especially for our erotic sexual nature. Belittled for the power of our emotions when faced with male energy that seeks to humiliate, to control.

Who amongst has not heard that demeaning statement 'You're too much'? It seems that women have been claiming equality and being shamed for it for eons. No wonder Lilith in us is dark and furious. Behind her naturally volatile energies, Lilith is a magical, gifted, at times utterly brilliant, Dark Feminine archetype in us. Yet we must meet her darkness willingly and with impersonal understanding, to release her brightest light. She symbolizes a central character in our process of full embodiment that is subtle yet felt viscerally. The insistent desire of the soul to fully express itself in human life beyond what are felt to be acceptable boundaries. In our current times of potent change, Lilith's mystery is key to our deepest creative life power. Her volatile energies illuminate innovative pathways to conscious embodiment.

Her-story

Lilith has many origins, fragments of her-story found in different cultures. Undoubtedly aspects of her nature have been lost in the mists of time, yet she has been part of cultural storytelling, art, and iconography for more than five thousand years. She is regarded either as a protective deity, or evil spirit, depending on where you look. The fact that she has remained alive in our collective culture for so long, indicates her prominent yet mysterious appeal.

Lilith's name is derived from several sources: the Akkadian Lilitu meaning 'of the night', also the name of a demon in ancient Assyrian myths; Laylah or Leila in Hebrew meaning 'night' and cuneiform inscriptions from Sumer, circa 3000 BCE, where the names Lilit and Lilitu refer to disease-bearing wind spirits.

Lilith first appears in Sumeria, in the Hymns of Inanna and the Epic of Gilgamesh (explored in Chapter 1) depicted on cuneiform tablets that were found in the desert city of Uruk, located 150 miles from modern Baghdad in Iraq. Clay tablets and cylinder seals from this site, dating from 3400BCE, are now known to be the first forms of writing. On these clay tablets, Lilith is mentioned as the handmaiden of Inanna. She is a beautiful maiden who gathers the men from the fields and the streets into the temple at Erech for the sacred sexual rites. In this role, she takes on the functions of priestess to Inanna.

Lilith appears later also, in the Epic of Gilgamesh, on comparatively more recent clay tablets dating from the 2nd millennium BCE. The Tree of Life, in its representation as The Huluppu tree, weaves its way through this Sumerian myth, as it does through many ancient cultures. It is a universal symbol found in many spiritual and mythological traditions around the world. Sometimes known as the Cosmic Tree, the World Tree, or the Holy Tree. The Tree of Knowledge connects heaven and the underworld, uniting all forms of creation. It appears in Norse religion as Yggdrasil, the World Tree. In both Chinese and Islamic cultures, the Tree of Life, or the fruit of the Tree of Life, is a symbol of eternal life. In Chinese mythology, the tree often depicts a phoenix and a dragon representing immortality.

Archaeological discoveries in Sichuan, China dating from around 1200BCE have revealed bronze trees containing these figures, along with fruit hanging in their lower branches. A Taoist story in Chinese mythology describes an ancient tree that produces a peach every 3,000 years. Whoever eats the peach is granted the gift of eternal life and happiness. It is like the Greek mythological story of Hera's golden apples of immortality that grow in the Garden of Hesperides.

Different aspects of the Tree of Life demonstrate the order and process of creation. In the Egyptian culture, the first couple (known as Earth and Sky) were said to have emerged from the Acacia tree of Lusaaset. The Egyptians considered this to be the Tree of Life, referring to it as 'the tree in which life and death are enclosed'. Similarly in Islamic belief, there is a tree known as the Tree of Immortality. It appears in the Quran as the tree in Eden from which Adam and Eve ate the forbidden fruit, just as in the Christian bible. In Buddhism, the Tree of Life is known as the Bodhi Tree and is believed to be the Tree of Enlightenment. In Judaism, the Tree of Life stands in the centre of a fruitful garden planted by Yahweh. It is the central symbol of the Kabbalah, a system for studying the different emanations and frequencies of life on the Tree of Life.

The tree is a common powerful symbol in Celtic belief systems also. It is depicted in multiple forms with the roots representing the 'other world', the trunk being the mortal world and the branches representing the heavens. The mortal world connects all worlds. Depictions of World Trees are also found in the cultures of the Maya, Aztec, Izapan, Mixtec, Olmec, the Bahai faith and Hindu cosmology.

The prevalence of the Tree of Life throughout world cultures demonstrates its potent representation of the whole of life in its differing stages of consciousness and evolution. It is also a mirror for the tree-like network of energetic connections within our human body. The tree therefore symbolises our individual and collective capacity of evolution, our connection to creation through the Earth, our interconnectivity with all life, and the in-dwelling spirit of divinity. We see interconnectivity represented in so many ways throughout nature. For instance, trees promote health and social well-being by removing air pollution, reducing stress, encouraging physical activities, and promoting social ties and community. It is now known that woodland trees act as mothers of life within the forests of our planet networking through their arms and roots. This fact of nature demonstrates how trees are not only symbolic of life, but they also actually provide us with the basic element of life that we need to even exist, namely oxygen.

We return to a more specific exploration of the Tree of Life, and Lilith's role with it as Original Woman, through the mythology of Sumer. In the story 'The Huluppu Tree' Inanna (see Chapter 1) discovers a tree on the riverbank by her palace. She cares for the tree, and it grows, yet all the time she is wondering about how she will get her bed and her throne — her symbols of power.

As Inanna tends the tree, a serpent coils in the tree roots, a bird makes its nest in its crown and Lilith builds her home in the trunk. The maiden Lilith, is depicted in a stone carving from that time as a female form with wings and clawed feet, connecting Heaven and Earth, perhaps alluding to her priestess-type role in the culture. The Anzu bird in the tree's crown is a mythical lion-headed eagle with supernatural powers also known as the divine storm-bird. The bird also has ancient symbology, representing unitary wholeness. It appears in various mythologies — as Garuda in Vedic texts from the Hindu culture, born from the Cosmic Egg at the beginning of time, Ba or Bennu in Egyptian mythology, and in the phoenix, sacred to the Chinese, Persian, Iranian, Lebanese, and Russian peoples. For the Sumerians, the Anzu bird represented the divine-human link as wholeness. All these bird symbols act as guardians of the soul's journey through incarnation and to the recognition of immortality. The serpent entwined in the tree's roots represents connection to earth energies and power of regeneration, also known as kundalini. These three beings making their home in the tree indicates its symbology as the Tree of Life.

It is said that Inanna wept, when these beings made their home in the tree, for it was no longer hers.

335

Eventually Inanna, longing for her symbols of power, makes an alliance with the warrior Gilgamesh that he will create her marriage bed and throne from the tree. This epic tale ends with the tree demolished, the serpent killed, whilst the Anzu bird and Lilith flew into the wilderness. Inanna had what she longed for, but in the process of getting it, the tree was destroyed.

As with the Garden of Eden myth, this Sumerian tale relates the separation of consciousness from the Tree of Life. Lilith is fully in the Tree, as are the Anzu bird and serpent. In some cultures, Lilith is also known as Mistress of the Beasts. As the tree is felled by Gilgamesh, unified consciousness splits. Lilith does not know she is unified, much as Eve in the Garden. And so, the journey to full consciousness begins, precipitated by the joint actions of Inanna and Gilgamesh. Meanwhile, Lilith flies into the wilderness. It's a theme we see repeated in a myth from the Jewish and Christian cultures.

In the Jewish culture, there are two different creation stories, both pointing towards Lilith and her expression. In one myth, God creates the Sun and Moon, shining equally as two great lights. When a dispute arises between them, God sent the Moon down to act as shadow to the Sun, its light diminished. Lilith arose from this shadow. In this same culture, in texts believed to originate from around 70CE and later (the time of the patriarchal rise), based on oral tradition, Lilith appears as the first wife of Adam. These texts state that Adam required Lilith to lie below him. She refused. She was called to being his equal partner, or not at all. When Adam would not listen to her demand for equality, Lilith uttered the ineffable Name of God, Yahweh (believed to be too holy to be spoken) and flew off into the desert.

On his desertion by Lilith, Adam immediately complains to God. One wonders why he did not simply go after Lilith. Human history may have been very different if he had, even given this is just an allegorical tale. On hearing Adam's complaint, God sends three angels to persuade Lilith to return to her mate. The angels discover Lilith by the Red Sea consorting with demons and bearing scores of demon children. She refuses to return. For her defiance of God, it was declared that every day one hundred of her children would die. Thus began Lilith's chosen exile rather than subjugation to Adam's will. Demetra George in her 'Mysteries of the Dark Moon' states that following her period of defiance, then mourning, Lilith made love with the water elementals, birthing many beings, thus giving rise to the collective unconscious. The collective unconscious contains the deepest aspects of our human shadow, and yet also, profound wisdom.

Similarities between the earlier Descent of Inanna and Lilith's role in the Epic of Gilgamesh, suggest that later myths reflect growing patriarchal controls. Inanna's descent and ascent (see Chapter 1) could be seen as the foundation of the Christ story, with its crucifixion, three days in the tomb and ascension. Lilith, with her ancient priestess role in the sexual rites as a natural aspect of the expression of man and woman on the Tree of Life, was now demeaned. She was labelled an unruly woman who would not conform, or as the serpent who tempts Eve. When it comes to the Christian creation myth, this labelling of Lilith as a troublemaker is taken even further, as God creates Eve from one of Adam's ribs.

In this Christian myth, Eve is created as Adam's helpmate, apparently submissive and dutiful, until she took a bite from the apple. Lilith appears as the serpent (sometimes winged, or as a woman with a serpent body) in the tree, tempting Eve, or giving her the apple. It's an image of Lilith reminiscent of the Huluppu tree from the Sumerian culture. In the Eden myth it is said she hisses 'Take a bite' to Eve. She's encouraging the innocent Eve to taste the fruit of the Tree of Life. This tree is also the Tree of Knowledge. Lilith's calling to Eve is to satisfy her curiosity, to know who she is and why she is here on Earth in a woman's body. The rest is history — literally his-story. For patriarchy, through religion, has portrayed that one simple act as the Fall, orchestrated by a woman.

As patriarchy further established itself, the story of Lilith was used as a warning to women. The message was: dare to defy authority, leave your husband, or ignore the rules of patriarchal religion, and you will be exiled. Yet Eve did not escape the condemnation of the patriarchy either, blamed for leading Adam and humanity astray by eating the fruit of the Tree. Despite their apparently bad behaviour, Lilith's connection to the Tree of Life as Original Woman is clear.

Lilith continues to appear throughout history. Her banishment also representing the distortion of the sacred sexual practices of the Goddess cultures that she represented. She was projected as a she-demon who married the king of demons and seduced men in their sleep, encouraging night emissions. Or she was alleged to endanger women in childbirth and kill children, especially newborns. Babylonian cylinder seals, charms and tablets from this time onward bear inscriptions and incantations of protection against her. Even now, amulets warding off her supposedly evil inclinations can still be found in Near-Eastern and Jewish cultures.

Dark Feminine archetypes with similar energy to Lilith are viewed with different eyes in some cultures and religions. Skull-bearing Kali in the Hindu pantheon, and Hariti, a demented and vengeful child-killer until her conversion to Buddhism, are worshiped as both death-wielding and life-giving. They are honoured as true representations of the Great Mother's innately sacred guardianship of life and death. In Tibetan Buddhism the parallel of Lilith is the Dakini, a manifestation of Prajnaparamita, the Great Mother of all Buddhas. Prajnaparamita represents original wholeness from which all life arises.

In the art world of western culture, Lilith is depicted as a female figure with the tail of a serpent in a carving on Notre Dame Cathedral, in Michelangelo's Temptation and Fall in the Sistine Chapel, Hugo Van Goe's Fall of Adam & Eve, in the giant rooftop mural of Lilith and Olaf in Klepp, Norway, in religious manuscripts, woodcuts and illustrations, as well as on amulets and charms. In literature she appears in Goethe's Faust, works by Keats, George Bernard Shaw, and C S Lewis, and in a poem and painting by Pre-Raphaelite artist Dante Gabriel Rossetti. Lilith has continued to infiltrate popular culture through novels and film until our present day. Despite being banished, she has continued to intrigue us through millennia. Lilith removed herself from society - perhaps she knew where it was heading - but somehow, we have not forgotten her. She lingers beneath the surface of consciousness, calling us home.

Black Moon Lilith's place in the Universe – Astronomy & Astrology

The astronomy of Black Moon Lilith is as mysterious as her energy. The Lilith I'm writing about here is one of four Lilith bodies or elements of our solar system. It is an abstract point, like the Ascendant or Midheaven in an astrological chart, the second centre of the Moon's elliptical orbit around the Earth. The Black Moon Lilith point and Earth are the double centre around which the Moon orbits. The Earth, as one centre, is physical, shining like a blue jewel. Black Moon Lilith is the other, invisible yet emitting a tangible oscillating frequency. In this astronomical relationship, Lilith can be seen as an etheric twin to the core energy of the Earth. She's a mysterious non-physical focus that holds space for life on Earth, much as Eve and Lilith hold complementary roles in some of our human creation stories.

The other three Liliths are planetary bodies. They are deserving of mention here, for they add to the allure of her mystery, along with her themes. They are Asteroid Lilith; Algol, also known as the Lilith Star; and the Dark or Black Moon.

The Lilith asteroid is one of a band of asteroids between Mars and Jupiter. They are considered fragments of a one-time planetary body, so can be viewed as facets of a larger whole. Many are named for goddesses and gods and are therefore ripe of archetypal meaning. Asteroid 1181, the most physical of the four Lilith bodies, orbits the Sun in approximately four years.

Algol, the Lilith star, also known as the Eye of Medusa (see Chapter 7), presents the Lilith energy in yet another dimensional frequency. As a fixed star, this Lilith is seemingly immortal, perhaps as a further collective dimension of Lilith. The Algol star is the second brightest star in the constellation of Perseus. Stars give off vast amounts of light, so they represent a centre of consciousness. As with others planetary bodies, they carry our human projections (stories, myths, qualities, beliefs, and fears) both light and dark.

Algol has a bad reputation in both Hebrew and Chinese cultures, considered to be 'most difficult' or 'negative'. It is a binary star, consisting of two stars that eclipse each other, said to represent Medusa's eye blinking. Algol A is three times as big as our Sun and twice as hot. Astrologers who study fixed stars link Algol with kundalini energy and collective rage arising from the repression of women and their Sacred Feminine connection. Algol is also purported to represent themes of death and resurrection.

The fourth Lilith, the Dark Moon, is even more mysterious than the one we're exploring. The Dark Moon is sometimes confused with Black Moon Lilith yet is different, purported to be a second moon that orbits Earth. Various orbiting moon-like objects have been seen by astronomers; one as far back as 1618 and another as recently as 2020. This planetary body has only been seen when it passes the face of the Sun. Why haven't we heard more about this second Moon? Is it physically there, orbiting our planet at a much slower rate than our visible Moon? This is of the nature of Lilith, elusive and mysterious, only known as a frequency in experience.

When it comes to the astrology of Lilith, it is usually the Black Moon Lilith point that is offered in chart interpretation, albeit not by every astrologer. The full cycle of this energy point is 8 years and 10 months. Due to its oscillation, there are two measurements for Lilith's placement:

true and mean. These measurements reflect her nature in us too: true and mean. They reflect what she represents: impersonal lunar consciousness, instinct and mysterious inner knowing, the demand for equality and sexual freedom, along with the experience of rejection or exile, with associated shame or rage.

Where Lilith is strong in a birth chart, she can indicate the darker side of sexuality, fertility, birthing and raising children: namely, abuse or rape, miscarriage or abortion, or the death of a child. Lilith signifies extremes of experience as a woman that we must face to awaken the knowing of our wholeness. She is the demand in us for equality and freedom as Sacred Feminine. Once we claim her energy, Lilith represents our capacity to belong utterly to oneself. She is known as wholeness expressing through both dark and light energies, the riches held in our shadows, a capacity for brilliance and a conduit for numinous creative energies.

My journey with Lilith

Relationship with a beloved male friend in Crete has always been one of profound growth. The challenge of being apart for many months at a time, yet so energetically intimate when we meet, is extreme. The moment I am in his presence, I feel his profound Masculine consciousness viscerally penetrating my energy field, even without any touch of intimacy. It's like I'm switched on through my whole body-energy, opening wide to his presence in every cell and beyond it. This brings ecstasy alive in me very naturally. Deep challenge is inevitable when I allow my humanness to get in the way of this profound unity. Transformation is a given, arising from such a profoundly intimate connection.

I had a late flight arrival, and he was not there to meet me. When I messaged him, he said 'Oh you are early; I will drive like a rocket'. He hadn't even left home, forty minutes away. He was on 'Cretan time'; I was fuming. I felt unvalued.

By the time he arrived, I had closed energetically. Not wanting to rock the boat, especially as we had not seen each other for almost a year, I had zipped up my fury, along with feelings of rejection. I had taken his action very personally. It was a lifelong theme with both family and partners to feel rejected. I knew this but could not move through it. The drive to my apartment was quiet, conversation stilted. When we got there, he pulled my suitcase from the boot and literally ran back to the driver's seat. With a brief 'See you soon', he was gone. I was devastated.

All week we kept missing each other. I would message, he would be working. He would message, I'd be busy. Life was shattering the dreams I'd had of a wonderfully reconnective time. Grief and aloneness began to arise at our lack of connection. I allowed myself to deeply feel it, connecting deeper into its roots. A new layer of loss began to emerge. It was connected to a past life with this Cretan man, bringing up raw painful layers of aloneness, isolation, and censure for being female. Alternating between deep grief, rage and terrible aloneness, Lilith was painfully alive in me.

Eventually we connected. Meeting for breakfast, we sat close whilst I shared. He was loving, listening deeply, and acknowledging my feelings and past-life revelations. His presence held me like a warm soothing balm. We spoke of how being apart encouraged the romantic dream in us, and how inevitably it must shatter. He shared how my closure had been painful to him, how he could feel the rage and disappointment in me and didn't know how to respond to it. I wept gently as I told him of my deep journey inward, our past life together. The pain of loss from that time was devastating. He heard and held it all with such love and presence, his heart response incredibly healing for me. Lilith in me felt utterly heard, accepted, and honoured in her rawness. His poet's soul met the pain in mine. Lilith was held by us both. In that tender holding, she opened her connective magic. The deepening flowed.

Lilith's Message: Be yourself, the whole of yourself, unapologetically, unashamedly! Demand to be known as equal but different, free to choose, determine and express what is true.

She's true & she's mean

The astronomy of Black Moon Lilith places her in a unique position when it comes to the Sun-Earth-Moon system. Her mysterious presence within the astronomy links our physical (Earth) and emotional nature (Moon), along with our life-force (Sun). She is of deep value in connecting us to the mystery of who we are as women and beyond it as impersonal Feminine consciousness.

Everything we rely upon for physical life on Earth comes from the Sun-Earth-Moon alignments. For our humanness, Earth is our ground of being. Our bodies come from the earth literally, from the union of sperm and egg (however that happens), the physicality of mother and father, and the foods that our mother eats whilst pregnant, that nourish both her body and ours, growing inside her. This rocky watery planet hurtling through space sustains us.

The Moon in astrology symbolises nurture and nature, how our mother matrix sets up our psychic, emotional and subconscious programming, particularly regarding our needs, and how we form identity. Women's menstrual cycle links into the Moon's cycle, much as the tides of our oceans. As the Moon waxes and wanes, as the tides of the ocean rise and fall, our inner tides of emotion, our moods, our sense of who we are and what's essential, fluctuate. The Moon energy is a strong element in our personal sense of self, with its roots in our physical and emotional needs. Initially, it is our experience of mother or caregiver and whether our needs are met or not, that informs this matrix within us. Where we are cared for and valued, physically and emotionally, when we are nurtured and fulfilled, we develop a core foundation of self-worth. We know that we are valued, that comfort is available to us, that we are safe and worthy of love simply in being alive. Where those basic needs are not met, we lack stability in knowing we are innately valuable, or lovable. We have a mother wound that needs tender holding and healing. Such a deep wounding to our core stability of self, although deeply painful, is Lilith's playground. She leads us towards impersonal wholeness.

Black Moon Lilith, being invisible, yet intimately connected to the Earth-Moon cycle, suggests a deeper level of natural energy flow within us that is less tangible. It is invisible and impersonal, beyond the Moon's personal energetic imprint within us. We could call this soul mothering, the Dark Feminine gift to us, expressed in the yearning to go beyond our personal self, to embody and intimately know our fullest potential as a soul. Whereas Moon is representative of the ego needs, Lilith goes beyond ego. She's about our soul essence, that which sits behind the ego. It is more subtle in its nuances and its calling for expression. Lilith is the Mystery of who we truly came here to be.

Lilith, as an absence, a void in the Earth-Moon cycle, represents the space of non-ego or what is beyond ego. It is the need and the calling within us to free up the unique brilliance of our soul essence. We could call Lilith an aspect of the Dark Mother (dark mater or matter), as Original Woman, in that she demands we go beyond the comfort of the Moon (personal mother), to face hidden aspects of self, to express the deepest mystery of our essence. Her purported role within myth and in the Garden of Eden suggests her mysterious presence holds secrets. Secrets that are aspects of the Tree of Life hidden within her deep nature which is our deep nature.

If we refer to her astronomy, Lilith's two placements — true and mean — provide clues to the twin aspects of her nature within us. She expresses both as profound darkness and radiant light, mysterious and magical, a soul calling to the true brilliance of our sacred nature. Yet she also expresses through the some of the most challenging shadow aspects of our human nature. These are the gateways to finer consciousness.

'Mean' is a label that not only reflects an average, but human qualities we have labelled callous, shameful, and unforgiving. Meanness is not a quality easily owned. We might prefer the true Lilith, the brilliant Lilith. But to know her, we must claim the mean one. Somewhere within, although we may resist or deny her dark aspects, we know they are key to who we truly are. Without using this key, without deep excavation, we do not have access to the wonder of her paradoxical nature, her dark-light brilliance. It is the extremes, the contradictions in us, that call us into connection with her. When Lilith is ripe in us, she's so visceral we are compelled to meet the dark to know the light. Her radiance is utterly compelling, both within us, and to the men who love her. She is key to our wholeness, and to theirs.

Eve's big sister

There is an English folk story that relates how lilies sprang from Eve's tears as she left the Garden of Eden. Lilies represent purity and are often associated with the Virgin Mary. Yet I cannot help but notice the strange resonance with the name Lilith. Would Eve have wept for her sister Lilith? I like to think so.

What do Eve and her big sister Lilith differently represent? Lilith was created equal to Adam, and she knew it. Wise to his request to 'lay under him', she asserted her equality; she stood strong in her knowing of what was true. Eve, being made from Adam's rib was an aspect of his physicality. How strange this story is when we know a man is birthed from a woman's body. It is also said that Adam named Eve, implying that he had power over her, for anything we name implies ownership. This creation myth seems to allude that Eve was made not only to be Adam's helpmate, but compliant, obedient to him.

Many of us have learned to play the role of Eve in our relationships. It is the collectively programmed path for many women, to be a supporter rather than a challenger. This has been fed by the patriarchal culture we have lived in for several thousand years and our ancestral programming as women. There is no doubt that we have a natural biological capacity for love, caring and nurture of those close to us, yet that is only one aspect of our Sacred Feminine nature. Even Eve came the point where she said, "I'm going to do this my way" and took a bite of the apple. Maybe Lilith had a quiet word in her ear? Maybe that's the natural way of evolution? Maybe she'd simply got bored with the peace of the Garden? Whatever her impulse, it was a catalyst for change. Women have been taking a bad rap for her supposed action ever since. For judgment of Eve's action has informed the culture of the Christian world for more than two thousand years.

Eve, when she's not being blamed for the Fall, is often portrayed as simple in her innocence. She is childlike, without experience. Yet the desire to explore, discover and know arises in her. Lilith as temptress or serpent, is portrayed as enticing Eve. Yet there is a different perspective: Lilith, who is also simple – simple in her authenticity – could be seen as trying to awaken Eve. She calls on her to act on her desire to experience and know, to activate her potential rather than simply be in the Garden. Lilith knows the journey to wisdom is through experience, not in innocence. An apple contains the seeds of life, but we must bite it to release them. We must ingest, digest, and process these seeds of life. Lilith was already aligned with her desire nature, as an equal partner in creation with Adam, so would not give way to his will. Eve had yet to discover desire and the power of her individual will. Was her big sister pointing the way? It would seem so.

Despite their different natures, Lilith and Eve share a similar fate. Both have been ostracised: one for rebelling, for demanding equality and freedom; the other for wanting to know, for apparently creating the Fall. Both disobeyed God in their own way. Without their actions, humanity would still be living in innocence, and ignorance.

Both Lilith and Eve were made scapegoats for man's desire for control. Rather than owning that desire for dominance of women and nature, patriarchal power-grabbing disguised itself through judging, humiliating and shaming women. Through his-story, through the distortion of the creation stories and through an assumption of power by men in the early church, they were labelled sinful. It was the teachings of Paul in the first century CE, that brought in concepts such as 'the Temptation', 'the Fall' and 'Original Sin' that contributed to, or actively generated, an anti-woman and anti-erotic agenda. Perhaps he was a misogynist? Yet recently discovered ancient documents, such as the Gospel of Mary Magdalene, point to women playing a strong role within early Christianity. What happened? The writings of Paul were compounded by the Council of Nicea in 325 C.E., when Emperor Constantine and church authorities are reputed to have edited or banned books that didn't support the agenda of patriarchal control. The truth of man and woman created equal but different, with differing roles in creation, was actively eradicated. The patriarchal agenda was strengthened through deception.

Lilith and Eve are two aspects of the one Feminine, expressing in different ways. We face their contradictory yet complementary natures within ourselves now. In our quest for self-authenticity, some of us will naturally tend towards Lilith's calling for equality, independence, defiance of the status quo and sexual freedom. Lilith is the dark aspect; the death-dealing sovereign power in woman that delivers an emphatic 'No way'. For other women, Eve's role as helpmate is a cherished desire. She is a creative aspect of woman, a nourisher. She values relationship, cooperation, service, and the field of growing relationship. Both roles are valid and valuable to us as women; they can be ultimately creative. Yet their presence within us is conflicted. Neither is good or bad, simply different, sometimes contradictory, and certainly relevant at different times in our lives as women. The importance is not in the difference but that we can act freely and move as our authentic nature guides in the moment.

As women we are constantly faced with the good/bad girl dilemma represented by the false archetypes of Eve and Lilith. To have to choose between the two is an artifice itself, a social construct based on erroneous beliefs about woman's nature. The dilemma is deeply associated with our notions about darkness being evil, rather than the polarity to light. Notions that have simply grown through the active promotion of false beliefs about who we are, arising from fear of our sexuality, along with a wilful discounting of the mystery and power of creation contained in a woman's body.

Woman's nature, as one with the Moon, is always fluctuating. It moves from lightness to dark constantly, our menstrual cycle flows with the potential of fertility and conception, pre-menstrual fierceness and releasing, and post-menopausal stillness and wisdom. The journey of archetypal Maiden innocence through Mother and Queen to Crone is similar. We carry different qualities of light/dark and its cycle at different times. To separate what appears to be good or bad, between Lilith and Eve is to suffer; we become split from our self. As the two 'original women' our quest is not to have to choose between them but to unify them within. To have the choice of expressing them naturally in our life's journey through our evolution in growing wholeness.

Growing wholeness naturally encompasses the extremes of a cycle, just like nature's flow from the bitter cold of winter to summer's abundance. Given that Lilith and Eve tend towards extremes of our female nature, what can we see about their potential union expressing as wholeness?

Here another archetypal figure within the Christian his-story is significant. She is Sophia.

Sophia is one of the central figures of Gnosticism, a Christian philosophical movement from around 100CE with uncertain origins. Gnosticism emphasises individual knowledge and wisdom, rather than dogma, as the path to oneness with the divine. Sophia is revered as Divine Female, Mother of the Universe, the equivalent to Jesus the Christ, as the Son of God. She is the embodiment of wisdom, also mentioned in the Bible as such. When we reunite the good with the bad, the dark with the light, as the natural journey of individuation, we discover wisdom. Wisdom arises through the experience of all aspects of life on Earth. And strangely, when wisdom becomes fully grounded in us, we also return to innocence, inner-sense. For me this represents the alignment of Lilith and Eve within us, fully connected to original innocence, resting in the divine, with the wisdom of experience in a human body.

Given the differing creation stories within humanity, ongoing scientific exploration into the origins of the Universe, different philosophical and religious beliefs, we must make up our own minds about the origins of life on Earth, or let it rest in mystery. There is one unquestionable truth however: from the union of sperm and egg, a child is grown and birthed from a woman's body. Despite patriarchal attempts to denounce and control women, this is fact. The truth of it has been vibrating deep in women's psyche and through our sister-to-sister connections, since time began. It is a growing recognition within our collective culture as we evolve that a woman's body is the gateway of creation.

Occasionally we may come across references (albeit hidden) to this natural power, in art, literature, in humanity's tribal and wisdom traditions. Michelangelo's painting 'Creation of Adam' on the ceiling of the Sistine Chapel is just one example. It seems to be depicting a deeper truth than the commonly held creation myth. Looking at it closely, one sees a female figure under God's left arm, surrounded by children, all held in what seems to be a great uterus, or perhaps a heart. Adam can be seen lying on what could be a female body, for there is a breast and nipple clearly seen above his figure. The Feminine is there to be seen, for those who look. Whatever name she is given – Eve, Lilith, Sophia - she is there at the beginning. She is with God.

Reclaiming eroticism as sacred lifeforce

Where did the Lilith archetype go during the time of the initial patriarchal suppression? Undeniably some women would have actively fought the cultural changes imposed within their community, or in their relationships and homes. Yet inevitably, over centuries, a new way of life and a new way of being for women came into existence. This change took many forms, over time, until it was firmly established then strengthened through religion.

The major cultural shift, after destruction of the priestess temples, was to personal ownership of property, land, and its resources, including ownership of women and their children by men. We might surmise that, over time, women's more strident voices became subsumed in the need for a home and food for our children, within this new, alien world that was emerging. The Lilith archetype in us turned inwards towards self-denial, to rejection of our angst and anger, cutting off our more visceral nature, or perhaps expressing our demands to the men in our lives in more subtle yet poisonous ways, simply for security's sake.

Or perhaps Lilith in us continued to express our deep wisdom, but we learned the danger of allowing her voice. The punishments for those who flouted patriarchal controls are well-documented – the death of Vestal Virgins who engaged their sexuality, the ducking of wise women, the burning of witches, the use of the scold's bridle and chastity belts. Violence as control was not uncommon. Has that changed even now? The cultural norm is consistent in its distorted perspectives and expression of double standards for men and women.

Equality is not just about women's rights, although that is vital; it goes much deeper. The legacy of distorted cultural perspectives on sex and power lie at the core of our lives even now. For example, a man is applauded for 'sowing his oats', a young girl encouraged by western culture to be sexual in her dress and manner and yet labelled 'easy' for exploring and expressing her sexuality. Equality is needed in many ways, but it is this root of judgment and control that really needs addressing. For women to reclaim the right to respectful acknowledgment of our role as creatrix of human life; for sexuality to be honoured as the expression of divine union. It is for us women to reclaim the innate sacredness of our body, to know sexuality as a natural way of divine connection. This is the reclaiming of Lilith in her vital role as gateway to our original sacred nature. It is to consciously embody a full acknowledgment and honouring of the Divine Feminine, aligned with the rhythms of Earth and Moon as well as Sun.

This is no easy task, for we live in a culture that is, in the mainstream, disconnected from nature, from the Earth and a human being's natural place within the oneness of life. Reclaiming Lilith involves a re-membering of this oneness, a full embodiment that must take place within our self and in our intimate relationships. We are called to heal our disconnections from our intimate self, body, and sexual expression, to address inequality in our life and relationships. It's not just about equality, our right to choose, or our sexual freedom, but a complete shift of perspective in all genders about our natural wonderfully erotic creative nature and the role of Masculine and Feminine consciousness within that.

The very basis of Life operating through eros – our desire nature - is known both through antiquity and new physics. In the Hindu culture, it is the dance of Shiva/Shakti; in Chinese philosophy, it's seen as the synergy of Yin and Yang; in particle physics, it's known to be the very basis of life operating through attraction and repulsion. Yet most human beings would not experience this dance of union consciously. If we did, we would know fulfilment beyond anything we might want, simply through connecting to that dance within our cells. We would also shift our relationship to desire as an external force of manifestation. It would become balanced. The paradox is, our lives and our partnerships lack the full aliveness of this dance of divine union, yet it lies at our very core.

Orgasm is a taste of divine union, albeit for an ecstatic moment. As is creative flow. It's the expression of Shakti's erotic life-stream in us. We both long for this union and taste it, albeit briefly or rarely. Its temporary yet alluring presence calls us. Many of us intuit we're here to experience the ecstasy of unity (although we might not call it that), yet when we try to hold fulfilment, it disappears. We discover it, only to lose it. This desire for fulfilment lies behind all our material demands; however they appear. Our pursuit of material comfort beyond what we truly need is its play, overshadowing the natural cycles that include loss, suffering and death. What we may not fully realise is that in our quest for comfort, we shun the full embodiment of our natural sensual connection to each other, to life and to the earth we walk upon. This has come through collectively distracting ourselves away from the messy, uncontrollable, bloody realms of menstruation, loss, illness, birth, and death – the realm of the Dark Mother. We have relinquished our true roots, both earthy and divine, through failing to fully embrace the natural cycle of life. As we have entered separative consciousness, as the Sacred Feminine way of being has been suppressed, so has the fullness of embodiment.

When life is suppressed, it becomes distorted. Life itself cannot be controlled, yet it can change shape under our human control mechanisms. We are witnessing and experiencing this distortion in our lives now. Having denied the pure aliveness of women's free erotic flow, our connection to our full participatory aliveness has diminished. Lack and separation now lie behind our desires; fulfilment is elusive. We forego our full abundance as Earth beings. When we live in the head and genitals only, sexuality is cut off from its natural erotic flow. It expresses in distorted ways such as voyeurism, pornography, and the control of women's bodies. Our disconnection from life has led to fantasy becoming a norm, violence thriving in the quest for a thrill, excitement replacing ecstasy, plastic becoming a poor substitute for flesh.

Anything natural that we separate from becomes a fixation. Its energy must go somewhere, for it is a force of nature. When we become fixated, obsession arises. As full erotic aliveness has been given over to the temporary relief of sexual release, unwittingly we suffer. The separation of body and mind providing momentary liberation from the pressure of living, yet only leading to the desire for yet another fix.

How and why did this disconnection from our natural state of living union come about? It is a question I ponder often. Is it truly the movement of evolution – many esoteric systems point towards unified consciousness becoming separative, so that a conscious return could take place i.e., that we would make that choice. Do we have to fall asleep to awaken consciously? As a woman, I know divine union is a real potential in partnership, for I have tasted it. And I am deeply called to live from that knowing of union. Yet collectively, the nature of our sexuality continues to be twisted by those who are afraid of it yet desire it, and women's open display of sensual beauty is deemed reason enough for rape and abuse. All the while, Lilith in us longs to be seen and known.

There is no doubt now that many women are calling with Lilith's voice. We are calling for an end to the cycle of corrupted desire, grabbing or violation, the wounds of abuse and shame, the distortion and use of our sexuality, the control of our bodies. To actively allow our desire nature, not only as a natural expression of being human, but as the vehicle to know and express our innate divine unity. Desire is where the physical and spiritual unify. How can erotic desire be 'sin' when it leads to human creation? Yet to fully know this as true, to embody our Sacred Feminine nature, requires we are willing to embrace the many faces of the Feminine, including her dark ones. We must cease to control them within us, as we call for that to end in our world.

The truth of Lilith is that she threatens patriarchal dominance, for she will not adhere to it. She destroys the status quo of our comfort zones too. Her demand is tangible in the longing for truth, both within us and in sexual union. All or nothing. She will not compromise it. For she is calling to bridge the divide between dark and light, to end separation, to return to the union that is at our very core.

In our time of awakening now, any awakened partnership will be experiencing Lilith's play. She calls us to bring relationships to impersonal union through the personal play, evolving consciously through the dance of dark and light. This kind of partnering goes beyond the dream of romantic love yet embraces that too. This is a tantric path i.e., fully embracing the dance of light and shadow in all areas of life, not just sexuality. It's to bring everything home to the divine. Having lived in Tantric community for thirteen years, I understand this is not an easy path. It is not for everyone perhaps. Yet Lilith's particular playground is relationships and sexuality, whether we recognise her or not. She has a strong and potent impact in partnership, often playing behind the scenes within power dynamics. She's alive in the mystery of potent sexual attraction, our calling to be seen, our rage at betrayals and those seemingly choiceless compulsive attractions that call us beyond any common sense. She plays where there is a recognisable soul meeting too, for she weaves her magic in mysterious ways. As Original Woman, Lilith is the dance of particles in our cells, attracting and repulsing constantly to create the play and drama of experience. Always she calls us towards the truth of wholeness, the embrace of dark and light within and in our relating.

Behind the calling of attraction, Lilith's real demand is for a meeting of equals - two whole beings expressing their divine nature. She commands mutual respect, to be seen and honoured as holy, whole unto herself. This potential may arise as a one-off sexual meeting that honours the potential experience of divine union. Or it may express as an evolving partnership that expresses the dance of Shiva/Shakti, where partners are devoted to expressing the sacred mystery of their self and their union. Lilith's calling is to embrace every aspect of life as Shakti, Feminine erotic flow, with Shiva, pure consciousness. If that worthy endeavour to make life in partnership conscious is our calling, we must face our deepest distortions. Every place where we actively create a separation is calling to come home to unity. We must transmute what feels deeply personal and often painful, for the sake of the whole. We must claim eroticism as the naturally aligned sacred nature of our life-force.

What's wrong with me?

The Lilith state in us is utterly vulnerable. Her seeming contrariness often acts as a necessary protection of her shame of woundedness. Lilith is renowned for her defiance. Defiance may be a clear stand for what is known to be true, yet it can also be a protective device, born of shame.

Shame is an insidious wounding. It's not like guilt, which is linked to our capacity for making mistakes, where accountability, self-compassion, forgiveness, and apology are needed. Shame arises when woundedness is inextricably linked to our state of being, rather than our behaviour. It expresses as: there's something wrong with me. We may not give it these particular words, but this feeling is deeply embedded in the female psyche. Over eons woman have been shamed for simply being female. We are the bearers of sexual shame for our entire culture. We see this in the onus projected onto women to adjust their behaviours to avoid predation or rape. It is evident in victim blaming. It is there in phrases that deny men's responsibility for their actions, such as 'boys will be boys', or in recent archaic laws against women's abortion rights. Making women the carriers of shame, makes us wrong from birth. It is the single most important weapon used in crushing the spirit of our naturally erotic and creative femaleness. It is a cover-up that has allowed Patriarchal control to thrive. It's a cover-up that's time is up.

These times require Lilith's fierceness, especially where we feel shame (often for no reason whatever). Not against patriarchy but in exposure of it. Lilith's energy, in demanding what was and is rightfully hers – equality, freedom in her sexual choices - is the key to transmuting shame. We don't need to dwell in shame. Or to judge our reactively defiant nature when it erupts. We don't even need to heal these aspects of being a woman. We simply need to recognise that we have been labelled through a twisted perspective. That we have carried that label both personally and collectively. Shame is the source of all self-hatred. It's never about behaviour but is rooted in the erroneous belief that our very being is somehow corrupted. In its absolute nature, the projection of shame makes us intrinsically powerless. It's a fait accompli that may be impossible to heal, but not impossible to embrace and act on. The truth is, we need to throw it out. We must say no to its continued projection wherever it comes from. In doing so, we are reclaiming the original woman in us, created whole, beautiful, fully available to express whatever is deeply true in the moment. The fact of our natural innocence and wholeness can shine through us. Self-hatred and shame naturally transmute as we refuse to carry their poison.

Shame has no place in our being woman. It is an insidious control mechanism used to demean us.

Turning our face towards the dark shadows of shame includes a need to break the silence, to talk about our woundedness, to call out the shaming blaming behaviours that are so rooted in our culture. It's time to throw off the cloaks of humiliation, to refuse the labels that still may fly towards us, to question how women are being defined, however subtle that may be. As we dethrone shame, so we claim our natural throne as sovereign beings – women, female, Divine Feminine, creatrix of human life on Earth. We claim our wholeness and in so doing, shine its light on our men, our partners in creation, bringing us into the potential of living unified consciousness here on Earth.

The play of poison and power

The Lilith archetype demands that we feel into and express a directly honest relationship with both our self and other. She goes beyond our personal Moon nature, to discover our deepest truth, the longing of our soul, the truth of our wholeness. Just like her astronomical position as empty space, the Lilith state calls for us to be naked, utterly transparent. It is a key to her magic. Her dance occurs through embracing the ecstasy that arises in deep loving and then, the extremes of our seeming separation. To go beyond the emotional immaturity of taking everything personally into a deepening understanding of the impersonal nature of evolving relationship. To live this, to embody this, allows the poison of pain to become the power of evolutionary partnership.

The themes we all face in partnership are not purely personal; they may belong to our personal history but in Lilith's realm they also belong to our collective imbalance, to the separation we have co-created over eons. Although the hurtful, dark, and edgy places where we fail to connect feel deeply personal, we all know them. When we embrace these raw edges with honesty, they allow us to enter the realms of deeper self-awareness and potentially, deeper union. When we flee their demand for exploration - either by escaping into Lilith's dark projections onto her own self or a partner, or by flying away into the desert, isolating our self in shame - we fail her calling for deepening union.

When the dark shadows in us become too much, we can be sure Lilith is involved. The Lilith archetype is always intimately involved in the dark thing we most reject or deny about our self, or project onto others. It's the core wounding about being female that expresses not just as 'I'm not ok', but as, 'I'm bad at my core'.

As pain arises, we might play 'bad girl', giving Lilith free rein to pour out scorn, rage, or venom. We might even enjoy it. Lilith in us can be ruthless, using our sexuality as a weapon against our self or others, using manipulation or even violence to control or punish. Lilith at her extreme is vengeful, full of toxic rage, energetically castrating males with her words or behaviour. In relationship she's present in darker emotions such as jealousy and vindictiveness, the desire for revenge, or the compulsive need to emasculate to feel powerful.

Where we are not actively in touch with her energy, we may see Lilith through a mirror. This mirroring can play in our resistance to, or judgment of, an openly sexual woman, a flirt, someone we consider to be too full of ego, dark, closed off or angry. We may project Lilith out onto the 'other woman', or in jealousy onto a more uninhibited women, demeaning their expression whilst subconsciously desiring to be more open in our own sensual nature. We project the pain of rejection or disconnection on another. Or we may use the energy of pain against another, becoming bitter and blaming, man-hating, bitchy, or undermining, actively creating separation. None of this is wrong in itself; it's simply the play of pain. Yet it's wisdom to recognize that projective behaviour simply takes us deeper into the darkness. Underlying the play of these distorted, yet clearly excruciating, raw expressions of unacknowledged pain, may lie a deep fear of sexuality, vulnerability based in sexual trauma and abuse, or a distorted belief in our own 'badness'. For even as Lilith in us points towards the shadows in our self or another, creating separation, the paradox is she's longing for union.

When Lilith is strongly activated in us, her energy can feel like a tornado. We may try to play 'good girl' - trying not to rock the boat, accommodating abuse through fear, or for the security of being taken care of – but often we simply cannot. Seething inwardly, Lilith will erupt somewhere, often in the most innocuous of circumstances, leaving everyone wondering 'What just happened?' Both the suppression or projection of what is raw and painful, distort it. Pain withheld becomes poisonous, whether we withdraw and isolate our self, or throw it out towards another, or both. We see this in the coldness of women who disconnect their life-giving sexual energies to punish a partner. It's evident in the self-harming behaviours of abuse victims, or the perpetually jealous, insecure partner. It's the grip of shadow that we perpetuate as self-destructive punishment of our self or another. Lilith is often involved in repetitive cycles of emotion or conflict, particularly in relationship.

Many of us recognise these deeply disconnected, often savage, places within us, if we are honest enough to admit it. Lilith's vitriol is inextricably linked to our cyclical nature. She's present in our pre-menstrual emotion, post-natal depression and menopausal 'couldn't give a shit', our shame or rage when cat-called or sexually harassed, or when our feminine intelligence is put down. She plays wherever we cut off from the visceral poisons in our body-mind system. She rages where our longing to be seen and acknowledged is denied. Just as Adam dishonoured Lilith's longing to be his equal, and would not face her rage in exile, we also deny her when we refuse to see and acknowledge her existence. Our denial of her darkness creates the very environment Lilith took herself off to, the desert. We lose our creative juiciness, our fertility, our innate connection to the full cycle of ourselves as Feminine. We become dry and barren. Rejecting Lilith's shadows, or her longing, is akin to rejecting our very life-force, for life is constantly flowing between light and dark. We are actively foregoing the power to be whole, continuing the patriarchal play in denial of the Dark Mother.

Without doubt, Lilith in us is contradictory. Regardless of her longing for utter union, she can also reject or push it away. She is the ultimate contradiction in us. All the Lilith stories in us involve the themes of her myth: disappointment, humiliation, flight, and desolation. It is in how we respond or react to these very human experiences and emotions that reveals Lilith's play as true or mean within us. We can be in the poison of our painful hanging on, like Lilith 'mating with demons'. Or we can recognise the games we are playing and come to honesty. When we are true, there is power found in the pain. If we are called to full awakening, it is necessary for us to transmute these often-multi-layered poisons – simply by being with them fully as impersonal movements of shadow within our wholeness. In doing so, we free up the original power of purity at the core of the distortion. We are then revitalized naturally in our always-available pure life-force, reconnected in our wholeness. The potential is also that we open the gates for our sisters, and the men who love us, as through Lilith, we are evolving for ourselves and for unity.

In her embodied expression, Lilith's willingness to face the shadow, and to challenge her partner in the same, is her greatest gift. She's not looking for a weak Adam-type archetype, who will not meet her demand. She calls a man to step up, especially through her seemingly negative behaviour. She challenges him in his presence. 'Is he present enough to hold even this?', she demands. She wants a worthy consort who will challenge her, meet her fire, and hold her accountable when she's being mean rather than true. She wants a man who is not afraid of her poison. In partnership, if Lilith in us is not honoured for her wise knowing birthed in the shadows of life, she may hiss and spit, or rage, or she may withdraw. Lilith is a master at solitude, either in retreating inward, or in leaving, where her partner will not meet her in truth. Her raw expression or withdrawal can cause a man to run too, yet it is his radical evolution where he's willing.

In these evolutionary times, many women have given up hope of conscious partnership or have chosen to step away from inauthentic relating rather than compromise. Yet the longing to be met in both our light and our darkness still deepens. Many women long for a mature partner of deep presence to engage this potential. A partner who will recognize and transmute their own patriarchal conditioning. It takes courage and willingness to engage full erotic embodiment against the perceived comfort of a quiet life. It's a tension you may recognise in your own attractions or relationships. What will it take for us to step into this evolving relationship potential collectively? Is that even possible? It is not a comfortable ride. It is the play of the Dark Mother's mystery. Lilith thrives in what's discomforting, bringing the poison of personal challenges to impersonal evolution. No conscious relationship can evolve in unity without engaging her.

Exile as the price of self-belonging

In the Jewish creation myth, Lilith did not blame Adam, or rage at his demand for her to lay under him. She simply flew off into the desert and refused to return. The symbology of the desert is pertinent to how Lilith plays through our human dramas: how we can isolate and blame our self, turn rejection and humiliation inwards as a weapon against self. Lilith's mating with demons is a clear allegory for the inner experience of seething with hatred, resentment, or rage. It's self-annihilation in the form of self-destructive thoughts, psychic splitting off, or an endless recycling of bitterness. Although Lilith's isolation is designed to protect from further pain, paradox reigns here too. For her lonely place of safety is also the place of her potential revitalisation.

The theme of 'original loss' is strong in the mythology of both Lilith and Eve. Both knew expulsion from the Garden; Lilith from her own volition;

Eve from her apparent wrongdoing. If we see the Garden as symbolising a state of innocence, natural wholeness, our Being, then it's clear why this expulsion is necessary. If we are here to evolve as co-creative beings on a planet of free-will, then we must experience the outcome of our choices.

Lilith, as original woman, represents our natural creative beingness. Her first experience, with Adam, established the pattern of the 'defiant one' archetype, compelled to act and react where she experiences a misalignment with what she deeply knows to be true. She is the absolute refusal to collude with an agenda she feels to be dishonest. As Original Woman, naturally connected with the truth of her wholeness, she stands for where we are called to be utterly original in our expression of self. As such, she expresses through both raw urges and subtle knowing. She is free thinking and utterly alive. She appears wherever we are forced to break out, or confront repression, often despite a strong desire to fit in or belong. She breaks the rules that do not align with her deep knowing. Then she retreats. She is called to deep union, but not at the price of her integrity.

Lilith's energies require we become direct and honest, bringing the apparent causes of anger and resentment into the open, even at the expense of acceptance. She is an active rebellion against subservience, imposed codes of conduct and correctness. Defiant in her refusal to conform; she lives authentically, giving herself permission to be unbeholden to the standards of anything other than her own deep knowing. She owns her truth, especially when that truth is simply a clear 'No' without rational reason. Yet such a way of being has its price.

As humanity faces a collective deconstruction of the social structures, belief systems and norms that are meant to serve us, the need to claim Lilith from her exile becomes stronger. Like children, who depend on parents for the rules and guidelines, we must mature beyond the need to be told what to do, how life is or should be, by any external system. With the obvious demise of patriarchal cultural paradigms, and with it, a clear lack of evolutionary leadership in the mainstream world, it is the time to rise beyond the system. This means, we are on our own. The discovery that we can no longer trust the system to take care of us, or its leaders to let go of self-serving behaviours, means we must actively take responsibility for our own lives. The calling to belong to our deeper self-authenticity, our wholeness, then gives rise to the potential for gathering with others of similar energy. Firstly, we must enter the desert though, for to come into congruence with oneself is the precursor to authentic connection with those who reflect this consciousness. Exile is the price we pay.

Lilith's experience in the desert symbolizes what takes place when we reject the norms put forth in relationship or by society. We must remove our self from what we cannot bear, where everything in us screams 'I simply cannot do this'. Often Lilith is present not as knowing, but as a rejection of something that is anathema to us, as a visceral reaction to dishonest, or a more obviously disrespectful or abusive experience. We might withdraw, perhaps in defiance, perhaps in pain, or we might choose to challenge. Whatever the circumstances, we must face exile from the sources of love that constrict our evolution, as well as sources of conflict. We must lose our sense of belonging, sometimes leaving our loved ones, perhaps our community – either literally, or through internal withdrawal - to connect with our own truth and strengths. Lilith's strong responses are our guides to what we may not initially or consciously recognize as misaligned. Gut reaction, a sudden loathing or rage, visceral embodied feedback, or psychic withdrawal, are her means. She can express as outrage but also is known through our despair. Despair at a way of living devoid of truth, deep meaning, or truly intimate connection.

Primal and emotionally charged responses, especially from females, are unacceptable to cultural sensibilities. Lilith was made into a demon, labelled 'child-killer' and 'vampire' for failing to conform to society's expectation of submission and good behaviour. In our own lives we may be labelled 'too much', called crazy, pre-menstrual, and much worse, for failure to play the 'good girl' game. Even now it's not unusual for a woman to be humiliated by society for daring to break the rules – leaving her children, being sexually free, unashamedly herself. Rejection is the price we pay to find a deeper self-belonging. The price of being unconforming is high, not just mentally and emotionally but physically. For instance, women without a partner often have a lower standard of living, or they may be unsupported in their desire to have a fulfilling creative life and be a mother. When we break the rules of what is deemed to be acceptable, like Lilith we may become a scapegoat, a hook for our family or society's projections of 'difficult', 'bad girl', 'loose', 'perverse' and other derogatory labels.

Sometimes the price seems high for claiming and living our truth. The temptation to self-sabotage, or accommodate the distortions of those around us, is strong if we are dependent on others for our identity, security, or wellbeing. Lilith then asks: What price my authenticity? Both the longing to belong and the fear of aloneness can create self-sabotage. Lilith's desire for truth is sometimes contradictory to her equally strong desire for love. In the deep she knows she was made for union. Yet a half-baked unity, devoid of honesty, does not fulfil her. Sometimes it's necessary to become lost to find new life. This is Lilith's quandary.

Lilith's time in the desert was where she became lost, yet it was also her place of self-discovery. Her defiance even of God (for she refused the three angels God sent to persuade her back to Adam) meant she was utterly alone. She is still in exile now, until we claim her consciously. It was a choiceless choice for Lilith, the price of compliance being too high.

Her desire to honour herself as creative Feminine, to not compromise her equality to Adam's demand, outweighed the pain of her ultimate exile. Where was Adam in all this? Patiently (perhaps) waiting for God to sort it all out for him. No wonder Lilith refused God's plea to return. She abhors insincerity, cover ups, cowardice, or lack of presence, especially in a man. She simply could not compromise, even for God. And Adam wasn't man enough to win her.

And so, Lilith was utterly alone. This is where we must go to free Her. Strangely, as we do so, we may find the emptiness of exile becomes full. For Lilith is always contradictory. Firstly though, we face the empty space.

Saying no to say yes

The astronomical placement of Lilith as empty space is key to her magic. Yet it is magic revealed only when we claim her inherent emptiness. This is the challenge. For she is the void that occurs when we don't receive personal reflection of our value as woman, especially when we are being most true. It is the absence of acknowledgment that sparks her magic, yet also our pain.

Lilith in us seeks first the truth within, then the meeting of it. It is natural that we seek acknowledgment of our deepest wisdom, yet it's never guaranteed. Pain arises when our demand for truth to be heard, is unheard, denied, suppressed, or blocked, either through our own self-negation, or in relating. Many of us know that feeling of being non-existent, ignored, talked over, mansplained, or belittled. Dismissal of Lilith's voice in us, rejection of her wisdom as irrelevant, is fuel for Lilith's inner wound of rejection. When the demand to be seen is unmet, she retreats into her inner desert, or she spits her venom. Whatever her reaction, a profound yet stark truth is always revealed, if we choose to see it – that seeking validation from another is always a risk.

Lilith in us knows, we can only ever be truly filled and fulfilled by our authentic self, our divine wholeness. Everything else, including those close to us, are merely mirrors. Mirrors are fragile, they can be broken or removed. They are not reliable. Yet the authenticity of our self is always available if we choose to make the courageous journey to claim it. This is a key to Lilith. Her courage at facing her utter aloneness, the absence of reflection – even God's condemnation for not playing the game with Adam – is the making of her. This capacity for standing alone, even whilst in an intimate partnership, is the making of us as Divine Feminine in embodiment. Paradoxically, the empty space can open the mystery and fertility of our true nature.

Lilith's void is the natural state of being that arises when we let go of identity, or when identity is demolished. Her polarity to the personal self-knowing and identity of our Moon nature is absence. Absence is an uncomfortable state of being to our humanness. For humanness seeks to be known through identity, rather than recognising the truth of our unknowability, the innate mystery of our Beingness. This is where Lilith's play becomes paradoxical. She calls us towards our emptiness in order that we may move beyond it into our brilliance. Her challenge is we cannot do that personally, other than through letting go, for brilliance is a transpersonal state of being.

The temptation to our humanness when faced with this bridge across emptiness, is to attach to the states we know, even when they are distorted and painful. For many of us, the distraction of having an identity, even a painful victim identity, is preferable to being empty. With Lilith, identity often stems from our wounding, our perceived personal lack, the darkness of our shadows, rage, shame, the vehemence of being made wrong. When we make a habit of energising these states, we become locked in the darkness of her empty space, a self-perpetuating spiral of pain. Whereas allowing our self to be in the desert, to rest in her space of lack - an absence of self-knowing, her raw ache - opens a transitionary state of being that is creative rather that self-destructive. We must enter the emptiness willingly though, letting go of all self-concepts, to bring forth its fruits.

Lilith's very being is a raw ache. The ache of not belonging, the desolation of utter aloneness, promise not met, feeling shame, no longer knowing oneself. It is also the bleakness that patriarchy has brought about – a world where the Divine Feminine is forgotten, femaleness is corrupted, and women undermined. The temptation to fill this ache with something, anything, is insidious. We must make a practice of constantly reminding ourselves of the truth whilst also feeling the sensational reality of her presence in our bodies. We must say no to simply filling our emptiness with equally empty distractions. Although it may be unappealing, meeting her raw ache of emptiness births renewal. Saying yes to emptiness, is saying yes to her mystery, ultimately magical, filled with revelation of the truth of our Beingness. When we are empty, we're available for Grace to surprise us with its unexpected beauty and bliss, the supreme acknowledgment, often when we least expect it.

The desert in bloom

The mythology and stories about Lilith never bring her to wholeness. She is stuck with the labels of patriarchy. So, our assignment is to reclaim her, to change the programme, to not only bring light to the darkness but to acknowledge its raw beauty and value, to realise our wholeness beyond the separation of dark and light.

Lilith flies into the desert like a wounded animal. She chooses isolation with all its shadows, over conformity or subservience. In our own lives we may experience this in a physical fleeing from abuse, or an internal withdrawal from censure, humiliation, or rejection of what we most value, especially our being female. Withdrawal can bring on relief, lead to desolation or feelings of going mad, especially when everyone around you is telling you differently than you know deep within. It is this ache of misalignment, being utterly alone with our inner world, that is our guide in the desert of exile. It is this ache, this absence, that opens the gates for integration - not as a shift back to light, although that may take place in the natural rhythms of evolution - but as the capacity to fully be with our exile.

When we are willing to live with the absence of reflected love and approval rather than compromise for comfort, we discover our capacity to fully be with our self, no matter how it looks and feels. Children need validation; it is essential to their healthy development. This is our Moon nature. As we grow up, maturity calls us to make the switch to internal validation. We are forced to outgrow our emotional tendencies, held by the Moon, and recognise the impersonal universality of our human emotional experience, held by Black Moon Lilith. As this happens, we begin to develop an evolving healthy sense of self, represented astrologically by the Sun (with its natural influence on the Earth and Moon cycles).

In a healthy maturing process, we learn to take care of the Moon connection to our personal needs, emotional patterns, and compulsions, as a natural part of growing selfhood represented by the Sun. In a healthy spiritual maturing, we then move towards the appropriate letting go of self but presence of something more. We develop beyond the personal self into the Mystery of who this is in this body-being — divinely undefinable, yet tangibly present. The self is still present but becomes translucent, allowing the Mystery to shine. In this we discover a strength of authenticity that is way beyond personal, a living embodied connection to Source itself. Through this, the absence of harmonious connection with others, or their reflection, carries less charge in our lives. We begin to discover faith in our self as the Mystery within the Mystery. The presence of Lilith is beaming, as experience becomes more impersonal. The strength to face our rage and shadows of shame in new deep ways naturally arises through us. Her magic begins to gleam. We discover her defiance within us, with the knowing that as we embrace, face, challenge darkness, we transmute for us all. We become the action of radical self-love, a gateway for anyone willing to enter.

When we rest in empty space, Lilith is alive in us. Paradoxically, being willing to be utterly alone reveals the potential to truly love. We are not dependent on the mirror of love from another, yet that might appear. With Grace, the mirror shines for us everywhere. We magnetise fullness of life through emptiness and receptivity, living mirrors of life's wonder. Lilith's magic lives through us. Accepting oneself in wholeness, in the blackest, bleakest, deepest shadows, brings the desert into bloom.

Being sovereign

Sovereignty is a word often used now in new age and women's circles. It is said to be the power of self-determination, the state of being free from the control of another. To claim sovereignty, we need to be able to stand alone, to defy the status quo, no matter the perceived cost. It is a state of being that arises from our core truth, that which is so deeply integral in us that we simply must do or be it. This demand to be fully aligned is not an egoic state; it arises from the impersonal realm of Lilith in us. Belonging to truth being of highest value within oneself.

Lilith demonstrates her sovereignty as she leaves Adam and the Garden. We might imagine she was longing to experience union with the partner created with her, yet the price of foregoing equality and honour of her Divine Feminine nature was too high. Rather than exist in compromise, Lilith claims sovereignty, even defying God. She could do no other. For the price of acquiescence was too high.

Lilith, being wholeness, reveals to us that true sovereignty is not a personal attribute; it arises from impersonality. It is not a quality we can own personally, yet it expresses in a personal way. It requires clear alignment. When we are sovereign, we are aligned with the deepest source of truth within, life itself, expressing uniquely through our self as a unique being. This path is not an easy one. Being sovereign, aligned with one's deepest self, might be straightforward when alone, yet we live in a world of relationship. We must find the way of love with others whilst also following our inner map. The temptation, or need, to compromise can be compelling, sometimes essential. In relating we face the challenge of alone yet together.

In Lilith's realm, relationship lacks juice without sovereignty. She knows that conscious relationship relies on inner union. She in us also knows that compromise carries a heavy price to authenticity, and therefore does not feed conscious relating. Consequently, Lilith is the one (in any gender) in relationships that calls for the deepest truth, both from oneself and from a partner. She in us is prepared to face the fiery furnace of dismissal or rejection, no matter how painful, rather than compromise inner knowing. Lilith in us viscerally knows the ache of deep heart wisdom denied by another, but it does not destroy us. She will not compromise her embodied knowing for anything, even God.

This uncompromising quality in Lilith is a quandary, for it can convey the deepest shadows of woman's pain as easily as truth. She represents split off, victim aspects of women's energy, arising from eons of cultural projection. These distortions have painted female attributes, such as strength in our demand for honesty and integrity, as wrong, shameful, devious, even dangerous. They have made us inherently wrong, simply for being female, for asking awkward questions and especially for our deep irrational wisdom. These distortions lie at the core of our pain and self-disconnection. They often express as dynamic tension where we feel at odds with our self, as we struggle with familial or social judgments that define how we should look, express and act to fit in. Where Lilith is strong is us, we constantly walk the raw edge of reflection, questioning: is this truth, or this is my pain speaking? Either way, the constancy of staying with the exploration, allows revelation. Sovereignty goes beyond certainty. Sometimes it requires we simply allow our not-knowing to be as it is, to rest in the Mystery, knowing revelation arises beyond our personal timing. We must rest in the uncomfortable crucible of liminal space.

Conscious relationships naturally bring us an 'attachment or authenticity' dilemma, calling us to engage and trust those qualities within us that may not fit the current acceptable social models, or the agendas of those close to us. Resting on the edge of not knowing is not necessarily comfortable but it can be our truest action. Lilith in us seeks to break the boxes of belief and ideals that limit us, that deny the deep instinctual knowing of the Feminine. No wonder her key expression is defiance, making a stand. Yet the question we must constantly hold with Lilith is: What am I standing for? Am I really standing for truth? Or is my defiance rooted in rebellion and vengeance for the sake of it? Here we are called to confront the core of the dilemma Lilith delivers. To stand for truth – even to discover what it is - we must face and embrace what currently covers it: our fury and shame. In meeting the depths of that darkness, sovereignty is a natural harvest. Becoming awake to our deep fears around power is a key aspect of this embrace. It is sign of maturity to know when fear lies behind our actions and responses and to dare to face its illusion.

To get in touch with Lilith's shadows now we must go back to the original wounding. It seems to be Lilith in the garden with Adam; his refusal to honour her as not only his equal partner, but as his love. Yet don't we also know that same scenario now? Our original wounding lies in every woman's experience of power imbalance, rejection, humiliation, being devalued simply for being female, irrational, premenstrual, crazy or whatever the derogatory label. It is in every woman's experience, hesitant to express our natural wisdom and knowing, or simply what we are feeling in any given moment. It is in every woman's experience of misogyny, being coerced or forced to obey through fear of violence, sexual wounding, or vilification of our natural eroticism. It's happening now. No wonder Lilith is wild and furious.

Embracing Lilith is the journey of claiming sovereignty, not as a static state but as an evolving one. Expressing her energies involves speaking and acting instead of hiding, repressing, and withdrawing. Yet it's also key not to judge our self when we do hold back. It's allowing what has been denied its voice, especially around being female. To address the misconceptions around our sexuality and our deep feeling nature. It is honouring the validity of our fiery reactions to shaming, manipulation, subtle innuendo and sexual power plays, and uplifting others to do the same. Although compassion is not a quality associated with Lilith, an open-hearted connection to her qualities, especially the rawest ones, opens the potential for compassion to be present. For it is in being broken open that we release the toxicity that blocks our most tender self-connection. Emotional maturity recognizes such breaking open as a gift, despite its rawness. It is a crucial element of being sovereign. For without being opened, how may we know what is deeply true? How may we know the deepest love?

Emotional maturity recognises how we think life, or relationship should look, is often not actually relevant to our evolution. It's the gap between what we long for and what we experience that compels us to transform. To be mature in relationship we need to be in right relationship to our evolution. We need to become increasingly aware of our values, what we desire, where we may compromise, where we need to confront, and the crux of what makes us individual. Of necessity, becoming an individual involves challenge and conflict, both inner and external. We are constantly faced with choices that involve different aspects of self and our relationships.

To be a healthy human being, our choices need to honour both our attachment drives and the desire for authenticity, our paradoxical longing for freedom and connection. This is not an easy path. Both are essential to our wellbeing, yet they make uneasy partners. It is the natural tension between them that consistently grows us if we allow it, creating true balance between individuality and deeply committed relationship. Lilith often presents herself in our dilemma between fitting in and standing out. Her role, within this natural tension of differing desires, is to break through to what is most real. To constantly question: where I am hiding, compromising, or avoiding, particularly in challenging what is accepted as normal yet is void of any real life. In doing so, Lilith finds her place within our psyche now, as a real feminist, spiritual warrior, and initiator, as the key to being whole and holy to our self.

Beyond sovereignty into the Mystery

Beyond her very human quality of defiance as a stance or shield, the fact of Lilith's astronomy draws us unavoidably into the world of invisible yet viscerally tangible realities. As we flow beyond the personal realm of Moon, we are inextricably connected to a numinous psychic sensitivity that links personal knowing with transpersonal reality. Lilith in us is this connection that opens subliminal senses to perceive subtle frequencies of the Mystery. There is little to be said about this, for to give it words distorts what is indefinable. Yet we can experience it.

The study of Lilith in astrological birth charts points towards both her shadow play, her radiance, and her astounding intelligence. One could even call it: her genius. The charts of well-known figures such as John Lennon, Steven Spielberg, Marilyn Monroe, Martin Luther King, Malcolm X, Frida Kahlo, Barack & Michelle Obama, Vincent Van Gogh, and Marion Woodman, to name but a few, feature this dark-light radiance of Black Moon Lilith. Often her astrological position reflects a place we experience a personal sense of lack or wounding but can also be a vessel for transpersonal brilliance. In those individuals in touch with Lilith, this brilliance radiates; there is something fascinating that cannot be defined. This numinous quality is enigmatic and impossible to hold as the ego self. If we try to, it backfires. We are propelled into Lilith's shadow. For Lilith's brilliance expresses through us, not from us.

To state that Lilith rules extremes of experience and expression would not be far wrong. For she holds a primal visceral level of raw experience that is difficult to express in words. She also pertains to a no-mind experience that is truly beyond words. Yet, as is her way, paradoxically, both can be known in an individual's energy field and body. They often express through magically transformative presence.

Being in touch with Lilith is enough for this transformative presence to emanate. It's not necessarily about healing the wounds that Lilith holds but expressing them alchemically. When we move through and beyond them into the empty space of the void - not just at mental and emotional levels, but psychically - what is potentially destructive expresses as creative genius or brilliance. It's allowing ourselves to fully be in the empty space where Lilith in us transmutes what we've labelled 'dark' into brilliance. It's a sign of true maturity that recognises, allows, and thus embodies this. That recognises this transmutative power as the wondrous play of Grace.

Lilith plays on the edge where genius resides. She lies on the edge of personal-impersonal consciousness, the synergy of Moon-Earth-Sun and beyond expressing through us uniquely. It's there that the paradox of wounded yet whole is known. As Original Woman, Lilith carries the blueprint of our original wholeness. We may intuitively know this, yet to live it as evolving consciousness requires that we face the shadows of our personal and collective denials. Her brilliant dark-light energy is calling. It takes both courage and commitment to meet her dark face. Yet when we do, we know beyond doubt, divinity is playing through polarity. We know; I am Original Woman.

Chapter 7

The Face in the Mirror –Medusa, Protectress of the Mysteries

The broken dream
is a stepping-stone
in the river
of love's longing.

Shards of promise
lie scattered,
debris strewn
on the shoreline
of heart potential
unfulfilled.

I look
and see my self
reflected,
each piece
a mirror,
broken
yet ripe

with the strength
of resurrection.

As I gaze
at the pieces
of self
revealed,
I realise
every piece
is a door
to the Mystery
of unknown life
arising.

I am not lost.
I awake
as the dream
dies
deep within me.

Cassandra Eve

Archetype: Protectress & Guardian of the Sacred Feminine Mysteries

Symbols: Snakes or serpents; hair; a mirror or mirrored shield; a mask; eyes; blood

Message: Confront your fears. Embrace your trauma. They mask the truth of life; they mask your power of renewal

Medusa themes: betrayal, violence, and violation; sex, death, and power; what we avoid; integrating traumatic experience; a shamanic journey; reclaiming our power and capacity for natural self-protection; inner alchemy

What the Medusa archetype calls for: Unlocking frozen places in the psyche; embracing trauma for your own healing and the sake of us all; reclaiming trust in yourself & your reactions as guides to the natural processes of life

The image of Medusa with her fierce gaze, snakes writhing around her head, is both well-known and striking. There is something compelling about her, despite her seeming ugliness. We are drawn to meet those glaring eyes. Perhaps they speak to our darkest places as women.

As with all Sacred Feminine archetypes, Medusa's terrible appearance cannot be taken at face value. Behind the mask-like features lie the alchemical mystery of the Dark Feminine. Once her darkness is engaged, Medusa can be a transformative magical goddess archetype. To know her beauty we must face some of our deepest darkest fears and pain; we must face our trauma.

Medusa is mainly known through Greek mythology, but there is a plethora of mythic and historical pointers to her energies. As happened with many goddess figures, the Greek story is a sanitised version of a more ancient tale, containing both mythic and historical elements.

Medusa is depicted in ancient cultures as the death aspect of the Triple Goddess, the dark face of the Moon. She is portrayed also as a fierce warrior, a priestess and protectress of the Sacred Feminine temple rites. The Temple of Artemis (built around 600BCE) on the island of Corfu reveals Medusa's protectress role in the early Greek culture. Its exterior holds a three-metre-high pediment of Medusa, with her children Chrysaor and Pegasus either side of her, along with two large feline figures. The body of Medusa stands out strongly and is carved in detail. Although the temple is dedicated to Moon Goddess Artemis, it is clear Medusa is playing a major role within the temple structure.

In her well-known Greek myth, Medusa is the only mortal of the three Gorgon sisters. Roman poet Ovid describes them in his Metamorphoses as 'harpies of foul wing'. Yet it is said Medusa was different to her sisters, either born mortal, or with graceful golden wings. She was deemed very beautiful, with much admired lustrous hair. Roman poet Ovid called it the "most wonderful of all her charms." Yet Medusa's beauty did not save her from her tragic fate. Her myth reveals how her destiny was inextricably linked with God of the Sea, Poseidon and Goddess Athena, and the hero Perseus. In it, we discover how her ancient role as protector of the dark Moon mysteries disappeared. Instead, Medusa became known as a monster.

Her-story

Medusa's origins lie in many ancient sources: bird and snake figures of the Neolithic period, Sun and Moon goddesses in Egypt, Sumeria, and the pre-Minoan culture of Crete, along with the Amazon warrior tribes of Asia and Libya. The mystery of her origins reflects her dual and sometimes contradictory nature of fierceness and beauty, victim, priestess of the sacred sexual rites, and monster.

The name Medusa means 'sovereign female wisdom' 'protectress' and 'the one who knows or rules.' It derives from the same root as the Sanskrit Medha, and the Greek Metis, meaning 'wisdom'. Metis is the mother of Athena, who is inextricably linked into the Medusa myth. In

Greek culture, Athena, Metis and Medusa together represent the new, full, and dark phases of the Moon. All are goddesses of wisdom, protection, and healing, in different ways.

In alignment with her dark Moon nature, Medusa's roots also lie in the Egyptian Dark Mother of Death, Neith (whose name means 'I have come from myself'), the Sumerian goddesses Inanna and her dark sister Ereshkigal, and the Libyan Triple Moon Goddess Anatha. The priestesses of Anatha are said to have had dark skin and dreadlocked hair. They wore fearsome masks to protect the secret temple rites of the Sacred Feminine from males, or the uninitiated. The masks also hid their identity when involved in sexual rites, keeping the nature of the sexual act impersonal. The blond blue-eyed Greeks may well have found these dark women in masks strange, even terrifying. Perhaps this is behind their demonisation of Medusa. The Amazon warriors of Eastern Europe and Libya were equally feared by them. They were the warrior guardians of the wild and Sacred Feminine and enemies of the Greeks. Known to be fierce fighters with terrifying facial tattoos, the Amazons had matted hair or dreadlocks. As the patriarchal takeover grew, they fought to retain the Goddess and nature-based cultures of matriarchy. It is possible that Medusa's origins lie most prominently in that region. The Greek historian, Herodotus, (560-420BCE) places her there, as does Roman poet Ovid (43BCE – 17CE).

Philosopher Joseph Campbell expands on this ancient mystery of the warrior goddesses. He links the Medusa myth to historical events, stating that the Greeks and other tribes overran the Goddess shrines and stripped the priestesses of their ritual masks. He describes what took place as follows, '...in the early thirteenth century B.C. is an actual historic rupture, a sort of sociological trauma, which has been registered in this myth'. He further states that the events and what lay behind them 'are registered yet hidden, registered in the unconscious yet unknown or misconstrued by the conscious mind'.

Whilst acknowledging her more obscure origins, much of what we know of Medusa comes from Greek mythology. Here she is known as one of the Gorgon sisters: monstrous winged female creatures, with snakes writhing in their hair, round-faced, flat-nosed, with large tongues, projecting teeth or tusks, and sometimes short coarse beards. The Greek poet Hesiod named the Gorgons, Stheno (the Mighty or Strong), Euryale (the Far Springer) and Medusa (the Queen).

Medusa is the most well-known of these Gorgon sisters. When depicted in art, her head is always the strongest feature. She has a ferocious face, sometimes with tusks, fangs, a forked tongue or bulging eyes. The snakes writhing around her head make her instantly recognisable. Famous artists who have been inspired by Medusa include Leonardo da Vinci, Rubens, Picasso, Rodin, and Salvador Dali, who portrays her hair like octopus tentacles. Picasso at least gives her a semblance of a body and a large red heart. Perhaps he saw beyond her supposed fearsomeness. Much ancient statuary, many bronze shields and vessels, coins, funerary urns, cameos, and mosaics have depictions of Medusa. She was a talisman of protection, those striking eyes symbolically warding off evil. Even now in Greek, Turkish, Jewish and some Asian cultures, it is common for people to carry an eye talisman to ward off the 'evil eye'.

Medusa has been an inspiration for poets through the ages. Percy Bysse Shelley on seeing Leonardo da Vinci's 'On the Medusa' wrote: 'Its horror and its beauty are divine. Upon its lips and eyelids seems to lie Loveliness like a shadow, from which shrine, Fiery and lurid, struggling underneath, The agonies of anguish and of death.' Whilst Mary Elizabeth Coleridge in The Other Side of the Mirror, speaks of the Medusa state as 'a woman, wild with more than womanly despair.... I am she!' Contemporary poet Carol Anne Duffy's poignant poem 'Medusa' is a potent example of Medusa's role in relationships both then and now. 'I stared in the mirror. Love gone bad showed me a Gorgon'. Formidable as she appears, one aspect of the Medusa legacy is to be a muse. We discover what's behind this contradiction as we explore her myth in more depth. For Medusa has children who bear gifts.

Two versions of the Greek myth of Medusa exist. They carry the common theme of rape or willingness in sexual connection, as encountered with

Persephone's myth in Chapter 4. In one myth version, Poseidon, God of the Ocean, appears to the young Medusa as a stallion, then mounts her as a mare. This version may stem from ancient art forms, where Medusa is sometimes portrayed as a female centaur, with the hindquarters of a horse, or with a horse's head. In another myth version, Poseidon appears as his mesmerizing God-self to Medusa, a priestess in Athena's temple, and either beguiles her, rapes her, or has sex with her (an ancient priestess rite) in the temple. The Goddess Athena responds to what she sees as a desecration of her sacred space by turning Medusa into a serpent headed demoness, terrifying ugly, much like her Gorgon sisters.

Why was Athena, a virgin Goddess, so enraged? Especially when the ancient temple rites included sexual connection. And why was her wrath directed at Medusa rather than Poseidon? Perhaps her own lack of sexuality is a clue. Perhaps she was secretly jealous. Athena, despite her ancient roots, is prominent in the time of patriarchal takeover. She is her father Zeus's daughter in that she favours the way of strategy rather than emotion. The result is that Athena fails to protect her priestess Medusa. She curses her with the snakes, stating whoever looks at Medusa will be turned to stone. She also actively supports her killing, as the myth goes on to relate.

Greek mythology is filled with tales of heroes. It was deemed a worthy task for a young hero to face the terror of monsters, like the transformed Medusa. Perseus is the Greek hero sent by King Polydectes to claim her head, including the snakes. The gods, always keen to meddle in human affairs, supported his quest with gifts: golden winged sandals, a helmet of invisibility, a curved magic sword, and a magic pouch in which to place Medusa's severed head. Athena gave Perseus a mirrored shield that he could use to see Medusa indirectly. This sealed her betrayal of her priestess. Clearly both men, gods and a goddesses wanted rid of Medusa.

Perseus killed Medusa, viewing her reflection in the mirrored shield, and wielding the magic sword to cut off her head. As Medusa died, her severed neck delivered up her twin sons (presumably conceived in her encounter with Poseidon): Chrysoar, a giant with a golden sword, and the beautiful, winged horse Pegasus. Then, fearful of reprisal from Medusa's Gorgon sisters, Perseus quickly pulled on the helmet of invisibility and winged sandals and fled, taking Medusa's head with him.

As Perseus escaped with Medusa's severed head, drops of blood trickled from her neck. The myth relates how oases grew in the desert and corals grew in the Red Sea where they dripped. It's also said that the droplets birthed a plague of poisonous serpents. Another version of the tale states how just one drop of blood from Medusa's right vein could cure and restore life, whilst one drop from her left vein could kill instantly. Athena later gave two vials of Medusa's blood to Asklepius, God of Healing, or to Hygeia, his daughter. Hygeia proceeded to make a healing balm from the blood that brought the dead back to life.

This Greek tale overwrites Medusa's more ancient origins as priestess, warrior protectress and guardian of the temple rites in the wider pre-Greek Asian and African cultures. As with many other ancient tales, rewritten by the Greeks, it is a telling allegory for a forceful patriarchal take-over, how growing cultural controls worked to decimate the role of the Sacred Feminine within the culture.

Our task as women now, if we are drawn to embodying our Sacred Feminine nature, is to disentangle this historical web of force and deceit, to penetrate the lies, to discover truth in our Sacred Feminine roots. As we face Medusa's fierce visage, as we engage the story and discover the meaning behind her sacrifice, we can claim the gifts arising from her challenging gaze, her serpent hair, her blood, and her children. She is a contradictory archetype to engage. To do so is deeply worthwhile, even essential.

If we explore goddess archetypes from other cultures, we find Medusa is not alone in her destiny or its circumstances. Tantric Goddess Chhinnamasta, an aspect of Goddess Parvati in the Hindu culture, is headless just like Medusa. Yet Chhinnamasta cuts off her own head. The self-decapitated nude goddess is mostly seen standing or seated on a divine couple who are making love. Chhinnamasta holds her severed head crowned with hair in one hand and a cleaver in the other. Three jets of blood spurt from her bleeding neck and are drunk by her severed head and her two attendants, Dakini and Varnini.

Kali is another goddess archetype from the Hindu tradition who carries the theme of blood mysteries. She is commonly depicted with a fierce face, wearing a necklace of skulls, a skirt of severed arms and dancing on the body of Shiva, her consort. Kali is a Keeper of Time, ruling the processes of destruction and death. She is yet another dark goddess archetype who holds potent keys to the mysteries of life and death.

Kali and Chhinnamasta are goddesses of contradiction, just like Medusa. They are symbols of both terror and transcendence. They stand for the life-giving and destructive energy of the Dark Mother, representing death and desolation as well as renewal and life. Just like Medusa, the stories of Kali and Chhinnamasta give emphasis to sacrifice, self-destructive fury and the potency of hidden mysteries held within their awe-inspiring forms.

Is Medusa a woman enraged and burdened with a terrible punishment she did not deserve? Or is she a symbol of female power? One that has been veiled for millennia. In our western cultural history, Medusa appears to be the archetypal victim, acted upon by Poseidon, Athena and then Perseus, but there is so much more to her myth than meets the eye. Medusa's story reveals a shamanic journey of death and renewal. There are keys hidden in her tale. They reveal how we may journey through traumatic experience to discover the heroine within. In so doing, we reclaim the power of the snake, ancient symbol of our life-force, and the blood, life-force itself. Some versions of her myth say that following her beheading, Medusa was returned to her previous beautiful self. Perhaps the spilling of her own blood brought about the miracle of her restoration to life. Or perhaps her sacrifice is a gift to us now, revealing the potential of our own emancipation from trauma.

Medusa's place in the Universe – Astronomy & Astrology

There are two planetary bodies linked with Medusa. The first is a bright stony asteroid discovered by French astronomer Perrotin on September 21, 1875. The second astronomical link to Medusa is the Algol star in the Perseus constellation, known as the Eye of Medusa. Algol is the second brightest star in this constellation and located in the curve known as 'Caput Medusae' referring to the head of Medusa.

Stars give off vast amounts of light and are therefore considered centres of great consciousness. They carry our human projections both light and dark, in the forms of stories, myths, qualities, beliefs, and fears. The Algol star has a bad reputation in both Hebrew and Chinese cultures, considered to be 'most difficult' or 'negative' and linking with Lilith (see Chapter 6) in Hebrew mythology.

Algol is a binary star, consisting of two stars that eclipse each other, said to represent Medusa's eye blinking. Algol A is three times as big as our Sun and twice as hot. Astrologers who study fixed stars link Algol with kundalini energy and collective rage arising from the repression of women and their Sacred Feminine connection. It is also purported to represent themes of death and resurrection.

The position of asteroid Medusa in an astrological birth-chart can show a victim experience, with the associated shame of victim-blaming, suppressed rage and pain. Medusa was punished after being raped, so she represents not only the trauma of experience but its aftermath. After Medusa was turned into a monster, she withdrew from the world, so this asteroid can also reveal what or how we hide away, along with a quest for true healing and redemption. Her placement can reveal distorted reactions to trauma, the need to claim it, or a gift in holding space for it in others.

Planets in aspect to Medusa show where her fierce energies may be supported to release or are challenged. Any planetary body that is linked to Medusa's position is called to rise to the power of their fullest nature, to transform the shadows, to birth magical renewal and strength. They are gifted Medusa's power of renewal as well as her traumatic inheritance. Besides carrying the personal elements of our pain as women, Medusa is a natural conduit to our collective experience. When her wounding is claimed in us, she holds deep wisdom based in our inherent sacredness as women, with a desire to protect and defend that for all women as a devotional duty.

My Journey with Medusa

In the early 90's I travelled in India twice, both times in the company of my former partner whose family origins are in Goa. Our first journey was for three months. For some of that time I was travelling alone, as we wanted to go to different places. The journey brought me face-to-face with the distinctive, sometimes shocking, contrasts of India. And unwittingly, into connection with Medusa's realm, in a truly sacred way.

India is a place of wild extremes; chaos and devotion walk hand in hand. It was a potent reflection for my journey at that time, as I was embracing deep relational trauma in my body. As I was so open, experiencing India's sacred heritage, along with its visceral challenges, was a shock to my entire system yet deeply moving. I found it exasperating, even repulsive at times, yet to my amazement, it was totally refreshing too. I had never seen such colour, so much life, so vibrant a place or people, such joy and pain openly displayed and expressed. I found the noise and the filth, the sights, and the stench, moved me to a depth of revulsion yet compassion unknown before. I was in tears every day and could not say why. I was simply moved by all my experiences. It was life in the raw, utterly heart-opening. I immediately fell in love with this vibrantly alive culture.

Being in a land of such ancient wisdom, I felt as if I could breathe in the very essence of life in India's air. I knew an innate spiritual presence in the land, the people, and their way of life. Behind the many masks: the arrogance of an obese elderly woman dripping with gold; the young mother lying in a gutter with a baby; the guy with no legs on a trolley who came to our rickshaw asking for alms, his eyes shining with Christ energy and the women in colourful saris digging the road, there was an innate joy for life. The many faces of everyday life, poverty, and trauma were all held in an innate trust in the divine. It was there to be seen, shining through the eyes of the people and in their zest for life.

Reverence and respect for the Feminine aspect of the divine, the Great Mother Goddess in all her forms, is everywhere in India. She was not just in the temples but on the streets, in their gaily decorated taxis and rickshaws, in the tilak daubed faces of the women. It was these women of India who had the most profound effect on me. I watched in awe as they carried themselves with a gentle dignity and soft femininity, evident even whilst performing the most menial of tasks. And of course, most of their lives were filled with challenge. There was an incredible natural strength emanating within their beauty. They embodied a grace that spoke of the Divine Feminine in all her aspects. It was wonderful to see. Often, I experienced a deep communion with women I encountered. We would inevitably discover some point of contact; a smile, a look, a touch that spoke of our knowing of the Great Mother behind and within it all. It was all that was required for us to deeply connect. I was being taken gently into a more natural connection with the essence of the Goddess within me and all women. I was experiencing holiness in the everyday; wholeness displayed and embodied.

Towards the last weeks of our travels my partner was drawn to spend time at the Ganeshpuri Ashram, north of Mumbai. As our relationship was in the fire of transformation, he felt it would support our deepening. I arrived there in a resistant state, well and truly stuck in my stuff. As often occurs, the ashram turned out to be exactly where I needed to be though. Our stay there brought forth a fierce initiation. It was an encounter with Medusa's energy in both her raging fury and her bright light, and an utterly unexpected awakening.

At Ganeshpuri, my partner soon fell into ashram routine - early morning chanting, meditation, and daily talks. He was happy to escape my mood. I was caring for his daughter and although I wasn't particularly drawn to the formal meditative routine, I was angry about not having the freedom to do my own thing. My resistance to being there, and my resentment towards him, became agonising. I was well and truly stuck in victim mode, seemingly unable to penetrate or transform my upswelling rage. Medusa's energy was burning in me, but I was also resisting it. Yet all was well; for unbeknown to me, I was in exactly the right state for a blast of light.

I was walking in the grounds with my partner whilst his daughter was out with new friends. The ashram gardens were stunningly beautiful, filled with peace. As we wandered, we came upon the Puja temple. It was constructed from pure white marble, completely open to nature at the front, and stunning in its simplicity. I was drawn into this beautiful sacred space. As I entered, I was struck by the clarity of a full-length portrait of Muktananda (the previous Guru in the ashram lineage) on the far wall. The beauty of his sacred presence seemed to tangibly emanate from this portrait. It was as if he was stepping out to meet me; his deep brown eyes meeting mine as I gazed at him. 'Yet more Indian eyes revealing something', I thought to myself. They were so intensely lifelike that I stood dumbstruck. Their gaze completely penetrated my being. Was I really seeing what I thought I was - a painting coming to life?

As I stood in awe, I suddenly experienced a bolt of energy hit my forehead and move through my body into the earth. It was as if I'd been struck by lightning. My mind emptied; my body fell to its knees. I lay on the temple floor, weeping with the love I could feel pouring through my body-being. My body was buzzing with an intense vibration of bliss; I was utterly obliterated in an ecstasy of feeling that I knew to be divine love. I knew the energy had come from Muktananda's eyes.

When I was able to move, my partner led me outside to sit in the temple garden. We sat under a statue of Christ, and I told him what had taken place. Being Indian, his knowledge of the processes of awakening with a Master was broader than mine. He said I had received Shaktipat - a transmission of Shakti, Divine Feminine energy - from the Guru. This could come directly from a living Master, or from a photograph or painting, as I had just experienced. Shaktipat is a catalyst of awakening. I had known nothing of this, yet clearly had experienced it. I was completely transformed. The rage and resistance that had filled me were utterly gone. I felt truly connected. In fact, I felt more connected than I ever had. I knew that I'd been touched by Grace through the energetic presence of Muktananda. As I sat with my partner in the gardens, I let myself totally rest in the place of peace I had so far denied myself. Nothing about my external circumstance had changed but I had been utterly transformed.

After my Shaktipat initiation, I naturally made space every day to meditate and reflect. I was still not drawn to participate in the ashram schedule, but I would go to the various temples and meditation spaces to simply rest in the peace of my Being. I was utterly in bliss whether in the sacred space of the temples, doing our daily washing, or caring for my partner's young daughter. Over a few days my initial experience of connection with Muktananda's presence intensified. I was blessed to feel his Being with me and hear his words of truth spoken directly into my heart. An inner dialogue developed that helped me to further understand my life's journey, particularly regarding its spiritual unfolding. Grace had found me. It was a transmission of awakening that changed my life.

As we started our journey home, I wept freely. I saw anew the blessings in the extremes of Mother India, the sights and events which had moved me so utterly: the liquid eyes of the leprous beggar who laid his stump of an arm on our taxi window and asked for rupees; the teenage mother asleep in a Bombay gutter, her tiny baby laying in the filth beside her; the shouts of joy of the women dressed in colourful saris bathing in the Indian Ocean; the seven year old boy trader so concerned to see me crying on the beach in Goa that he wanted to take me home; the dying dog covered with pus-filled sores to whom I gave my last drop of water; chatting with the women fruit-sellers on the beach. The colours, the sounds, the fragrance of Mother India stayed with me. I knew that I had been changed forever by her essence and her people. I knew that behind all the masks of poverty, filth and chaos, life was displaying its truly joyful divine presence. I knew I had been blessed to receive that directly through Muktananda. Life would never be the same again.

It is said that the eyes are the window of the soul. The eye has been used as a protective amulet in many ways, particularly in Eastern cultures, for eons. My experience at Ganeshpuri, and in daily encounters, affirmed without doubt that energy is both given and received through the eyes, sometimes with astounding effects. The energy of Shaktipat that came from Muktananda's eyes changed me irrevocably. I didn't know anything of Shakti, the Divine Feminine, or any of the archetypes such as Medusa then in my life. Yet it was after this awakening that the Divine Feminine energies began to emerge and pour through me. Following this first India journey, I started a women's sharing group. Over years, the flow of that opening expanded in many ways. It is still occurring. For the blessing of the Guru is eternal.

Medusa's Message: Confront your fears and your trauma. They mask the truth of life; they mask your power of renewal.

An archetype of collective trauma

Both as individuals and as a collective, we are conditioned in unhealthy ways and open to deeper consciousness. Our personal experiences contribute to individual patterning, mental-emotional imbalance, and illness, including conditions such as Post-Traumatic Stress Disorder;

broader experience leads to collective conditioning. Just as the hundredth monkey effect reveals the possibility of collective awakening, the impact of shared human experience creates deep underlying themes of fear, insecurity, and shutdown in society. A simple example of this is the legacy of two World Wars on the previous generations of our families. These individuals experienced life in ways most of us cannot begin to understand consciously now. Yet we also share in its burden through our genetic inheritance. Without acknowledgement of the horrors of war, undertaking the necessary healing work, these shadows continue to underpin our collective experience. They leave a legacy of deep fear and trauma in our human psyche. Medusa is an archetype that reflects this impact of collective experience on us now.

In these present times, we live in a period of transition like no other in human memory. It's clear a deconstruction of our Western culture is taking place. We do not know the outcome. Uncertainty rules for many people, fuelled by fear from the status quo, namely, our political system, financial sector, and the media. We can see the means of transition at play now – a pandemic, failing welfare and healthcare systems, political duplicity, inflation, the greed of the 1%, environmental devastation, the refugee crisis, every aspect of life is uncertain. What we may fail to realise is how historical trauma, personal and collective, also contributes to our experience of change now. As life as we know it is falling apart, memories of similar transitions in the collective psyche emerge too.

When we're facing change, no matter its origin, deeply seated trauma, and fear of its repetition can influence us without our awareness of it. Throughout our known history we have faced the devastation of our societies. History points towards a series of invasions that changed existing cultures overall and particularly, the status and role of women. Little is known factually about this transition from matriarchal to patriarchal culture. Yet it is commonly held that between 3000BC and 500BC approximately, there was a complete decimation of what were female-inclusive, or matriarchal cultures. Did that occur peaceably? Definitely not. The natural insecurity engendered by a transition was heightened by how violently the change took place.

Trauma from these times is still in our psyche. Many awakened women connect intuitively, or through past life experiences, to it. Trauma is still held in the land too, as I discovered through my experience in Crete (shared in Chapter 1), and in other places since. The legacy of collective pain is underlying our current stresses, fears, and healing processes. Its roots lie beneath the personal trauma we may have experienced. They play in many ways: through subconscious and irrational fears of change; subtle fears about speaking out to those with perceived authority, and in lacking trust in our own knowing.

We will all experience the collective legacy differently, according to our soul journey our frequency of awakening now, and our gender. For all of us, but particularly women, it is wise to recognise also that we live in a collective field of distorted sexuality now. The presence of low-grade sexual trauma is endemic in every female body, whether we are aware of it or not. We face the threat of unwanted attention, sexual harassment, abuse, or violence daily. Our bodies are adrenalized through this constant sexual attention. Archetypes like Medusa symbolise and hold deep memories of violation. They are powerfully triggered in the current collective vibrations of change. We are wired into the emotional components of this legacy of trauma and power distortion. The frequencies of long-buried fear and suffering are influencing us now.

Medusa represents a link to our ancient past, particularly through the transition to patriarchal control. She is symbolic of the dramatic change in women's status over a long period of time, a change that continues to this day. In my view, to make a conscious contribution towards evolution now, we need to not only explore but to reclaim archetypes such as Medusa. Without their re-possession, our conscious owning of the creative potency of the deep dark aspects of the Sacred Feminine, these archetypes continue to operate unconsciously, perpetuating in us themes of victimhood, powerlessness, and inequality. We must make the journey deeply inward, as well as actively in our culture, for conscious embodiment. In this collective movement, we will be drawn individually to different paths as we evolve, yet every man and woman's evolution feeds the collective in some way.

With the Medusa archetype we are called to explore women's role as priestess, particularly within the ancient temple rites that involved sacred sexual union. We must reclaim a living knowledge of our legacy. One of the ancient roles of priestess was to protect the mysteries of the temple practices, secret initiations including sexual practices, along with the natural processes of life held in women's bodies: menstruation, conception, pregnancy, birth, and death. The priestess, in her devotion and humility, acted as representation of the Great Mother's sovereignty over all life and death. The sacred rites she performed were generally protected through secrecy and involved attire such as masks and veils. This ensured their mystery remained untainted. They were naturally protected also by the culture's connection to, and reverence for, Mother Earth and her natural cycles, her elements, the food, medicine, and shelter provided by her bounty. She, the Great Mother, was held in awe and gratefulness as provider and sustainer of all life. She was known to be inherently present in the mystery of death.

In ancient cultures, Medusa represented the dark phase of the Moon cycle in Triple Goddess Anatha. Through association with Egyptian Neith, she stood for the death aspect of the Great Mother. The warrior tribes from the North that invaded the Mediterranean and North African lands from around 2500BCE and instigated the patriarchal changes to culture, lacked this earth-based natural understanding of the goddess's dark phases. Darkness and its gifts were anathema to them. They worshipped a Solar God, whom they saw as the source of all power. They feared the mysterious nature and cycles of the Great Mother Goddess, for they could not control them. The destruction of the temples, desecration of priestesses, distortion of ancient myths, and the control of women, were their ways to gain power.

The decimation of the natural world that we see now is rooted in the same distorted qualities of these takeover times, namely use, abuse, and control. Patriarchy views nature as a resource to be used and consumed, not honoured. This is rooted in the dishonouring of the Great Mother and the mystery of women's life-giving nature. It is established through the control and ownership of women's sexuality, property, and human rights. The rise of patriarchy involved not only the desire to dominate and control, subjugating the natural rhythms of nature and women, but aggressive assault. It is known now that those who instigate the act of war, use rape to systematically traumatise women – for traumatised women seldom fight back. It is the ultimate abhorrent act in gaining control, for rape so deeply scars women that they become disempowered, numb, and often, but thankfully not always, silent.

We know little about the actual events of patriarchal takeover, yet our healing process often throws up the trauma of rape, violation, and bloodshed. The existence of female warriors, the Amazon women, who were also priestesses, reveals how this takeover was fiercely resisted. The Amazons rode horses into battle and were described by Greek epic poet Homer as 'the equal of men'. It is highly likely these warrior priestesses were involved in fighting the invasions of northern tribes. They were already aligned to sacrifice in their devotional role. They understood service calls for a huge loss of self, perhaps even their lives. To fight in protection of what was sacred, although anathema to their peaceful ways, was natural for some. Yet they could not prevent the domination that ensued; they could not protect what they had vowed to safeguard. Such deep trauma created many layers of pain within us. It has left a legacy of powerlessness, even futility, rooted deep in the female psyche now.

The Medusa archetype derives from these violent experiences of change. It has been strengthened through a conscious intention by patriarchal and religious control to hide and distort the truth throughout history. The Greeks portrayal of Medusa as a monster and demoness encouraged later cultures to project their own fear of the dark aspect of the Sacred Feminine onto her, making her progressively more toxic. This was not only a rejection of her innate sacredness but its betrayal. It has left a multi-layered trauma in the psyche that is a shattering of trust in life, its sanctity, and perhaps even in the goddess, whose perceived role was to protect those who served her.

The Legacy of Change

Change is inevitable; we cannot avoid it. Sometimes it seduces us into new life, at other times, change is thrust upon us. One thing is certain, change is constant.

As we explore the Greek myth of Medusa, we can see that however change occurs, it can leave a legacy of suffering in the psyche that exerts a powerful influence on everything that follows.

Medusa is initially depicted through her myth as a young and beautiful woman, serving as a high priestess in Athena's temple. Her interaction with the God Poseidon, brought change no-one could foresee. But then connection with a god was always dangerous in mythic times. The god of the sea, storms, earthquakes, and horses was known as a master seducer and illusionist. Whether he appears to Medusa as a stallion, then mounts her as a mare, or as his mesmerizing God-self and beguiles or rapes her in the temple, the interaction was a catalyst that changed Medusa's life irrevocably. The transition that ensued took her from young woman and priestess to monster, then to death, freedom, and the birth of her gifts.

The possibility of change can be a beguiling force in our lives. It can act much like the energy of Poseidon (the planet Neptune's energy in our lives), charming us with its possibility. Despite our dreams, our hopes and positive affirmations, or our good intentions, we never know where change will take us though, even when it seems attractive. This is the very mystery of life that the Goddess represents. It is only with hindsight that we may see how what seemed to be promise led us into the Underworld. Or what seems to be challenging brought forth fruit. No matter its outcomes, change always involves a death of some kind. Sometimes we need to be tempted by an illusion (our own or one presented by another) to leave our old life behind. Sometimes a traumatic occurrence thrusts us there.

Like Inanna and Ereshkigal, Hekate and Persephone, Sedna and Black Moon Lilith, and many other Dark Feminine figures, Medusa must travel through the darkness. After her encounter with Poseidon, she is blamed by Athena for the desecration of her temple. Shocking as this is, we know how this works, for we experience it in the contemporary form of 'victim blaming'. This paved the way for Medusa to be ostracised as monstrous, cursed to turn whoever gazes on her to stone. Not only was she a victim but labelled now as a monster. Medusa's traumatic experience was amplified through being cut off from any care or support. She was left utterly alone, bereft of understanding or comfort. As Athena exiled her from her temple, she retreated to a cave where she hid in shame. Is it any wonder her legacy to us is one of self-loathing? The distorted wounding that many women feel and that states, 'It must have been my fault somehow'. It's a wounding that is actively fed by the patriarchal systems perspective on women.

Victim blaming layers trauma on top of trauma. It compounds the wounding of the original experience. There is not only denial of the reality of what has taken place, its tragedy and horror, but the apportioning of blame on the one who has suffered. Current parallels include rape victims being accused of 'attracting' or 'asking for it'; mothers ignoring the obvious signs of abuse being displayed by their children; a collective culture that allows genital mutilation in the name of cleanliness or control, or anywhere we turn a blind eye to discrimination simply because it's too challenging to speak out or fight for what's just. Patriarchal culture has encouraged more than a blind spot when it comes to power and its abuse. This applies not only not to women. Denying the underbelly of life, or laying blame elsewhere, is the epidemic that actively avoids response-ability for our traumatising culture.

In the Medusa myth, the Goddess Athena plays the victim blaming role. She is an aspect of the Sacred Feminine that coolly denies her instinctual and mysterious nature in favour of creative holistic intelligence, rationale, and strategy. Athena's roots lie in the deeper ancient mystery of the Divine Feminine, nonetheless at the time of patriarchal takeover, she represents the growing need of women to cut off from their belly knowing, intuition, and earth-connected wisdom. Athena's roots lie in the ancient Mother Goddesses, yet she was objectified by the Greeks who reinvented her as an unwavering, rational goddess of wisdom and warfare, closer to a female version of her father Zeus than the instinctual, powerful Feminine deities from whom she evolved. Athena was a product of her time, as all mythic archetypes are. Over hundreds, even thousands of years, she has led women to develop intellect as an equal quality to intuition, to enter the patriarchal world.

Athena has been seen by many, especially within feminist movements, as a betrayer of women's rights. Following her treachery to her priestess, she supported the male hero Perseus in taking Medusa's head. She sacrificed the sisterhood of woman, that of the priestess, for the sake of the emerging cultural shift. She compounded Medusa's trauma and cut herself off from her roots in the goddess wisdom that had prevailed for millennia. It is no wonder Medusa is portrayed as fierce and raging, for Athena's cool rationale is a clear example of women's inhumanity to woman at the time when she most needs her succour. Cruel as it seems, this is Athena's role. For she portrays the evolution of women's intelligence away from purely instinctual knowing towards a holistic intelligence that includes rationale. She symbolises the need to actively cut off from instinct to develop new forms of intelligence.

At the inception of patriarchy, the evolutionary pendulum was swinging away from earth-based participation mystique towards individuality. Athena's cool head was needed to forge a place within a growing male-dominated culture. We see this way of intelligence thriving in many women now, especially within the corporate and political worlds. It is essential to being active in the patriarchal world, but as with all personal attributes of change, the pendulum swings to an opposite extreme before coming to balance. This polarisation of instinct and rationale is played out between Medusa and Athena. It still plays out now in our psyche and is at the crux of healing trauma. We must reach our wounding where it took place, in the instinctual realms within us, not through intellect.

Participation mystique allows the needs of the collective to take precedence over those of the individual. This was (and still is) the primary way of being of the tribal and earth-based cultures. The further we go back in time, the more we see individuality disappearing into collective consciousness. In primitive psychology, there is no concept of an individual, only collective relationship. Instinct is the primary active force of this way of being. It operates through gut feeling, giving us subtle direction or warnings. It's the animal nature deep inside us that is still awake and alert on a primal level. It's the natural law of the tribe that operates as one. It is our inborn connection to one another, our planet Earth, and its natural rhythms.

The arrival of Athena – born from her father Zeus's head – is symbolic of the shift in intelligence available to women as the priestess cultures were decimated. It represented the arrival of growing individuality. For that to be accomplished, women had to pay the price of change. Their existing roles and ways of being, both internal and in the culture, had to be destroyed for evolution to precede. The dark face of the Moon had to be denied so that greater consciousness dawned in humanity.

We are still involved in that evolutionary process. The pendulum swing to an extreme of rationale - that had to deny its predominantly instinctual way of being to establish itself and grow - can potentially return to balance now. This is the crux of our evolutionary process right now, and to renewing our relationship with the natural world. It is no coincidence that we are seeing a rise in trauma-based healing. The deeper shadows of instinct are being claimed. Such change is demanded, as we face the consequences of our disconnection from the earth of our roots, our beautiful planet Earth, and the resulting environmental challenges. The Athena archetype has delivered the gifts of the mind to women. It has presented us with many new possibilities, despite our losing our roots. Now we are all (men and women alike) called to address how we may have gone too far in detaching from our true grounding that comes from our Earth connection.

The synthesis of higher intelligence and instinct is calling us now. It is essential. For Medusa's myth reveals how her betrayal, as instinctual Feminine, leaves her stranded within our collective consciousness. As instinct is our animal nature, the demand for change lies in our relationship to Earth, as well as our inner environment. In the main we have forgotten the mystery of the darkness, not only from our need to reach for the light of consciousness, but from the fear of what our bodies hold as trauma. We cannot avoid Medusa and her sister goddesses. They are always present – in the dark mystery of birth and death, and the life transitions we cannot avoid. Medusa is frozen in time. No wonder we are compelled to meet her gaze. She needs us to reclaim her.

What lies behind our masks?

The betrayal of our instinctual nature and the Earth by the patriarchal system, is a core theme through our recent human history. Slowly but surely, we have learned to adapt to social norms (albeit unwittingly, or unwillingly) that deny our response-ability for the legacy we leave future generations. Also, we are only just beginning to acknowledge and understand the impact of our collective past (war and other traumatic occurrences) on our actions now. We must reclaim the energies of our collective legacy, to discover conscious ways into our collective future.

In his book A New Earth, spiritual teacher Eckhart Tolle writes about the collective dimension of the pain body that carries thousands of years of repression and abuse. It reflects the need to acknowledge how far away we have come from the basic human values of care and respect. The core values of the Sacred Feminine nature – receptivity, creative power, nurture, flow, the diverse expression of the life/death cycles, and our unity with life in all its forms – have been denied in favour of control and suppression of various groups of individuals, not just women. The ages of slavery, colonialism, racism, and religious supremacy, industrial, technological, and military might, all demonstrate the need for dominance that colours the patriarchy.

Many of us are aware of this legacy of patriarchal dominance. We live with it, and within its systems. Gradually, sometimes dramatically, we are awakening within it, claiming the right to create a different world, an Earth-honouring way of life that respects all life no matter its form. For this to happen fully, we are called to recognise and stretch beyond the shadows of the patriarchal systems in so many ways. Yet crucially, we are called to claim the wounding that the patriarchal shadow has perpetuated. We must enter it. The gaze of Medusa reminds us. She knows the pain of our inner darkness, the rejection of what we don't want to see or deal with, personally and collectively.

The legacy of denial in the patriarchal system is as damaging as the system itself. It is endemic. Through it, we end up not only carrying our woundedness, but also the shame of being ostracised from the care of

427

our culture, due to the intensity of that wounding. Projection is an insidious aspect of this separative distortion. Others, especially those in need who may threaten our own security, are perceived as a threat. In this coping mechanism based in security consciousness, we are all doubly wounded, for we lose the capacity of deep care connection and compassion we all long for. In our trauma, collectively we are isolating ourselves from the very connections with each other that we need.

Despite the massive challenge of these times, there is hope. As the system fails again and again, the potential redemption of collective pain is calling. Change is taking place, albeit slowly. Recent revelations about the Irish Mother and Baby Homes, the extensive sexual abuse in sports and the film industry, the outcry at Putin's invasion of Ukraine, the duplicity and deceit of politicians, are showing us the depth of our collective denial. We can no longer deny our denial, even though we may feel helpless in its wake. If we're awake, this is not a justification for blame, but a call to step up individually. For we are all responsible to bring light into the darkness of what has been hidden. Revelation is one of the keys.

Revelation takes courage. The price of being speaking honestly, awakening consciously within and despite our patriarchal culture, requires clarity; it takes strength and integrity. Deep in the psyche, we have unconscious memories of the price paid for bucking the system.

The fear that arises for breaking the collective rules is often overwhelming. Yet we must act, in our own sphere and the collective, in small and larger ways. Deep layers of collective trauma lie behind what seem to be our individual fears, doubts, lack of confidence in being fully oneself, or in speaking out. We know there is potential for yet more trauma in our calling to move beyond it. It's a quandary. Yet to face this seeming lack in our resources, and the fear, is our contribution to a new way of life, a new world. We must unlock the deeper shadows, to truly create renewal. For when we step out of our comfort zones, we feed the power of renewal for us all.

Trauma of any kind may freeze us in time, as can fear. Whether our reaction at the time of facing danger is to fight, flee or freeze, there is also the underlying force of shock to face, embrace and heal. Medusa represents the raw power of these instinctual responses to any threat. Her gaze says it all. It's her most potent symbol. She looks both terrified and terrifying. Gazing at her face, we somehow know her, even whilst we may be denying her. Described as fierce, penetrating, cold, even demonic, her visage gives us clues to the residue of unhealed trauma. Whilst the eyes cannot lie, our faces can often be hidden by masks in a misalignment of appearance and psyche. If we're perceptive, we can see this in the smile that lacks warmth, the numb gaze of one who has detached from her body, the mask of pretence that hides a broken heart. It's as if we have made an unconscious collective agreement to hide what's really going on. We want to hide the shadow's distortions and we end up wearing its mask.

This collective collusion is revealed in a 1970's opinion poll showing the collective perspective on beauty. It found that beautiful people are judged to be more popular, more successful, more loved. So, beauty is also a mask that hides the truth. This research is probably as true now as it was then, if not more so. For the advent of social media has brought more collective attention to how we look, and more so, to how our lives appear.

One of the ugliest myths in our culture is that your beauty is your worth, as is your social media platform. Being accepted and loved is a primary need for us all, so the connection between being 'beautiful enough, 'good enough', and 'successful enough' is strong. This natural need to feel loved, to be seen, has been twisted into the need to be someone special. Or to know ourselves through a reliance on the opinions of others. To keep up appearances, many human beings are now wearing masks of some kind. The facades are perpetuated by collective social mores, particularly through the fashion and beauty industries. Many other wonderful human qualities now pale under the illusion of beauty or success. Through this focus purely on appearances, the patriarchal mindset fails to recognise the damaging outcomes of emotional hiding, protecting or denying our vulnerabilities; or concealing the state of our mental health through fear of judgment and shame. It's a collective epidemic that results in a culture devoid of honesty, true care for our self and each other. Even in awakening, the risk is that spirituality becomes yet another measure of success. It takes deep consciousness to be awake to the more subtle distortions of trauma behind these displays.

The collective delusion in these times is a signal that many human beings are inhabiting Medusa's trauma freeze state, even in subtle ways. Major life stresses, such as facing a pandemic, cause aspects of the psyche to split off or freeze. We become numb, so lost to ourselves or the intense processes of change we're undergoing, that we no longer recognise what's happening in our inner world. We don't recognise the masks we are wearing. Confusion, exhaustion, brain fog, the feeling to avoid certain situations, shutting down or dissociating, cutting off from the body's feelings, or from others, these are all symptoms of underlying freeze state. Psychology has a term for this state of internal collapse - 'Medusa state'. It happens where we have dissociated from dissociation itself. Life can look 'normal' but occasionally there is an explosion, or the individual acts through repetitive behaviours that are comfort based but are in fact deeper cut-off strategies. This happens when our system feels flooded. Given our current collective circumstances, it's possible to see how even this distorted, disconnected state could become the norm for many people. It's a deep paralysis of the fight-or-flight response. Without knowing it, we can be living in a state of psychic petrification.

When we experience a threat or a shock, the body experiences a huge surge of hormones. If we don't de-stress, this energy gets trapped in the body leading to chronic emotional and physical tension, often with long-term health effects. Untransformed energies not only inhibit our full health spectrum, but they get passed down the family line, genetically or psychically. In my own journey to full well-being, I am transmuting the legacy of the Irish famines that colour my mother-line's fight for survival. I have more than enough food yet that inherited fear of not having enough is still there in the psyche. My fridge is nearly always full. This reveals how the collective trauma we have faced clearly influence our individual choices now.

Fight or flight, being the active reactions to threat, allow the energy of shock or fear to move. These reactions may naturally leave us shaking once the threat is removed. They are more of an open response towards release of trauma than freeze is. Nonetheless the energetic imprint of all harrowing experience may leave residues that must be reclaimed to enjoy fullness of life now. How we respond to trauma itself also has impact. Self-blame, especially when compounded by victim-blaming, leads to overlays of toxicity following a wounding. There is the original event, what we say to our self about it, and then what others add (if we have the courage to speak about what's taken place). Many women claim a legacy of silence following an assault, or simply dismiss seemingly minor violations – that touch of a hand on the lower back, the subtle yet not so subtle put-downs – simply because of fear that their wounding will not be received with acceptance. It's a habit that brushes off an invasion, albeit a subtle one, with 'It's ok, or the inner 'It's not worth making a fuss about.' This clamming up adds layer after layer of deadening to our psyche. It's a numbness that covers the naturally fierce, protective nature of the Dark Feminine.

Many women are afraid to claim power now because we are locked-up in the trauma from our past, personally, and collectively. The same can be said for some men. There are aspects of us all in exile, just as Medusa was. Resolution and integration of our many human facets is complex. If we want to be free and whole, we must commit to engaging what is frozen in time.

In her myth, the gaze of Medusa turns those who look at her into stone. It's a potent analogy for trauma freeze. Freezing can show up in many ways through our nervous systems. It is a common response when we're faced with anything beyond the norm, with that which takes us beyond the edge of our current resources. We may simply pause for a moment to regroup, or we literally freeze with fear, like a rabbit caught in headlights, feeling powerless in the threat of the unknown or dreadful possibility presenting itself. It is not uncommon for us to be turned rigid, and then powerless, by our fears.

It's important to recognise that freeze is an appropriate and natural reaction of our survival system. It creates a pause wherein we may choose an appropriate response to what is occurring, yet because we have lost our natural connection to instinct, we can tend to get stuck in the freeze state. At its ultimate, the fear of fear itself paralyses us; we are turned as if to stone. The mind goes blank for we have moved from Athena's realm of rationale into pure, often terrifying, instinct. There's reason behind the saying 'scared stiff'. We become literally rigidified in the face of the unknown, or the terrible possibility we think is on its way.

The freeze response masks our alternate inbuilt survival responses - fight or flight. It's a shut-down that at some point will call for release. It's a natural reaction that may disarm the threat, save our life, or not. Freeze is the least active mechanism of the body's survival reactions yet potentially it's the most dangerous, not only to our long-term health but to the legacy we leave in the collective psyche. When animals have faced a threat, once safe, the body shakes. They literally shake off the experience and reset their energetic balance; they de-stress.

For humans it's not so simple. Many people's current lifestyles are so adrenalized through pressure that unless we have taken on conscious practices to transform stress, we may live in a constant state of underlying trauma. This state expresses as a psychic numbing where we cut ourselves off from feeling, simply because to feel is to be overwhelmed. We create a spiral that circles from fear through denial and suppression to numbness. The paradox is, in trying to protect ourselves from feeling, this spiral cuts us off from the source of our power for life, love and joy. Many of the traits traditionally seen as female, like compliance, submission, and caretaking, are rooted in trauma, based in the need to be safe. We all need to feel secure as a foundation for resourcefulness in meeting change. Where we have fooled ourselves, is in believing paralysis is safety. In valuing unnecessary security over a life fully lived, we literally abandon our gift for fullness of life.

Devastation is a doorway

Behind the unacknowledged legacy of collective trauma lies devastation. Within the wilful negligence of our environment lies our own desolation. It is vital we acknowledge this, for our self, for each other and our Earth. Acknowledgement may seem to be without power, yet its potential is to recognise, within the heart of our deepest wounds, lies redemption. We connect consciously to the truth of our vulnerability. We are not immortal; death is always present. For that is the cycle of life of which we are part.

Vulnerability often makes us uneasy, simply because it is the edge of the unknown. It arises from the truth that what we know and love, where we feel secure, is ever-changing. Endings are ever-present. Vulnerability is the state of openness that acknowledges, life is change and there is no control of that cycle. Strangely, when we acknowledge this, we are free to choose a new response, for our energy opens in flow. The truth is, we always are vulnerable. To face the fact of this is to open a door into empowerment. It is to stretch beyond the patriarchal system's roots in control.

To claim our natural state of open vulnerability means we must face the truth. The worthy task of facing our darkness is to reach right into our core. It is to bear witness to the horrors of our lack of humanity. To become accomplished in self connection and the repossession of what we don't want to face. When we don't fully claim our inner states of being, we remain possessed and obsessed with avoiding what we fear. When we face what we fear, we just might discover there is always light in the darkness. For in truth, we are the light of consciousness entering that disowned place. To unlock our freeze state, we need to admit our avoidance of the shadows, slow down, and learn to listen.

As we become awake to avoidance, the need to bear witness, to acknowledge the hidden pains of our human history, in our self and in each other, is key to the redemption of our collective pain-body. For just as our own experiences may lead to freeze or switch off, we can also control our responses to what we see as overwhelming in others. Another's trauma can literally make us switch-off and go numb, perhaps feeling empathy but lacking response through fear. We can be turned to stone, rendered powerless in the face of another's devastation, or their plea for support or release. Unless we have reached similar places in our self, another's suffering can seem to disconnect us from the innate power of being our self. It can propel us into the need to fix it, close it down, switch off, rather than simply bear witness to another's tragedy. A tragedy we have all experienced at some point, simply in being human.

This lack of connection can manifest as dissociation, a psychic numbing to our own and others pain. Closing to protect ourselves, we also lose what connects us. The risk then is we objectify others. We embody Medusa, turning others to stone by stripping them of their humanity, the very thing that will connect us. Both dissociation and objectification cut us off from empathy; they turn us to stone, either through self-inflicted paralysis or by holding others away. Dissociating helps us to feel safe through anaesthetising. It cuts off feeling, helping us feel able to tolerate life, but lacking the capacity to fully engage it. We become practised in judging (sometimes very subtle), separating, and avoiding, to stay in control. Control that denies our need to grieve and heal.

Aliveness and the capacity to grieve are inextricably linked. We need to grieve well to be fully alive. The Dark Mother holds this capacity to face devastation and grieve, just as she holds the potential of birth. In many cultures, rituals of mourning are commonplace. In Sicily a group known as the 'Prefiche' were the community mourners. They dressed in black, reflecting a connection to the deep earth, to winter and the Dark Mother. They led the community in grief, crying, wailing, howling, chest pounding and tearing their hair. They expressed to open the doorways of grief for others, so loss could be fully acknowledged and expressed. This rising wave of feeling would sweep the dead to the other side. When the Christian Church became established in Sicily, the Prefiche were amongst the first groups to be outcast. Their open way of expressing grief was seen as a threat to control. It was an outright denial of the Dark Mother's role as giver and taker of life. It was a repudiation of the truth that resurrection occurs here in nature through the Sacred Feminine, that death is both an ending and food for new life.

Grief often holds a fire of fury within its black heart. For freeze state covers both our pain and our anger. Many of us fear rage. We have been conditioned and threatened out of expressing it; we have been punished, put in the scold's bridle, shamed for the power of our emotional expression. Yet feeling is life-force, in its full range of expression. To remain frozen requires huge amounts of psychic energy. In keeping the lid on the shadow – what we are told is unacceptable –

we fail to claim our birth right, fullness of life. Our oneness with nature demonstrates this. Storms are an essential aspect of life. They clear the land of what is no longer needed; they open space for regeneration. They are an inherent aspect of nature's cycles.

Storms are great cleansers, but we cannot make them happen. The freeze state is so primal, we can't force or fix our way out of it. Trying to fix our instinctual states can induce a deeper freeze state. Our survival systems reintegration as a natural state within the body occurs though a process of de-stressing, through relaxing. True healing happens through safety, without pressure or demand, through caring for our self with deep compassion and patience. As when caring for a sick child, we need kindness and patience. We need to allow feeling or give space to lack of feeling. It is caring acceptance that reconnects us to the Great Mother, in whose loving hold we may reach deeper layers in the psyche. In this process, it's essential to reconnect body awareness: breath in the body, presence with warmth to our self, nurturing our senses, soothing, relaxing, embodying consciously. Connection to nature is a support for trauma release too. In her myth, Medusa's direct gaze causes the turning to stone that our freeze state mirrors. But this physiological reaction in our system requires an indirect approach. Perseus's mirrored shield reveals this. Our approach to trauma needs subtlety and sensitivity. It takes care, and it may also take time.

The power in our eyes

There is a saying, attributed to Imam Ali, cousin and son-in- law of the prophet Muhammed, 'What you hide in your heart appears in your eyes'. This is a truth. The eyes cannot lie. They are said to be windows to the soul; they hold its secrets.

When we look in another's eyes we connect with their aliveness, or lack of it, where they are willing to meet us in connection or may be hiding. When we cannot meet another's gaze, we reveal our discomfort. We betray our lack of trust, appropriately or not. Our common phrases, 'catch someone's eye'; 'a sight for sore eyes'; 'the apple of his eye'; 'if looks could kill'; 'looking daggers'; a 'dirty look', are just some examples of the truth behind our eyes. We are always transmitting with our gaze. The eyes speak.

There are many veils of projection about Medusa's gaze. It has been labelled monstrous and terrifying. In her myth, Medusa's gaze was literally petrifying. Yet behind this depiction lies a deeper mystery. What her expression was, and what it became through the Greeks, differ. Symbolically, it is reminiscent of a priestess mask, as Medusa may have worn physically in her role in Athena's temple. These masks were worn as protection of the Sacred Feminine mysteries of the Moon, blood, magic, and the cycles of birth and death. They were used to protect the uninitiated from knowledge they were not ready for and to

440

depersonalise the priestess who wore it and her partner within the sacred sexual rites. This prevented individuals from attaching personally to the sacred act of lovemaking and initiation. The priestess masks were often red, taken on and off as required in different practices. The colour red links them with blood, a symbol of life. Also, to the power of menstrual blood, that through patriarchy came to be seen with fear and disgust. Menstruating women were rumoured to have powerful magic. As patriarchy took hold, these sacred aspects of women's lives were labelled unclean, or even, evil.

Masks are worn for many reasons: to hide or disguise, to entertain, to deceive, also to protect. Masks cover the truth of facial expression, they hide the subtle body signals we subconsciously perceive that lead to connection, or not. Masks can be physical or simply a habitual way of holding expression. Human beings, like animals, have many ways of displaying and hiding that operate instinctively. For instance: looking someone directly in the eye is powerful. It potentially opens a more honest connection yet can also be perceived as threatening. Have you seen the Maori Haka? The ferocious expression of the dancers is spine-chilling. The direct look of an individual who truly knows their self can be equally challenging. It can give rise to a powerful feeling of being seen through.

To be truly seen can be empowering, yet to that in us that wants to hide, it is disconcerting. There is a clarity in a direct encounter that is penetrating. It cuts cleanly through all the layers we may be trying to hide. If we're not ready or available for such a direct gaze, it can turn us as if to stone. The feeling of being seen through, of being naked, especially when we hold shame in our system, can be too much. If we can open to such directness, the potential is that our mask crumbles. The invitation to openness offered us may force or encourage us to confront what's afraid of exposure. The shaktipat transmission I experienced at Ganeshpuri was such - a direct shattering from the Divine. It utterly penetrated the pain I was holding and opened a door of renewal. My defences crumbled in the clarity and bliss of love. I was freed to move on.

What we look at, or look away from, provides clues to where we sit in our consciousness. Disregarding what we find challenging, either internally or in an encounter in our world, is an aspect of denial. Passive by-standing or observing without engagement, can sever us from the simple act of caring. Disregard implies a choice (conscious or not) to devalue or deny something as insignificant when it is significant. In our western cultures, particularly British, we have been trained in politeness, or simply in protecting ourselves from what is unpalatable: a homeless person in a doorway, the sight of a road accident, an argument in the street. Archetypal psychologist James Hillman suggests that "The eye and wound are the same". This connection reflects that what we refuse to see, or deny existence to, is a violent act. It is a cold-hearted refusal that compounds trauma to the psyche, both our own and others. It is Medusa in us, turning our capacity for care to stone. In so doing, we not only become dehumanised, but we deny the much-needed act of compassionate response towards what we are witnessing.

The physical eyes are not our only means of seeing. In the chakra system - the theory of subtle energy centres in the body that is first mentioned in the Hindu Vedas (1500-500BCE) — there is an invisible third eye situated in the centre of the brow between the physical eyes. The third eye is the source of intuitive or psychic vision. It is one of the sources of shaktipat; others being a sacred word or mantra, a touch or even the transmission of a pure thought.

The third eye is called Ajna in Sanscrit, meaning 'command', 'perceiving' or 'authority'. In yogic metaphysics, the third eye is the centre where we transcend the duality of a personal 'I' that exists independently. It's where we move beyond the five senses into the truth of unity. As such, it is where our personal experience falls into the unified experience of being human and yet also where we transcend that. It propels one into the truth and as such, opens a clear consciousness of self beyond trauma.

There is yet another centre of seeing in women. A sensitive woman can 'see' with her vulva, with the secret knowing held in the most intimate places of her body. Energetic and physical links between the throat, the vulva and vagina are now being recognised. The vulva is a similar shape to the eye. It is just as sensitive, perhaps more so. When a woman experiences vaginal trauma, connection to her deep intuitive wisdom is damaged. What is very natural, but often unacknowledged natural wisdom becomes distorted through unhealed pain, particularly sexual wounding. This aspect of 'sight' is cut off, becoming dulled or frozen. Or we may intuitively feel the wisdom arising from our sexual centre but doubt or deny it.

Simply being female in a patriarchal society can create a repression of energy in our body. Closure is encouraged through our cultural sensibilities. It is rooted in feeling insecure, not knowing how to be and behave within a culture of social norms that sexualises women, that constantly affirms a woman's sexuality exists to serve men or sell products, or that a woman in her sexual power is easy.

Living within a sexually distorted society means that the most sensitive parts of our female bodies are constantly under assault energetically. This can also happen through invasive screening that is considered essential, such as mammograms and cervical smears. At the very least, these procedures are emotionally intense. If we don't acknowledge this, speak up for our needs, acknowledge where we need support, our lack of self-care can get stuck in the uterus, vagina, and throat, adding to the trauma legacy already there. The direct gaze of Medusa confronts us to face this legacy. Look in her eyes – they are both demanding and imploring! She asks that we face our disconnection from body feedback directly, simply by feeling body sensation, listening, becoming sensitive to our ineffective coping mechanisms, through somatic therapies and massage, movement, and dance. She asks that we dare to claim the full intimacy of being in our beautiful bodies.

The mirror's reflection

Just as the eye is purported to be the window to the soul. A mirror provides another means of seeing. Mirrors reflect, so represent our capacity to reflect on both the big picture and the personal. They offer a potential for clarity. The word mirror derives from the Latin 'miror, mirare,' meaning 'to wonder at, to be astonished.' Looking at the stars in the night sky is like looking in a mirror. The potential is we realise our cosmic nature, for we see both dark and light.

In ancient cultures the Sun was celebrated as Feminine in its life-giving nature and was associated in some cultures with the goddess. Amaterasu, the Shinto Sun Goddess in Japan, is one such archetype. A mirror is one of her sacred objects. In China, bronze mirrors are used to chronicle astronomy and cosmology, reflecting the movement and rhythms of the natural cycles. Perseus used a mirror-like shield to avoid a direct confrontation with Medusa. The mirror reflected her monstrous image so he would not be turned to stone.

Integrating the darkness of deep trauma is not easy. Mirrors are essential. It takes courage and willingness to face the brutality of its existence, the murky shadows of our human experience. It's not unusual to feel powerless in facing our powerlessness. Right timing is an aspect of this process. Facing our trauma depends on our individual life rhythms and resourcefulness, our devotion, our willingness to go there, or simply whether we've had enough of feeling powerless. Who knows when that timing arises for any individual? Working with astrology, I know the rhythms of our evolutionary cycles have relevance, both personally and collectively. There are times we cannot avoid diving deep. It doesn't take much intelligence to see we are all being called to face the shadows of our distortions and disconnection in the 21st century. Whether we choose to or not is an individual matter, yet with collective impact. Where we do make a conscious choice for healing, we need a mirror.

In slaying Medusa (and releasing her from her frozen state) Perseus wielded both a sword and the mirrored shield given him by Athena. Here the myth points us to another crucial factor in reclaiming Medusa's legacy. What we cannot face directly can be reclaimed indirectly, through a mirror. For what we cannot see, we cannot heal.

446

The mirrored shield used by Perseus, is brightly polished on both its outer and inner faces. It reflects both the truth and the potential for clarity that exists in reflection. Its brightness and reflective capacity help clarify our perspective on our self, either through self-enquiry or through the supportive reflection of another. The mirror is where we can recognise with clarity: I am operating instinctively here; I am running from, reacting to, or fighting the past. This clarity arises from questions such as: Is this real? Or is it simply a mirror image of the past that only has the power I give it?

The mirror of inner reflection supports us in seeing what is really taking place, as does that held by another, for instance, the support of a professional. One who holds dispassionate reflective space for deep exploration and healing. The gift of the mirrored shield from Athena to Perseus reflects the support of this detached perspective. Perhaps it was Athena's means to redeem her betrayal of Medusa with a quick death.

A mirror offers us a reflection that can help us to move on. It does this through bearing witness to 'what is' right now. It's a perfect reflection of things as they truly are, not as we might wish them to be. We can play the role of mirror for ourselves and for each other. This involves a capacity to hold space with loving acceptance; to simply be a reflection that leads towards redemption. To have pain or wounding witnessed opens the grace of connectivity, loving acceptance, empathy, or

447

compassion. As we receive this, an opening through and beyond trauma can begin to occur. The healing potential is we feel validated, held, and loved, both in our wounding and beyond it. In that, we can discover the courage and self-respect to continue to face our disconnection from our shadows, our terror and trauma. We may also discover the truth, that deep healing, wherever it occurs, is for all who have experienced suffering. It both heals the psyche and feeds it with love; love arising from unconditional acceptance.

Off with her head!

The focus on Medusa's head through the ages is intriguing, given the links with Athena, whose archetype holds the evolution of Feminine intelligence. What can Medusa reveal to us about intelligence? And what does the act of beheading represent other than the fact of death?

And then there's Medusa's hair, comprised of writhing snakes. How might we understand what these snakes-for-hair mean?

Hair is one aspect of our body with a multitude of meanings, a fundamental part of our appearance and how others see us. At the very least the state of our hair speaks of cleanliness and self-care, yet it also conveys powerful messages of self-expression. Hair is often associated with a women's sexuality, as are snakes. Because of this link, the need for women to hide their hair is an element of patriarchal control still alive today.

How we wear or hide our hair can reveal ethnicity, beliefs, lifestyle, group or tribal alliance, and sometimes socio-economic status or religion. Hair symbolism is the subject of several anthropological studies, particularly regarding tribal initiations, marriage ceremonies, mourning rituals and magic. In some cultures, hair is considered the seat of the soul and to retain the properties of its owner even after cutting. It could therefore be used in amulets, charms, or curses. Anthropologists have even put forward the theory that long hair represents unrestrained sexuality, short or bound hair is linked to repressed sexuality, and a shaved head means celibacy. Nuns cut their hair off when they take orders; monks shave their heads. Head shaving is also used as a means of humiliation. Both totalitarian governments and prisons have used hair as a means of social control, using head-shaving as part of a process of dehumanisation, stripping individuals of their identity.

In western culture women's hair has a particularly strong sexual connotation. It is linked to hair in other parts of the body, especially the pubic area. Our collective memory of the serpent power of sexuality is linked to women's long hair. Medusa depicts this with her snakes-for-hair. What snakes represent before and during the patriarchal take-over provide us with clues to the deeper sub-conscious connections.

Serpent energy is widely known in esoteric circles and through Hindu philosophy or religion as kundalini. Kundalini is primordial cosmic energy within the body. Historic symbolism depicts it as a coiled serpent resting at the base of the human spine, at the muladhara, also known as the root chakra. It is illustrated as two serpents intertwined as they climb the spine. The shape of the serpent coupling is almost identical to the design of our double helix DNA.

Some yogis consider kundalini to be the flow of energy within the network of the energy body and that there is no anatomical equivalent. Others relate the flow of kundalini to the flow of messages along the nerve fibres in the physical body. Most agree however that kundalini is a spiritual-psycho-physiological power that is centred within the sushumna, an energetic channel that connects along the spinal cord.

Whilst an individual is not consciously awake, kundalini energy is the static form of creative energy that serves to vitalise the whole body. When awakened and uncoiling, this electrical power moves in a spiral; hence the symbolic description of 'serpent power'. As kundalini is aroused (through spiritual practices or sexuality), it steadily increases the vibrations within the physical body and all its subtle bodies. This vibratory activity cleanses and transforms stuck energies in the bodies whilst also energising the consciousness of the evolving individual. Hindu philosophy states that kundalini practices raise an individual's level of consciousness towards enlightenment. There is no evidence in Western culture that ancient priestess rites were based in this knowledge, but it is an interesting synchronicity.

The symbol of the serpent or snake is sacred to cultures and religions globally. It has long represented life, health, and renewal. In religion, mythology, and literature, snakes often represent fertility or a creative life force. The ancient Chinese connected serpents with life-giving rain. Traditional beliefs in Australia, India, North America, and Africa have linked snakes with rainbows, which in turn represent fertility, or the union of Heaven/Earth. The spirituality of the Eastern Mediterranean and more recent Mayan cultures had snake Gods and Goddesses. There are snake temples in Buddhist Myanmar too, where snakes act as the protectors of the temple. Similarly, the Hindu religion of India has snake temples where they are associated with fertility and rebirth.

In the Greek culture serpent energy is associated with medicine. The ancient Greeks considered snakes sacred to Asclepius, the God of medicine. He carried a caduceus, a staff with one or two serpents wrapped around it. This has become the symbol of modern physicians. For both the Greeks and the Egyptians, the snake represented eternity. Ouroboros, the Greek symbol of eternity, depicts a snake curled into a circle or hoop, biting its own tail. The Ouroboros symbol originated from the fact that as snakes grow, they shed their skin, revealing a shiny new skin underneath. As such, they stand for rebirth, transformation, immortality, and healing.

As guardians of the Underworld, snakes hold the hidden wisdom and sacred mysteries of death and the Great Mother Goddess, who holds both life and death. The Nagas of Hindu and Buddhist mythology suggest a more obvious synthesis of the snake energy and humanness. They are regarded as semi-divine mythical beings, half human, and half cobra. They have the capacity to take wholly human or wholly serpentine form, potentially dangerous but often beneficial to humans. The Nagas reflect the dual nature of serpents in human thought, that they symbolise both evil and renewal, fear and wonder.

Snakes were a natural aspect of ancient temple culture. Snake pits have been discovered in temple sites in Greece and the Near East. It is believed that snake venom, in tiny amounts, may have been used as an hallucinogen. The connection between serpent energy and the rising of kundalini in sexual practices may have been known also. The renewal of a snake's skin was potent symbology for the rejuvenation possible through ritual lovemaking.

Snakes also have a reputation as symbols of death or evil. The serpent that tempts Eve and Adam into disobeying God is seen as such yet if we explore deeper, there is another meaning to this biblical myth, related to sexual power. The differing ancient stories about Lilith and Eve as Adam's wives portray this (see Chapter 6). The serpent is either cast as evil or a symbol of knowledge and wisdom. Some Christian saints are said to have driven away snakes as a sign of miraculous powers given to them by God, for instance St Patrick in Ireland. This is yet another representation of the powers of the patriarchy, particularly in the Christian religion, controlling sexuality through the concept of sin.

Given this link between Medusa's hair, snakes, and sexual energies, it may be more easily understood how different cultures and religions have required women's hair to be covered since patriarchal times. Until at least the 18th century, the wearing of a head covering, both in the public and while attending church, was customary for Christian women in Mediterranean, European, Middle Eastern, and African cultures. Women who did not cover their hair were regarded as prostitutes or morally loose. Even today, head coverings are the subject of volatile debate between women who do not want to wear them, or at least to have a choice, and the patriarchal system that thrives on control.

This need to 'cover up' certain aspects of our bodies or nature, or even denude our bodies of hair, reveals the distortions in our cultural mindset around sexuality. Disconnected from its natural power of rejuvenation, and its creative potency, we have become disempowered in the naturalness of our bodies. Both men and women are constantly receiving distorted messages about beauty, youth, what's normal or desired. This begs the question, is the current fashion of shaving all body hair also an act of disempowerment?

The recent trend for labiaplasty is a more extreme example of disempowerment. It shows the extremes women are prepared to go to, either to fit in, or to please their men through having a neat 'clam shell' shaped vulva. It's clear that as we distort our bodies, conforming to cultural trends that have no basis other than fashion, we are displaying a deep lack of self-confidence in our bodies and our sexuality. Medusa's fate was to have her serpent power distorted and ultimately destroyed, through her beheading. We are acting in a similar vein voluntarily. Cutting off the ancient serpent wisdom of body, energy, and sexuality through conforming to society's distorted norms.

This split between naturalness, instinct and intellect is represented in the mythic relationship between Athena and Medusa. As Medusa's head was cut off – removing both of her old identities, the priestess and victim – the split was firmly established. The old ways of the priestess were betrayed by the calling of Athena towards a new way of intelligence. Instinct was being replaced by a move towards rationale and strategy. My view is that it's an evolutionary movement, but that does not mean there is no loss or pain associated with the change. As always there are paradoxical, even contradictory, elements at play.

454

Beheading was the means of Medusa's death and yet also her release. To sever head from body is not merely to kill; it symbolically disconnects mind from body, intellect from instinct, rationale from earthy wisdom. The face is the most personally expressive part of the body. The experience of the senses happens through the head too: seeing, smelling, hearing, tasting, breathing, laughing, and crying. It is what others recognise first. Beheading is therefore not only a brutal show of power, through violence, that delivers a trophy to the perpetrator, it is the claiming of that individual's personhood. For women, this is what patriarchy meant; the denial of their right to be themselves.

It is clear through the dilemmas of our current collective culture that patriarchy is the shift from nature-centred awareness towards the development of intellect and individuation. Yet we have gone beyond the evolutionary impulse of individuation into disconnection from our roots. Perhaps the experiment has gone wrong? Perhaps we needed to lose ourselves in the extremes of an individuation process to finally take responsibility for what we're creating? There are no easy answers. And how can we really know? We only have a partial limited view. Yet our disconnection of head from body is obvious. It is at the very root of our current issues.

In our post-modern world many individuals believe solely in the power of the mind, believing their thoughts are a true reflection of reality.

Science posits that consciousness exists inside the brain rather than the other way round – the brain being the instrument of consciousness. Much as science attempts to explain away the mystery of life, to deny the spiritual beingness of nature and Mother Gaia, our cultures have become mentalised, objectifying life in the attempt to control it. In so doing, it is clear we have become disconnected from the very source of our life-force. In many ways, we need to metaphorically behead ourselves, to integrate the tools and power of the mind into our body-being. To return to body-wisdom, which is Earth connection.

Beheading kills yet also releases the soul from the body through death. It is said that in her death, Medusa found freedom. Similarly, we must lose our heads to heal. We are called out of the intellect into the emotion, sensation, and body-feeling of our wounding. This potentially leads us to a fuller aliveness. Only through being in the body can we truly heal.

Beheading calls us to recognise that whilst thought has its place, it is not useful in our healing process. We must strip away our illusions about being powerless. When we live in the head alone, we inhabit a powerless place. When we let go of our thought processes as being the only reality, the potential is we come back to body awareness. Body awareness opens the somatic experience. This becomes a guide towards wholeness through trauma release. As we get more in touch with our body, the integration of new frequencies of expression and action is natural. We become more fully embodied as consciousness, with mind, feeling and body serving as vehicles of our true nature. We are freed, just as Medusa is liberated by Perseus's sword. Her death is her freedom, whilst her streaming blood becomes both a potent life-giving medicine and a power for death.

In her myth, Medusa is dead yet free. 'So what?' we might say. As her body lies head-less, her soul is released from the burden of trauma, her children emerge from her severed neck. There is new life. Death brings renewal. For death and life are always unified in the Dark Mother. They are the eternal cycle, constantly changing forms.

Much like the processes of change we try to deny, death is a subject many of us avoid, especially in our Western cultures. In a society based on expansion and growth, on being happy or successful, the gifts of loss, are largely ignored, and certainly met with denial until we are brought face-to face with the fact. Our experience of a pandemic is perhaps the wild card that brings the fact of loss home to us globally. Evolution requires death, not just physically. It requires that we sacrifice that which no longer serves our lives. Medusa's beheading was a sacrifice to evolution. Cutting the thread of bondage to an old, albeit valuable, way of being at that time. It was a symbol of transition: instinct to intelligence.

The sacred link between death, sacrifice, and rejuvenation, largely unheeded in mainstream western culture, is more well-established in Eastern culture and religions. In the Hindu religion the symbology of beheading relates to cutting the thread of bondage to identity. The seemingly terrifying goddess figures, Kali and Chhinnamasta, represent losing the mind to experience true freedom. They stand for the fundamental transformation of a human being, letting go of identity (seen in the face, and held in the mind) and what we perceive as reality through conditioned belief, to experience true freedom of consciousness.

In depictions of Chhinnamasta in particular, the cut head does not appear lifeless. It is feeding a stream of blood back into her own body and those of her two attendants, just as finer consciousness feeds those who encounter it. Likewise, Medusa's death, opens the possibility of new life through her children, unlike Athena who bears no children yet in a strange coincidence, was born from the cleaving open of her father's head. There is no mention of Zeus suffering through this violent act of 'giving birth', or of blood. Yet the release of Medusa's blood is an integral aspect of her myth, bringing forth the renewal from what is otherwise a terrible tale.

Blood is life

Medusa is the life-force of being human, along with breath. Both are intimately linked in the health of a physical body, yet for women, blood carries a far deeper significance. From the hormonal surge of menarche to the release of menopause, blood is an integral aspect of our being woman. It carries the gift of giving life through our bodies. It requires our surrender to the messy discomfort yet mysterious power of menstruation, the wonder and uncertainty of pregnancy, to the power of birth, and the release of menopause. Throughout our lives, our women's body are subject to change over which we have no control. It is the making of us and is also our undoing. We carry the processes of birth, life, and death within. We live them viscerally.

This flow of change is deeply embedded in a woman's make-up. Just like nature, we are fluidity: body, mind, emotion, and physical energy waxing and waning with the tides of the Moon. Just as blood is flowing constantly through our veins, we also retain or release it according to the tides of our fertility. In our natural way of being, we are the fullness of flow we know in the natural rhythms of the seasons, from darkness to light, Dark Moon to Full Moon, rest to rejuvenation. The ancients may not have understood this flow in the ways we do now, yet each aspect of life was given its full place in the cycle. The Dark Goddess aspect of the Moon's cycle was both venerated and feared for her power, for the inevitability of death's triumph over life represented in her dark phases.

The sacred mystery of life in nature was both feared and revered. The mystery of women's life-giving nature an acknowledged aspect of that, honoured in the temples, along with the revitalising power of sexuality. The associations with blood were living. In the temple cultures the priestesses' masks were generally red, as were their robes. The life-giving force of blood is red, yet the term 'scarlet woman' has come to carry negative connotations.

Reverence underlaid with fear is not an unusual response to life's mysteries, including our female bodies. It is reflected in a mixed bag of beliefs, rituals, superstition, taboo, and reverence towards women's menstruation in different cultures and religions over eons. The ancient reverence for the blood mysteries, women's role in creation, the power of life and death held by the Great Mother, was replaced by fear during patriarchy, perhaps purposefully. Denial of the mysteries of life occurring through women's bodies paved the way for its takeover.

In later periods this was amplified by the need of science to discover, categorise, and prove. What could not be controlled had to be destroyed or denigrated. Women's natural power of life, once given veneration, became viewed as inconvenient, unclean, something to be dealt with, and more recently, medicalised. Menstruating women were isolated through fear of their 'power for evil'. The ancient rites of seclusion for menstruating women to rest and rejuvenate, became distorted as rejection of their unclean nature. This was a profound denial of the Dark Mother aspect of life, the phase of Dark Moon, winter with its times of storms or famine, death as well as life.

Pliny the Elder reflected the growing fear of women, as patriarchy was establishing. A piece on the power of the vagina and menstruating women in his Natural History published in 77AD states, "There is no limit to the marvellous powers attributed to females. For, in the first place, hailstorms, whirlwinds, and lightning even, will be scared away by a woman uncovering her body while her monthly courses are upon her. The same, too, with all other kinds of tempestuous weather; and out at sea, a storm may be lulled by a woman uncovering her body, merely, even though not menstruating at the time". This piece acknowledges the connection of women's menstrual cycle with the power of nature, albeit distorted. It is coupled with fear too, "Contact with menstrual blood turns new wine sour, crops touched by it become barren, grafts die, seed in gardens are dried up, the fruit of trees fall off, the edge of steel and the gleam of ivory are dulled, hives of bees die, even bronze and iron are at once seized by rust, and a horrible smell fills the air; to taste it drives dogs mad and infects their bites with an incurable poison." One wonders what kind of encounters he had experienced with women to write in such a way. Certainly, it indicates the growing beliefs at the time. As patriarchy established control, in an endeavour to align purely with the

461

one Sun God of light, or the growing Christian religion, the dark tides of the natural cycles were pushed into unconsciousness.

Menstruation myths from these times reflect the shift to control of women that patriarchy established. In the Abrahamic religions the separation of menstruating women from their husband, families and tribe was motivated by an idea that a menstruating woman is unclean. This originates in part through the Bible and Eve's supposed transgression in Genesis. It's compounded in the Book of Leviticus, where there are lists of required and forbidden activities for menstruating women. Similarly, in most modern Muslim communities, there are forbidden activities for menstruating women, such as entering a mosque, praying, or having sex.

Conversely in the Hawaiian and Polynesian cultures menstruation as seen as the most sacred time for women, a time of spiritual power. Hawaiians lived with a matriarchal culture until the 1800s therefore we can assume this belief was rooted in their ancient ways. Their word 'tapu' – with its meaning of sacred or spiritual and thus requiring special circumstances - gave rise to the modern word 'taboo' with its distortions from the original meaning. In Polynesian cultures menstruating women were regarded as 'tapu'. They were distanced from the community in menstruation huts, like the ancient 'red tent' practices in the pre-Muslim Middle Eastern cultures. In this sacred space, women had seclusion from the tribe and their usual care-taking roles. They could enter the darkness of rest and woman-space, rejuvenating and nourishing, emerging to serve their families once more, with their inner world replenished.

In other cultures, there are mixed messages about menstruation according to class or caste. For instance, in Indonesia high-caste women enjoy both menstrual privileges and restrictions, whereas low-caste women are ostracised, even at times being banished to sit on a trash heap.

In her mythology Medusa's blood carries this contrast of life and death, good and supposed evil. After her beheading by Perseus, drops of blood trickled from Medusa's neck. Her myth relates that some drops birthed oases in the desert and corals in the Red Sea, others gave rise to a plague of poisonous serpents. It also relates how just one drop of blood from Medusa's right vein could cure and restore life, whilst one drop from her left vein could kill instantly. After Athena received Medusa's severed head, it is said she gave two vials of her blood to Asklepius, God of Healing, who was the son of Apollo and a mortal woman. Asklepius or Hygeia (his daughter) made a healing balm from Medusa's blood that was purported to bring the dead back to life. In this we see the rejuvenation theme of Medusa's energies at play again. If we view 'bringing the dead back to life' metaphorically, it reveals how our engagement of trauma-based energies is essential for our fullest well-being. In this, Medusa surpasses the intellectual rationale of Athena every time, for although Athena's gifts were essential to evolution, Medusa connects us to the very core of being alive. Perhaps it is only now, having the extremes of both archetypes, that we have the potential to bring them together.

Interdependent powers of life

Those of us who have seen a Sheela-na-gig figure carved on a church must question: exactly what is a female figure exposing her large vulva and pulling back her labia, doing there? Is it a remnant of the ancient pagan religions? Is it a warning against lust? Is it serving as a protective function? Is she, Sheela-na-gig, the female counterpart of the Green Man? Or symbolising the Cailleach (the old woman or hag) who has both life-giving and death-wielding powers within nature and human lives? Sheela-na-gigs in western and central Europe can be accompanied by male figures at times. There are several in the UK including a male figure who appears to be masturbating (St John's Church in Devizes) and an animalistic man with a huge erection crawling towards a Sheela-na-gig, plump and fecund with her legs held apart (St Mary and St Andrew's Church in Cambridgeshire).

Exposing the vulva, or the lifting of skirts, known as 'anasyrma', has been used throughout history, either as a method to ward off evil, or as a force of protest, to shame men for their actions. The Irish hero Cú Chulainn, who lived around 0BCE, faced a horde of women walking naked on his path when he threatened to do battle with his fellow Irishmen. None of Cú Chulainn's friends or counsellors could convince him not to go to war yet the naked women, led by their chieftainess, Scannlach ('the Wanton') succeeded.

Similar stories emerge from the Mediterranean culture. The ancient Greek historian, Plutarch in his treatise on the "Bravery of Women" dedicated to his friend Clea, recorded the use of anasyrma on the Persian army when fleeing from a battle. Their women lifted their skirts, apparently saying, 'Whither are you rushing so fast, you biggest cowards in the whole world? Surely you cannot, in your flight, slink in here whence you came forth.' The Persians were so shamed and humiliated they returned directly to battle. There are tales of anasyrma in Greek mythology also. Bellerophon, the great hero and son of Sea God Poseidon, turned tail and ran at the sight of the Xanthian women's display.

Using the vulva to shame men and their actions is still in use today. in 2002 Nigerian women shut down oil production and stopped its expansion, simply on threat of exposing their genitals. The Pussyhat Project founded by Krista Suh and Jayna Zweiman, and the Women's Marches, made similar statements of protest shortly after the 2016 US Presidential Election.

It doesn't take much intelligence to recognize the similarity between Medusa's snake hair and pubic hair. Freud is not the only psychoanalyst to interpret her serpents this way. In Freud's interpretation, decapitation equals castration. The fear of Medusa is based on a psychological castration of males by females, particularly where there is still 'mother attachment'. According to Freud, the sight of hair-covered genitals (or any similar representation) freezes the immature male in terror of the father's retribution. Obviously, this is open to interpretation. His treatise 'Vagina Dentata' (vagina with teeth) was never finished. Clearly, he had his psychological patterning to transmute in his attitudes, emotions, and sexuality. A quote from his letters to his fiancé, Martha Bernays, certainly suggests what those were, "Even a marriage is not made secure until the wife has succeeded in making her husband her child as well and in acting as a mother to him". This desire for both mother and lover in a partner demonstrates a conflict within intimacy that often underlies sexual connection now. It is an aspect of our growing maturity in conscious partnership to recognise its play.

Sexual connection is charged with our most primal fears and desires. The deep desire to share love, or simply connect our animal bodies, has its own drive. It is the power of life itself, with its constant calling to create. Or the distorted need to dominate. The power of sexuality opens the gates of intimacy, a most vulnerable space within, where every kind of feeling and emotion may arise. The fact we may lose control, that we need to lose control, to fulfil the true potency of lovemaking, is a risk to our very human sense of security. We become naked in more than one way. For in true lovemaking, in vulnerability, we face the loss of self that is essential to unity.

Medusa's play in sexuality is not obvious at first. Apart from her interaction with Poseidon, the myth does not openly address this aspect of our lives. Yet myth carries multi-layered symbology always. The mention of Medusa's gaze turning men to stone, has sexual connotations. The power in a women's eyes can turn a man 'to stone', either through desire, resulting in an erection, or through rage, potentially generating fear, numbness, or impotence in a man.

Collective male projections around sexuality and desire can generate fear that has a powerful effect on male physiology and psychology. Desire for a woman's beauty and juiciness is also permeated by fear of the power of that beauty. Desire can be overwhelming. It takes us beyond rationale into our primal drives. Our phrase 'mad with desire' can be seen in many different lights. Much as a woman can act as muse through a sexual encounter, so her energy can also overwhelm. The potency of women's passion and fierceness, particularly during orgasm, can be awesome yet also petrifying to a man who wants to control her. The power of sexuality can give rise to all kinds of complex reactions and behaviours. As we address the legacy of patriarchy, the need to unravel the inextricable links between sexuality and power, fear, violence, and control, is evident.

For men and women to embody the potency of conscious love, our instinctual wounding must be brought to finer consciousness. It is a collective task we cannot avoid as we evolve. One that is growing as women are standing together to say, 'No more!' to power plays, particularly through sexuality, or to state 'No control!' with our bodies. Patriarchal abuse of power has both distorted and disrupted our natural body systems, much as it is doing with our planet. It is necessary to engage our full body awareness and projected judgments if we desire true freedom. This journey is different for men and for women.

The Greek myths are full of heroes. The hero's quest reflects a man's journey of maturing. Psychologically, it symbolises a young man's drive to prove himself, to discover his true freedom, the meaning and significance of his life as a man. Aspects of the quest relevant to sexuality are to free himself from emotional ties to his personal mother. Then he is energetically free to love a woman fully.

In ancient times, this quest for freedom was rooted in an honouring of 'Mother' in the Earth. Men recognised their dependence on the Great Mother. This knowing provided a holding space for a man within his culture, within the honoured cycles of life, as he was detaching from personal mother ties to discover his place in the world. As patriarchy became rooted in culture, disrupting women's sacred roles, inevitably men's lives were also uprooted. Their innate understanding of life's interdependence disappeared. They had gained control, only to lose their true power of life within Life. The Great Mother was no longer honoured as the deep holding space for a man's life. This disruption of connection now has many outcomes for men. In terms of psychological and sexual maturing, it means that potentially a man's need of his personal mother is more difficult to break. The psychological task to consciously discern the placement of 'mother' and 'lover' within his psyche, to separate the two, is more challenging due to this schism with 'Great Mother'. It requires deep honesty and detachment from his little boy self to birth maturity of presence. It requires the love and support of conscious women.

The solar hero – symbolising conscious man - matures by destroying his need of mother, wiping out his boyhood patterns of immaturity and powerlessness. He is also required to face the collective subconscious fear of death from the old king rites, where sex with the high priestess or queen meant death by execution for a man. Through these sacred rites his blood was given to ensure the fertility of the land. This rite was the mirror of women's surrender to her monthly bleeding. The sacrifice of his blood was to feed the land that fed the people. These ancient rites are far behind us, yet their subconscious memory can still subtly impact behaviour, especially in sexual connection. A man needs his full presence to go through these energetic frequencies and fully meet a woman in lovemaking. In presence, he consciously engages the kundalini serpent power - represented by Medusa's snakes-for-hair - for transformation, rejuvenation, as a unifying power with his love and for their evolution.

To mature through and beyond these subtle yet charged influences in the male psyche requires clarity and fierceness of detachment. This is suggested in Medusa's myth through the sword of Perseus. A sword is a common symbol for cutting through, with clarity and precision. It represents the mature presence and strength needed to cut through the mother-ties. It carries the symbology of intense focus required for detachment.

The erect penis is a similar sword-like symbol when connected to a man's presence of consciousness. It can cleanse a woman's vagina of pain. It can open her body, yet also take her beyond it. The penis also has an eye. Perhaps it is to see psychically in the dark of the vagina? In the Medusa myth, Perseus's sword takes her head off. An erect phallus, used consciously, metaphorically can take a woman's head off, opening her more fully into her heart and body by 'blowing her mind'. Or bringing her energies down from her mind into embodiment.

To the ancient Greeks, love and sexuality were inextricably connected with the creation of their three worlds: Earth, Heavens, and Underworld. Greek myth contains every element of sexuality; incest, homosexuality, lesbianism, trans, bestiality, polygamy and intermarriage were accepted as purely natural aspects of life. If you travel to Greece now it's not unusual, particularly on the island of Crete, to encounter the bare-breasted figures of Minoan Snake Goddesses, plus statues of males or satyrs with sizeable erections. Greek dances, passed down through eons, celebrate the fertility of women and the land, especially in springtime. They include graphic demonstrations of diverse sex acts. Greek mythology expresses similarly, revealing a conscious connection to the instinctual layers of the psyche. Yet rape and abduction are commonplace; in later myths they are symbolic of the patriarchal takeover. Medusa's rape is just one of many demonstrations of the shift of power. Yet her beheading is unusual. The Greeks viewed beheading as a most honourable form of death. Perhaps through this perspective, we may see Perseus's act, as sword-wielder, not only as the means of Medusa's release, but also as honouring her sacrifice.

The Tantric systems of Hindu and Buddhist cultures connect beheading with the theme of sacrifice also. I've already mentioned Chhinnamasta as a similar archetype to Medusa. Chhinnamasta becomes Chhinnamunda in Buddhist texts, where she is also the one who cuts off her own head to feed herself and her two attendants. In some iconography, Chhinnamasta is depicted standing on a love-making couple. They are Rati, a goddess associated with sexual desire, and her consort, Kama, the God of Love. Frequently the background scene is a cremation ground, with distant hills and a river. There is also a serpent and flowers; the whole scene set amidst a fierce storm of thunder and lightning. The symbolic depiction of lovemaking is astounding. It mirrors how we symbolically die in the opening to love; how we must fully let go to experience its sweetness. It depicts the fierce spontaneity of passion, like lightning striking the earth and the sweetness of loving, like a flower giving off its perfume.

Chhinnamasta is associated with the quality of self-sacrifice as well as the awakening of kundalini – the serpent energy of spiritual awakening that lies at the base of the spine. She is considered both a symbol of self-control and surrender, and an embodiment of sexual energy, depending on interpretation. Chhinnamasta symbolizes the Great Mother in her aspects of life-giver, life-sustainer, and life-taker. Iconography in both Hindu and Buddhist systems reveals her varied conflicting aspects of creating and nourishing life through blood and sexuality, yet also how she destroys through violence and death. An alignment with Medusa as dark aspect of the Triple Moon Goddess is clear. Both Medusa and Chhinnamasta represent the journey of life in its entirety of possibility and experience, where all life events, including death, are an aspect of unified consciousness. Chhinnamasta, much as Medusa in her death, is revealing the power of transformation and rejuvenation, freeing the mind, and opening the body. The Feminine sacrifices herself and her blood, drunk by her attendants, and so rejuvenates and renews the Universe.

The symbology of Chhinnamasta signifies that life, death, and sex are interdependent. Like nature, she shows us that new life arises from that which dies. This cycle is revealed also in Medusa's myth. Through her death, new life is born. Through her sacrifice, and in partnership with Athena, she is playing a role in women's evolution: that of encompassing creative intelligence. Medusa's unwitting partnering with Athena, although seemingly tragic, opens a gateway towards wholeness. Such is the nature of life, seemingly tragic at a personal level, for the benefit of all collectively.

Reclaiming the sanctity of trust

In our current times, human beings live with a legacy of damaged trust. Our collective history has led to a cultural worldview based in fear and lack. It's a perspective lying behind the destruction of our natural world and potentially leads us to our own extinction. Our need to reclaim trust in life's processes, despite our inevitable losses, is key to our evolution. It redeems the extremes of patriarchal mindset that have come to govern our lives.

As we evolve, the necessity as I see it, is to engage and understand the duality of light and dark, life and death with deepening awareness, to recognise they are opposing yet complementary aspects of life. Both are essential to each other, for without the forces of destruction and death, there would be no possibility of renewal. The essential shift in this is to realign our perspective on the energy of darkness, what we might label as negative: loss, pain, suffering and death. It's to recognise that darkness is merely the absence of light. We cannot avoid it, for it is an integral and natural aspect of life on Earth. As we evolve the potential is, we recognise we are the light of consciousness seeing and penetrating the dark phases of life on Earth. Loss and death are natural aspects of our lives. The rhythms of day to night to dawn, summer to autumn and winter then spring, dry to wet, loss to renewal, are the way of life here on Earth. The cycle is always moving, the wheel of life incessantly turning. To be mature is to realise every aspect of that cycle has its place within the whole.

The Medusa mythology engenders in us diverse reactions to what we see as a dark experience. The human tendency is mostly to reject or dismiss that which we fear, but in so doing, we are denying our power of change. We are actively foregoing the power of life and evolution that is gifted to us, simply through the fear of what our darkness may hold. Particularly in our collective culture, we mainly avoid unwanted experience through resistance, or we reach for the light whilst burying what we think is unacceptable. This occurs through playing victim to the shadows, or in absolving responsibility to others for our wellbeing, A clear allegory for our collective attitude lies in how we fill the Earth with our rubbish, abdicating responsibility to be care-takers of our home, or feeling powerless against the forces of consumerism. Yet the tide is turning. There is a ground-swelling of conscious change taking place within people, despite our fears. Many are consciously facing the challenge of these times: the biggest one being that time is running out. We are embracing the darkness of our collective actions, individually. In so doing, we face the ultimate conundrum. That the darkness holds both our shadows and our mystery.

Reconnection to the instinctual layers of our being in a healthy way is the potential of Medusa's legacy. Her myth reveals that even through deep trauma, redemption, release, and new life are possible. The main task lies in learning to trust ourselves and the flow of life's natural processes, despite their mystery and our fear of them. This starts with honesty, honesty to oneself. It's to acknowledge 'Yes, this is what I see, feel, know or experience right now'. Core honesty is an open acknowledgement of life's dark edges. It happens when we allow ourselves to get back in touch with our body and the disowned aspects of our emotions. It requires willingness to listen deep; to become aware of visceral reactions, including the ones that don't look so pretty. It requires we become awake to the multi-layered nature of our shadows:

their energies, our fear and judgment of them, our resistance to them. Integration and embodiment begin with acknowledgment.

Many of our strongest reactions, arise through the Medusa themes: the dishonouring and demeaning of our woman nature; rape or sexual assault; betrayal and the treachery of patriarchal perspectives. Even the most subtle experience – a word or remark, an uninvited hand placed on the body, or a certain look - may carry the energy of belittling, shaming, or demeaning that we already carry in our female psyche. It may carry the distorted sexuality of 'You're mine to use", albeit subtly. We do know these energies; we have had enough experience of them. We know our reactions too: fury, withdrawal, or even playing along. To be truly free, we need to discharge and liberate our reactions - just like the Earth releases through storms, earthquakes, and other natural means. Like the wrathful goddess archetypes reveal to us, our reactions are natural energies. They are there to guide us (and often to compel us) into renewal. Like nature's storms clear the land, albeit through devastation, we must sometimes rage, to clear the space for growth.

Our culture has not actively encouraged or supported women to be forthright and call-out the often-subtle distortions of patriarchy. If we don't trust our reactions, or risk allowing them through fear of where they might take us, we never cross the boundary that frames our self-doubt as acceptable. If we don't face the shadow in our self, we are ill-equipped to question or challenge the darkness that comes towards us from others when it does. Other archetypes are active in this shadow-play, for instance Eris (see Chapter 2). Her disruptive energy disturbs our system, but it happens for good reason. Disruption doesn't arise to compound our wounding but to highlight the potential of transmuting it. Experience, especially experience we can't control, has a function. Without it, we do not learn and grow. We do not mature to fulfil our sacred potential.

When we allow experience to grow us, even when, especially when, it is challenging - and when we trust that such experience has a purpose - we acquire the gift of embodied wisdom. This occurs only through the engagement of experience, or our energies of reaction, as they arise. The means of engagement varies according to the circumstances and our state of being at the time. Sometimes we may reflect a put-down or invasive move on us straight back with a clear response. Sometimes we may need to remove ourselves and work with the energy inwardly, especially if there is a threat of danger. A psychic invasion of our personal space is more subtle, but there are ways to engage this too. The action of taking an event or experience inward can be the natural movement of our receptivity. If we make space to take care of it consciously. It's not necessarily an avoidance, but a means of subtle energetic engagement and release.

In avoidance we don't grow wise; we simply stagnate. Many women find it challenging to respond authentically when faced with demeaning or sexual energies, for fear of violence. We find it difficult to share our experiences through the possibility of humiliation, the fear of victim-blaming or judgment. With hindsight we might discover different ways we could have expressed, yet in the moment, underlying fears or memories, family patterning, lack of cultural support and embedded trauma prevent it. It's a quandary, for if we don't engage the energy we've received with awareness, it compounds whatever wounding is already there. It stays in our system, poisoning it.

If we don't trust our reactions as pointers towards growth, we enforce victim consciousness on ourselves through a lack of embodied capacity to respond. Without the willingness to fully face this lack, without judgment, however it expresses, the challenge simply continues. We keep attracting similar scenarios, until we engage differently. Our natural capacity of healthy self-protection remains undeveloped, stuck in self-doubt and powerlessness. Yet awareness is everything. Even if our responses do not shift, awareness guarantees the light is coming on. Awareness is a sign that trust is building inside. As we allow that to grow, with conscious self-loving practices, new response embodies naturally. Now and again, it surprises us. For it simply appears, expressing through us in right timing. Our task is to trust the natural processes within us. Not to force growth, but to allow it, to trust it's gestating deep within us, like seeds within the earth. Trust allows those inner seeds to find their own right timing; it's a protective function of the psyche.

The sanctuary of self-love

Medusa carries the energy of protection, both personally and for women collectively. She carries the priestess legacy, safeguarding the mysteries of the Sacred Feminine. To reclaim our natural capacity to protect our self, our sisters and children, nature, and the Earth, we must face and embrace Medusa's other legacy: the violent overthrowing of a sacred way of life. We must reclaim the sacred, bringing love to our human frailties and wounds. As we reclaim self-trust from our experience of being wounded, we begin to recognise it as a sacred commitment to oneself. It is a sanctuary. Trust opens our capacity to safeguard our self, not from the need of defence but as a natural expression of self-love and self-respect. It reconnects us to a natural reverence for all life. We are called to safeguard the sacred nature of life. This applies to our own well-being and that of our sisters, to the sacred mysteries of life, death, and rebirth through menstruation, conception, and birth. It applies to the natural rhythms of life on Earth, how all life, including ourselves, is intimately linked to the Moon cycles, and beyond that to the gift of life through our Sun.

Seeing ourselves as sacred, worthy of love and respect, simply through being alive, is essential. Learning to trust our self in the face of our own experience is a practice. Especially if our experience, or our caretakers, have not equipped us to do so. It's a quandary, as the fact of trauma, or an emotional wounding, is inherently disempowering. To go through and beyond this, we must unlearn what the mind says a particular experience means about who we are. This is an inside job initially. We must get on our own side, turning internal criticism into awakened self-responses, deconstructing judgment with recognition of our own learning processes. When we don't have our own backs, life in the world is tough. When facing the Medusa wounding, (and we all do to some degree) our task is to shine a light in our shadows, to name them for what they are – agents of growth.

Trusting our instincts supports our capacity for self-love and the task of protecting our self. This applies not just physically – for instance, senses on alert as we walk down a dark street at night – but daily, in terms of being awake to that which devalues our being female. When we don't trust our instincts, or the subtle levels of our sensitivities that indicate 'Something's not quite right here', we feed our victim state, simply through a lack of willingness to listen and engage our knowing. Healing our wounds involves not closing our eyes to our subtle knowing, to our own or another's suffering. It involves removing the mask of 'I'm fine', the habit of discounting oneself, and engaging experience from a new place. This requires core honesty, the capacity to initiate and hold difficult conversations, sharing our heartbreak with each other. We cannot change or heal our dark shadows without going there. As we dare to, as we discover through vulnerability that we are all wounded in some way, the light of trust starts to emerge brighter.

Transformation is a multi-layered process that takes time, yet with grace, with consciousness, it can happen in a moment. We don't have to carry our stories of devastation indefinitely. According to Harvard brain scientist Dr Jill Bolte Taylor, an emotion can be perceived, fully felt, and dissolved in just ninety seconds. There's a ninety second chemical process that happens in the body that will fully clear the arising emotion. This is astounding. It reveals that ongoing emotion is often underpinned by choice, as is a lack of self-support. We choose to keep energising the feeling or the habit. Emotional attachment to a story about 'my wound' creates an emotional loop that simply keeps looping. Fully engaging our healing allows the layers to dissolve as they naturally rise, often triggered in simple daily interactions. It's our resistance towards fully feeling, or our attachment to mental constructs of identity based in the feeling, that create the loop. We become attached to the story as 'mine', energising a victim role and response. We are literally possessed by our story, rather than taking possession of it consciously.

To dismantle the patriarchy, we must take apart and transmute what we have inherited through it. The only way to do that is in allowing our instinctual energies to free up, with courage, in boldness. It's a dangerous edge to walk. Yet a woman who loves herself is a dangerous woman. She's a threat to the old order, daring, in that she challenges distortion. Dangerous in her love of honesty and her respect of 'equal but different'. This is not just a women's issue. It is time for all of us to learn new ways. For men, the focus is in claiming their Sacred Masculine presence, their life-honouring presence, their desire for purpose in service to life and our planet Earth. As we all withdraw energy from the patriarchal structure, with its hierarchical basis, we will naturally return to honouring the whole web of life and to the sacred union that is our birthright.

Inner alchemy

Encountering Medusa within oneself is a shamanic initiation. She demonstrates that facing and embracing death is key to new life. Whether we name her shaman, alchemist, or initiatory guide, Medusa requires that we journey deep into the Underworld of our human experience, both personally and collectively. Her beheading symbolises rebirth, arrived at through the confrontation with fear that is central to shamanic journeying. Facing Medusa is an initiation on the path to individuation that ultimately thrust us out into life utterly renewed.

Perseus was well-armed by the Gods in his quest to kill Medusa. It seems she was the victim of his actions. Yet perhaps her yielding to his sword, was of her own free will, an intentional act. In choosing death, she was granted new life, for her children are born from her beheading. As her soul was released into freedom Pegasus, the winged horse, and Chrysaor, the giant with a golden sword, are born. The purity at Medusa's core takes form through the children who come from her body. These two very different offspring of Medusa are expressions of the polarities of both her spirit and the instinctual survival response she so clearly represents. The magical winged horse Pegasus represents flight; Chrysaor, the warrior giant, symbolises fight. The birth of Pegasus and Chrysaor represent the birth of new consciousness – magical inspiration and strength. Yet like Medusa, they also represent how instinct has its shadows. They are contradictory figures even as they are inspirational ones. As we claim Medusa's legacy, we can choose how we embody them.

At birth, Pegasus, symbol of purity, imagination, and magic, immediately takes flight towards the Heavens. Pegasus is a figure of beauty and inspiration, known to the Greeks as a muse, stimulating the beauty and lightness of music and poetry. Yet his shadow demonstrates the flight response from trauma – escape towards the light, spiritualising what is calling for deep feeling and transformation. This flight towards the light is based in avoidance of the shadows and pain of trauma. It's a denial of the need to feel the sensational reality of the body to fully heal. Feeling to heal releases dense emotional frequencies held in the body. It opens vulnerability. In later mythology it is said that wherever the hoof of

Pegasus struck the Earth, beautiful springs appeared. These springs represent the potential of rejuvenation, the lightness of spirit possible when trauma is fully released and new energy grounded (his hoof opening the Earth). He stands for the deep soulful expression that occurs when we have transmuted the survival orientated flight response.

Chrysaor, meaning 'he who has a golden sword', was Medusa's second child, released on her beheading. In Greek mythology he is seen as a warrior giant, or in some sources as a winged boar, being highly favoured by Ares, the God of War. Chrysaor represents the fight element of our survival instinct. The fight response can express through a pure animal reaction of rage, charging in when danger or fear arise. In a healthy response, it's the expression of warrior energy that operates as protection. According to the few documents that make references to Chrysaor, he eventually became the King of Iberia, one of the Greek's western provinces. He stands for the inner warrior-king as the ultimate protector. His golden sword cuts through danger with conscious intent; gold representing his connection to the solar life-force.

Together Medusa's children represent both the unhealthy and transformed polarities of flight and fight. Flight transformed, with its upward flow, opens inspiration and leads to rejuvenation. When fight is operating consciously, it expresses as self-possession. Both can be symbols of revitalisation. These two children of Medusa also suggest the gifts of integrated left and right hemispheres of the brain: inspiration and creativity, clarity, and action. This links with the evolution of intelligence that Athena represents, the predominance of instinctual reaction making way for the evolution of integrated creative intelligence.

If we take the long view of human evolution, we are simply in one of its phases. Our evolution over eons demonstrates (from the limited knowledge we have right now) the shift from participation mystique (no individuality) into patriarchy (individuality but with females controlled) into conscious co-creativity, equality, and humanity (the Age of Aquarius). In this, the potential is both empowered individuality and living collective consciousness. Medusa's part in this movement points towards the reclamation of trauma locked in the psyche, so we may move towards wholeness. The gifts of Medusa's instinctual knowing may then consciously weave with Athena's contribution of creative feminine intelligence.

Medusa and Athena carry different qualities of Feminine intelligence, both of which are essential to our lives as women. Athena's role in the play of patriarchy, her betrayal of Medusa and her gifts, is now coming full circle. Athena was not drawn to sexual expression, or she denied it. Her place was in the world of men, not as partner but as friend and strategist, and as protector of the people. Her role has eventually brought women to a new way of being in the evolutionary cycle, operating from rationale yet also with creative intelligence that honours the whole as well as the goal. This is ongoing. Medusa's role as priestess was intimately connected to the ways of the Feminine and her rhythms. More than that, as priestess she carried the wisdom of sexual union as a pathway to the experience of divinity as union. She draws Sacred Masculine consciousness down towards physicality, into deeper communion with the Feminine as form. It's an initiation that draws an immature male into the mysteries of life and love in her very body. It's a sacrament of which she is guardian.

The snakes around Medusa's head are a potent symbol of the wisdom that can come from our sexuality and the instinctual levels of the body. The regeneration that snakes represent through shedding their skins points us towards Medusa's power of life through death, darkness, and rebirth. Yet snakes need the light and warmth of the Sun to build their life-force. Similarly, our sexual energies need the light of consciousness to find their healthy place within our wholeness. In some representations of Medusa, particularly those that are carved, what artists have depicted as snakes, also appear to be the rays of the Sun. The Sun symbolises our fullest life-force and brightest light. That which opens as kundalini (the serpent energy) rises through sexual union or spiritual practice towards the fullest light of consciousness. In its rising, the whole body is regenerated; it brings whole-body creative potential to life. Body, instinct and all the vehicles of our body-being are unified.

Many cultures have Sun Goddesses. The Aztec Coatlique, whose name literally means Snakes-Her-Skirt, looks like Medusa. She offers us deeper insight into the links between serpent energy and the Sun's light. The Coatlique sculpture in Mexico City's National Museum of Anthropology is one of the most well-known representations of her. The sculpture stands over ten feet tall, towering over onlookers. Numerous snakes writhe across her body, forming her entire skirt, her belt and even her head. Two enormous snakes curl upwards from her neck to face one another. Their split tongues curl downwards, appearing to create a single serpent face. She is a potent, even terrifying figure, much like Medusa; the twin snakes emerging from her neck indicating that she was decapitated. The resemblance to Medusa is uncanny. Even more compelling is the recent interpretation being offered for Coatlique's appearance that is based in myth. The Aztecs believed there were eras of the Sun, signifying evolution. In this myth, several female deities sacrificed themselves to keep the Sun in motion, effectively allowing time itself to continue. They were responsible for preserving the rhythms of the Cosmos through the sacrifice of their lives.

Our exploration of Medusa's myth and associated goddess figures now brings us full circle, back to the Triple Goddess. Just as Sun, Earth, and Moon flow in different yet complementary rhythms to create the Moon cycle we see in our night sky, the Triple Moon Goddess brings the cycle into an evolutionary spiral. In the ancient Triple Goddess symbology,

Athena stands for the glimmer of the New Moon, its new cycle requiring foresight, courage, and strength. Metis, (Athena's mother swallowed by Zeus) represents the light of the Full Moon, carrying the gifts of fullness, fruition, and mothering. Medusa stands for the Dark Moon, our psychic capacity to face the darkness and regenerate. As they swirl through each other in the full lunar cycle, each playing her unique role, so together with the Sun, the light of our consciousness, they also spiral us through our evolutionary process.

This evolutionary process is a spiral that we constantly move up and down to grow consciousness. As we integrate the dark flow of the cycle represented by Medusa, wisdom dawns in us that feeds the emergence of a new cycle, the New Moon light, carried by Athena, whilst Metis carries the fullness of expression. Without each other, their fullness is denied. Medusa's evolved instinctual intelligence complements Athena's creative intelligence in the world. Medusa protects Sacred Feminine values, whilst Athena calls us to engage the patriarchal world to rebalance it. In their alliance the dark wound of patriarchy is being dismantled piece by piece. This is our task, as individuals and together.

Medusa is perhaps the ultimate guide to our transformation from darkness to light, serpent medicine, shedding the skins of the past, bringing consciousness and healing to our world. Her seemingly monstrous appearance is seen transformed in the Nemi fountain, near

Rome in Italy. Here her beauty is clear, as is the fount of renewal she stands for, clear, sweet, fresh, ever present.

Glossary

Archetype: a model or pattern of a particular way of being, held within
Asura – demon in the Hindu tradition

Asura: demon in the Hindu tradition

Being: one's essence

Body-being: the whole of one's nature – body, emotion, will, mind, soul

Boon: reward

Chakra or chakra system: the theory of subtle energy centres in the body that is first mentioned in the Hindu Vedas (1500-500BCE)

Collective: the whole of humanity

Conditioned self: the ego; the identity we take on and believe; the result of our childhood programming and experience

Creatrix: as opposed to Creator i.e., Divine Feminine energy of creation

Crone: wise woman; a post-menopausal woman

Dakini: female practitioner of a Tantric path

Dark Goddess: the goddess archetypes that carry the destructive, or death-wielding aspects of the divine, classed as shadow energies by patriarchy

Dharma: a Buddhist term meaning true behaviour, action, or way of life

Divine Love: love beyond our human capacities

Earth Mother: the innate intelligence in the Earth, Gaia

Eleusinian Mysteries: rituals enacted in ancient Greece to honour Earth Mother Ceres and to reveal to the people the natural cycles of birth, life, death, and rebirth

Enlightenment: a state of oneness with the divine

Feminine/Divine Feminine/Goddess/Deep Sacred Feminine: interchangeable terms for the receptive, nurturing, loving aspect of the divine expressing through women and men; Shakti

Form: physical object or manifestation

494

Gaia: the Greek name for the Earth and the natural intelligence of our Earth

Grace: divine intervention or blessing

Great Mother: the ultimate Universal or Cosmic Goddess symbolising the fertility and abundance of the Earth, out into the Cosmos, and encompassing all other goddess archetypes.

Her-story: past events and knowledge as portrayed through myth and story, art, music, culture, tribal and oral traditions as opposed to the supposedly factual accounts of history (his-story)

Hundredth monkey effect: a theory put forward by Ken Keyes that once an animate system reaches a critical mass, new behaviours automatically transfer through consciousness.

Kali Yuga: the age of strife, discord, and conflict in Hindu philosophy, spanning 3102BCE to 2020CE

Knowing: our non-rational connection to what is deeply true

Kundalini: spiritual life-force within the body that rises through the chakra system

Masculine: the Sacred Masculine frequency of the Divine; Shiva consciousness; presence of stillness

Masters and Mothers: divine beings incarnated in bodies

Matrilineal descent: ancestry traced through the mother's line

Mystery: life in its unknown quality

One: a state of unity

Olympians: Greek god & goddess hierarchy

Pandora's jar: character in Hesiod's writing who carries a jar containing misery & evil

Pantheon (Greek or Roman Pantheon): collective noun for the deities of a particular people or culture

Participation mystique: a term introduced by philosopher Lucien Lévy-Bruhl to describe a psychological connection with objects, people, or ideas where the subject cannot clearly distinguish himself as separate but is bound by identification. The relationship is both unconscious and undifferentiated.

Patriarchy: a system of society or government in which males hold the power, the father or eldest male is head of the family and descent is reckoned through the male line.

Patriarchal: pertaining to patriarchy – a goal oriented linear process for society based in control

Priestess: a woman devoted to serving the divine in whatever form is sacred to her

Realised Consciousness: consciousness opened to its true nature as divine

Sacred Feminine: the divine expressing in goddess forms

Scold's bridle: a torturous device used to silence women

Self: the divine within as opposed to self, meaning ego

Shadow: unhealed aspects of self, often suppressed, rejected or unconscious. The disowned self—the parts we think are unlovable, unworthy, or unacceptable

Shakti: Sacred Feminine energy or goddess figure in the Hindu religion

Shaman/Shamanka: one who acts as an intermediary between the natural, human, and supernatural worlds

Sheela-na-gig: stone carving of a women exposing an overly large vulva often seen on English, Irish, French, and Spanish churches, towers, castles, and ancient wells.

Shiva: Sacred Masculine energy or God figure in the Hindu religion

Sky Gods: the divine worshipped as solely being in the Heavens

Source: life as divine energy

Spiritual bypassing: avoiding pain by using spiritual concepts to deny, invalidate or escape our human realm

Subtle Body: psycho-spiritual or energetic constituents of living beings, according to alternative health, esoteric and mystical teachings. Each subtle body corresponds to a subtle plane of existence, in a hierarchy of being that culminates in the physical form.

Sushumna: an energetic channel that connects the subtle bodies with the physical along the spinal cord

Tantra: the embrace of every part of life, including sexuality and death, as sacred

Tantrika: female practitioner of the Tantric path

The Collective: the whole of humanity

The Titans: ancient Greek god/goddess pantheon

Transcendence: moving beyond the normal or physical level of existence or experience

Triple Goddess: Great Mother Goddess with her forms of Maiden, Mother & Crone

Underworld: the Greek & Roman culture's 'hell' world. In psychological terms: that which lies in our shadow, or unconscious

Woman: the archetype of consciously awakened Sacred Feminine energy in women's bodies

Yahweh: the ineffable name of God in the Hebrew culture

Yin & Yang: the twofold nature of universal energy: expansive and contracting, seemingly opposite or contrary forces that are complementary, interconnected, and interdependent

Yogi/Yogini: Hindu practitioner of spirituality

Bibliography

Suggested further reading

These are books that have informed, inspired and enlightened my journey with the Divine Feminine Archetypes. I honour the wisdom they carry.

Bolen, Jean Shinoda – Goddesses in Every Woman
Bolen, Jean Shinoda – Goddesses in Older Women

Estes, Clarissa Pinkola – Women Who Run with the Wolves

Gainsburg, Adam – The Light of Venus

George, Demetra & Douglas Bloch – Asteroid Goddesses, The Mythology, Psychology and Astrology of the Re-emerging Feminine
George, Demetra – Mysteries of the Dark Moon, The Healing Power of the Dark Goddess

Trista Hendron, with others – My Name is Medusa
Trista Hendron, with others – Original Resistance, Reclaiming Lilith, Reclaiming Ourselves

Kempton, Sally - Awakening Shakti

Massey, Anne – Venus, Her Cycles, Symbols & Myths

Monaghan, Patricia – Encyclopaedia of Goddesses & Heroines

Small, Jacqueline – Psyche's Seeds

Stone, Merlin – When God was a Woman
Stone, Merlin – Ancient Mirrors of Womanhood

Marion Woodman, Elinor Dickinson – Dancing in the Flames

Wolkstein, Diane & Samuel Noah Kramer – Inanna, Queen of Heaven & Earth

Printed in Great Britain
by Amazon

17837856R00292